PHOTOSHOP® CS4
DOWN & DIRTY TRICKS

Scott Kelby

Editor of *Photoshop User* magazine and
the world's #1 best-selling Photoshop author

PHOTOSHOP CS4 DOWN & DIRTY TRICKS

The *Photoshop CS4 Down & Dirty Tricks* Book Team

CREATIVE DIRECTOR
Felix Nelson

TECHNICAL EDITORS
Cindy Snyder
Kim Doty

TRAFFIC DIRECTOR
Kim Gabriel

PRODUCTION MANAGER
Dave Damstra

GRAPHIC DESIGNER
Jessica Maldonado

STOCK IMAGES
COURTESY OF
iStockphoto.com

Published by
New Riders

Composed in Frutiger, Museo, and ITC Studio Script by Kelby Media Group, Inc.

Trademarks
All terms mentioned in this book that are known to be trademarks or service marks have been appropriately capitalized. New Riders cannot attest to the accuracy of this information. Use of a term in the book should not be regarded as affecting the validity of any trademark or service mark.

Photoshop CS4 is a registered trademark of Adobe Systems, Inc.

Warning and Disclaimer
This book is designed to provide information about Photoshop CS4 Down & Dirty Tricks. Every effort has been made to make this book as complete and as accurate as possible, but no warranty of fitness is implied.

The information is provided on an as-is basis. The author and New Riders shall have neither the liability nor responsibility to any person or entity with respect to any loss or damages arising from the information contained in this book or from the use of the discs or programs that may accompany it.

THIS PRODUCT IS NOT ENDORSED OR SPONSORED BY ADOBE SYSTEMS INCORPORATED, PUBLISHER OF ADOBE PHOTOSHOP CS4

ISBN 13: 978-0-321-56317-0
ISBN 10:   0-321-56317-4

9 8 7 6 5 4 3 2 1

www.newriders.com
www.kelbytraining.com

This seal indicates that all content provided herein is produced by Kelby Training, Inc. and follows the most stringent standards for educational resources. Kelby Training is the premier source for instructional books, DVDs, online classes, and live seminars for creative professionals.

For my longtime friend Jim Workman,
without whom I wouldn't have written
my first Photoshop book, Photoshop
Down & Dirty Tricks, *nine years ago.*

Acknowledgments

I consider myself very, very blessed. Each day I get to work with such a wonderful group of people, and when I'm not working, I'm surrounded by family and friends whom I dearly love, and all of whom come together to help enrich my life in so many ways. There's not a printed acknowledgment I could write that would honor them in the way they deserve, but one of the benefits of writing a book is that at least I get to try.

Kalebra: My wonderful, beautiful, amazing, hilarious, fun-filled, loving wife. You're the greatest thing that's ever happened to me, and asking you to marry me almost 20 years ago was clearly the single best decision I've ever made. Your spirit, warmth, beauty, patience, and unconditional love continue to prove what everybody always says—I'm the luckiest guy in the world.

Jordan: My little buddy—you're just the greatest. A father couldn't ask for a more fun, more crazy, more lovable, or more loving son than you. I'm so thrilled and proud of the little man you're becoming, and I'm so delighted that you've been blessed with your mom's heart, compassion, and spirit. You have an incredible life ahead of you, and I can't wait to see the amazing things you'll accomplish along the way.

Kira: My little princess. It's just like mom said it would be—I'm wrapped around your finger, and yet I couldn't be happier! You've warmed my heart in a way that only a little snuggly angel like you can, and the fact that you're a little clone of your mom only proves that you're going to be an amazing woman of character, grace, and heart. Daddy loves you very, very much!

Jeff: I can't tell you what a blessing it's been having you as a brother. You've had a tremendously positive impact on my entire life, and I could never repay you for all you've done, and continue to do. I love you, man.

Corey Barker: I'm deeply indebted to you—not just for the wonderful job you did on the 3D chapter here in the book, but for the half-dozen or so times I came to you when I was stuck on a particular step, or when I needed help on how to achieve a particular look. You totally saved my butt. You are an immensely talented and gifted individual, and I'm honored to have you as a contributor to this new edition of the book. Thanks man—you rock!

Jean A. Kendra: I can't thank you enough for your constant support, understanding, and the freedom and help in accomplishing my goals, but mostly for your friendship. It means a lot.

Dave Moser: I've truly valued our friendship all these many years, and I'm thrilled with all the fun and exciting things we're able to do together. There are few people with your passion, guts, integrity, vision, and unflinching dedication to quality, and I'm glad I get to do all of this with you.

Felix Nelson: If you had nothing but your amazing Photoshop talents, you'd be in the top one-quarter of one percent of Photoshop designers in the world, but your creativity, talent, ideas, discipline, and humor put you in a league all by yourself. Thanks for everything you do—here in the book, in leading our creative team, and for your friendship and dedication.

Kim Doty: As my in-house Editor, you don't have an easy job (keeping me organized and focused), but you do it with such a great attitude, and sense of calm, that everything just somehow comes together. You make doing these books a lot of fun for me, and even though you hate doing it, thanks for bugging me to get all those little "stragglers" turned in on time. You're the best (and you even let me use three exclamation points in a row)!!!

Cindy Snyder: Thanks for all you do to make sure the projects in the book look and work just like they're supposed to. Testing my stuff, much of which is written really late at night, has got to be a hoot, and a challenge, but you always rise to the occasion, and for that I'm very grateful.

Jessica Maldonado: The look of my books all comes from you and I'm so grateful that you're the one designing them, and that our company got lucky enough to find you. I brag about you to anyone who will listen, and your creative layouts and ideas are only matched by your wonderful attitude and your unwavering dedication to each project. Thank you for giving my words such a wonderful-looking stage to play upon.

Dave Damstra: If they ever have a competition for the best page layout guy in the business, I'm sending you to steal the show. Having you lay out my books is definitely a strategic advantage and you set the standard, not only in your work, but in your amazing attitude in life, as well.

Kim Gabriel: I don't have to tell you—it ain't easy putting together one of these books, but you keep a lot of plates in the air, you keep the trains running on time, and you do a marvelous job of keeping it all moving ahead. I can't thank you enough.

Kathy Siler: You've made my job so much more enjoyable, and easier (partially because you do so much of it for me), and you do it without ever breaking a sweat. Also, it's great having someone who always looks out for me, and there's no way for me to completely thank you for all you do to make sure I have time to write these books and still have fun doing it, but thank you.

My Home Boys: A big thanks to the creative geniuses who walk the halls at Kelby Media Group and fill them with lots of laughter, incredible images, and inspirational creativity, including: RC Concepcion, Brad Moore, Jason Scrivner, Matt Kloskowski, Dave Cross, and Larry Becker.

New Riders and Peachpit Press: A big thanks to my wonderful Publisher Nancy Aldrich-Ruenzel, marketing maverick Scott Cowlin, and the entire team at Pearson Education who go out of their way to make sure that we're always working in the best interest of my readers, and who work hard to make sure my work gets in as many people's hands as possible.

Ted Waitt: As my Editor at Peachpit, it's such a pleasure working with someone who "gets me" and what I'm trying to do for my readers, and why things have to be a certain way (hey, it all counts). I'm really honored that I get to work with you.

Adobe: Thanks to all my friends at the mothership, including: Kevin Connor, John Nack, Mala Sharma, John Loiacono, Terry White, Addy Roff, Cari Gushiken, Julieanne Kost, Tom Hogarty, Jennifer Stern, Dave Story, Bryan Hughes, and Russell Preston Brown. Gone, but not forgotten: Barbara Rice, Jill Nakashima, Rye Livingston, Bryan Lamkin, Deb Whitman, and Karen Gauthier.

iStockphoto.com: My personal thanks to the great people at iStockphoto for enabling me to use some of their wonderful stock images in this book. I totally dig you guys!

Most importantly: I want to thank God, and His son Jesus Christ, for leading me to the woman of my dreams, for blessing us with two such wonderful children, for allowing me to make a living doing something I truly love, for always being there when I need Him, and for blessing me with a wonderful, fulfilling, and happy life, and such a warm, loving family to share it with.

Other Books by Scott Kelby

The Adobe Photoshop Lightroom 2 Book for Digital Photographers

The Adobe Photoshop CS4 Book for Digital Photographers

The Photoshop Channels Book

Scott Kelby's 7-Point System for Adobe Photoshop CS3

Photoshop Killer Tips

Photoshop Classic Effects

The iPhone Book

The iPod Book

The Digital Photography Book, volumes 1 & 2

The Mac OS X Leopard Book

The Photoshop Elements 7 Book for Digital Photographers

About the Authors

SCOTT KELBY

Scott is Editor, Publisher, and co-founder of *Photoshop User* magazine, Editor and Publisher of *Layers* magazine (the how-to magazine for everything Adobe), and is the host of the top-rated weekly video podcast *Photoshop User TV*, and *DTown TV* (the weekly video podcast show for Nikon dSLR shooters).

He is President of the National Association of Photoshop Professionals (NAPP), the trade association for Adobe® Photoshop® users, and he's President of the training, education, and publishing firm Kelby Media Group, Inc.

Scott is a photographer, designer, and award-winning author of more than 50 books, including *Scott Kelby's 7-Point System for Adobe Photoshop CS3*, *The Adobe Photoshop CS4 Book for Digital Photographers*, *The Photoshop Channels Book*, *Photoshop Classic Effects*, *The iPhone Book*, *The iPod Book*, and *The Digital Photography Book*, volumes 1 & 2.

For five years straight, Scott has been honored with the distinction of being the world's #1 best-selling author of all computer and technology books, across all categories. His groundbreaking book, *The Digital Photography Book*, volume 1, is now the best-selling book on digital photography in history.

His books have been translated into dozens of different languages, including Chinese, Russian, Spanish, Korean, Polish, Taiwanese, French, German, Italian, Japanese, Dutch, Swedish, Turkish, and Portuguese, among others, and he is a recipient of the prestigious Benjamin Franklin Award.

Scott is Training Director for the Adobe Photoshop Seminar Tour and Conference Technical Chair for the Photoshop World Conference & Expo. He's featured in a series of Adobe Photoshop training DVDs and online courses at KelbyTraining.com and has been training Adobe Photoshop users since 1993.

For more information on Scott, visit his daily blog, *Photoshop Insider*, at www.scottkelby.com.

COREY BARKER

Contributing author Corey Barker is an education and curriculum developer for the National Association of Photoshop Professionals, and teaches at major Photoshop events like the Photoshop World Conference & Expo. He has a regular column in *Photoshop User* magazine and *Layers* magazine (the how-to magazine for everything Adobe), and is co-host of the highly rated podcast *Layers TV*. Corey is also Executive Producer of the highly popular tutorial and blog website PlanetPhotoshop.com. He is an award-winning illustrator and designer with over 14 years of industry experience, and is an Adobe Certified Expert in Photoshop.

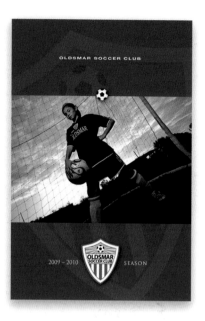

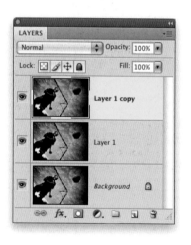

Nine Quick Things You'll Wish You Had Known Before Reading This Book

It's really important to me that you get a lot out of reading this book, and one way I can help is to get you to read these nine quick things about the book that you'll wish later you knew. For example, it's here where I tell you about where to download something important, and if you skip over this, eventually you'll send me an email asking where it is, but by then, you'll be really aggravated, and well—it's just gonna get ugly. We can skip all that (and more), if you take two minutes now and read these nine quick things. I promise to make it worth your while.

(1) You don't have to read this book in order

This is a "jump-in-anywhere" book. I designed it so you can turn right to the effect you want to learn, and start right there—you don't have to start at Chapter One and work your way through it in order. *By the way, the screen captures here are just for looks, so the pages don't look empty (they're a sneak peek at some of the projects you're going to learn). Hey, how things look really matters!*

(2) Practice along with the same photos I used here in the book

The idea behind this book is to show you techniques that you can apply to your own work, but while you're practicing, you might not have the exact image you need for a particular technique right there at your fingertips, so I made some of the same images you see here in the book available, so you can practice along using them. The photos are either ones I took, or royalty-free stock photos from our friends at iStockphoto.com, who were gracious enough to allow me to make their wonderful stock images available to you for download. There are also a few images created by my contributing author, Corey Barker. You can download them at **www.kelbytraining.com/books/CS4DD** (see, this is one of those things I was talking about that you'd miss if you skipped this and went right into the book).

Now the story can be told....

L'ÉGOUT

100 ml

(3) I tried to use fonts you already have on your computer

A lot of these techniques, since they're based on real examples, have type as a part of the design, so in most cases, I tried to use fonts that come with Photoshop CS4 and get installed automatically when you install Photoshop. In a few cases, I had to use fonts you may not have, and in those cases I made a layered Photoshop file with a rasterized version of the type available for download from the book's downloads page (see #2). That way, even if you don't have the font, you can still do the technique.

(4) If you're a more experienced user, don't let this thing drive you crazy

I wrote this book so any user, at any level of experience, can jump right in and do these same effects. Because of that, the first time I mention to do something in a project (like create a new layer), I spell everything out so nobody gets left behind. But I only spell it out that first time in a tutorial, then later I just say "create a new layer." If you can't remember how you created a layer just two or three steps ago, maybe learning Photoshop shouldn't be your biggest concern. Anyway, if you're more advanced, don't let the fact that I spell everything out throw you. Again, it's just a few extra words, and you can bounce right by it if you already know how to do it, so don't let it slow you down.

(5) The intro page at the beginning of each chapter is not what it seems

The introductions at the beginning of each chapter are there to give you a quick mental break between chapters, and honestly, they have little to do with what's in the chapter. In fact, they have little to do with anything, but writing these quirky chapter intros has become kind of a tradition of mine (I do this in all my books), so if you're one of those really "serious" types, I'm begging you—skip them and just go right into the chapter, because they'll just get on your nerves.

(6) Why I give you specific sizes and resolutions for each project

It's because those sizes work with the low-resolution source images you're downloading to practice with. We usually couldn't make the high-resolution versions available (for copyright reasons), but luckily these 72-ppi low-resolution images look perfectly crisp and sharp onscreen.

(7) Corey's contribution to this book

In the Extended version of Photoshop CS4, Adobe really improved the 3D capabilities they introduced back in Photoshop CS3 Extended. I really wanted to include some of these cool new 3D effects here in the book, but the problem is I'm not a 3D guy. Luckily, I work with the amazing Corey Barker (who is a 3D genius guy) and I asked (begged) Corey to write the 3D chapter, and it totally rocks! Not only did Corey write the book's 3D chapter, but he also created some bonus videos for you. Check them out on the book's downloads page (again, see #2 for the Web address).

(8) Read the lead-ins at the beginning of each individual project

Those short little lead-ins up at the top of each project are worth reading. Sometimes, they just tell you what the project you're about to work on is based on (and that helps frame it in your mind), but often they explain a key concept that will help you better understand the project. Either way, they're very short and worth the few seconds it takes to read them.

(9) This is a special effects book that's not really about special effects

You probably bought this book to learn a bunch of cool special effects (and you will), but although this appears to be a book about special effects, it's really a book about learning the "other side" of Photoshop (the parts beyond the most common stuff, like color correction, sharpening, Camera Raw, and stuff like that). Of course, when I wrote the first edition of this book (nine years ago), I thought I was writing a special effects book, but through the years (and the three other editions of this book), I've received literally thousands of emails and letters from readers who've told me that this is the book that they feel really unlocked Photoshop's power to them and took their understanding and use of Photoshop to an entirely different level. I also heard the same thing from educators around the world, who use previous editions of this book as their classroom textbook on Photoshop. Because of that, in this edition of the book, I give a lot more of the "why" about particular things you're doing—much more so than in any previous editions of the book. Also, some of the projects are a little more ambitious (and have more steps) in this book than previous editions, but don't let that scare you away—just follow the steps and you'll be able to do each and every effect. Lastly, because this is really about learning Photoshop at a whole 'nuther level, I really encourage you to do each project, even if it's one where the final image isn't one that you might use in your line of work. You'll still find techniques and concepts in there that you can apply to your work in other ways (and you'll learn things you wouldn't have otherwise learned, and that's a good thing, right?). Anyway, thanks for taking a few minutes to read this, and I really hope it helps you to get the most out of the book. Now, let's get to work!

CHAPTER

Miracle Photo

photo effects, part 1

These chapter intros are all named after either song titles, movies, or TV shows, and this chapter is named after the song "Miracle Photo," by a band called Ruth (which is an all-guy band, which is what makes the name cool, right? Because if it was an all-guy band and they named it Mike, it would sound totally uncool, unless of course, no one in the band was named Mike, which would then make the name cool again. Now, if they were named Mike and really wanted to take it up a notch, they'd have to concoct a story about how their first agent was named Mike, but then he was killed in a freak combine accident, or that Mike was the club owner of the first paid gig they ever played as a band, but then he was killed in a freak combine accident). Anyway, when I first saw the name of their song "Miracle Photo," it reminded me of those stories you hear on the news where a farmer out in the Midwest finds a potato in the shape of Elvis's head, and people come from hundreds of miles around to see it because they feel it's some sort of message from beyond, like Elvis is trying to contact us through starch. You might think I'm crazy, but I believe that's exactly what these bizarre discoveries are, which are too eerily coincidental to be any-thing but authentic communications from beyond the grave, and in this particular situation, I think the message is clear— stay away from combines.

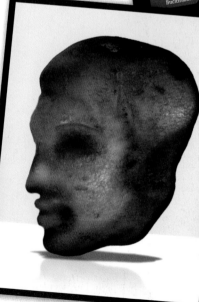

Desaturated Portrait Look

This desaturated look is one of the most popular looks out there right now in high-end portrait photography, and you also see it used pretty often in automotive shots, or any type of photo where you want a really dark and dramatic sky. The challenge in adding this effect is with your subject's skin tone—sometimes it looks great, and sometimes it makes your subjects look washed out, but you won't know until you see the final image. In this project, you'll learn what to do if you run into the latter.

STEP ONE: Open the image you want to apply the effect to and then press **Command-J (PC: Ctrl-J)** to duplicate your Background layer. Press that keyboard shortcut again to duplicate that layer one more time (so you have your background and two copies above it, as seen here).

STEP TWO: Go to the Layers panel and hide the top layer from view by clicking on the Eye icon to the left of the layer's thumbnail. Click on the middle layer (shown highlighted here) and then press **Command-Shift-U (PC: Ctrl-Shift-U)** to remove the color from this layer. Now, go up to the Opacity slider and lower the Opacity to 80% (as shown here) to let just a tiny bit of the color come back into this layer.

STEP THREE: Make the top layer visible again by clicking where the Eye icon used to be, then click on this top layer to make it active. Change the layer blend mode of this top layer from Normal to Soft Light (as shown here), which adds more contrast to the image, and brings back more of the color. Now, you could just flatten the image and be done right at this point, and a lot of people will do just that, because they like how the desaturated skin tone looks. Generally, I like to go another step or two to bring back most, but not all, of the original flesh-tone skin colors. So, if you want to learn how to do that (it's easy), then go on to the next step.

STEP FOUR: Press **Command-Option-Shift-E (PC: Ctrl-Alt-Shift-E)** to create a new layer at the top of the layer stack that is a flattened version of your image, and then get the History Brush tool **(Y)** from the Toolbox. I always think of the History Brush as "undo on a brush," and if you started painting over your entire image with it, it would return it to how it looked when you first opened it. We're going to use this brush (in the next step) to bring back the original skin tone of our soccer player, and the original purple and yellow colors in her uniform.

Continued

STEP FIVE: From the Brush Picker in the Options Bar, choose a medium-sized soft-edged brush, then take the History Brush and start painting over the soccer player. Make sure you paint over her uniform, as well (as shown here). When you're done, the original skin tone and uniform colors are back, but now, with the rest of the colors desaturated, her skin color looks a little too vibrant. There are two ways to fix this: The first is to undo your painting with the History Brush (press **Command-Z [PC: Ctrl-Z]** if you only made one continuous brush stroke or **Command-Option-Z [PC: Ctrl-Alt-Z]** if you made multiple brush strokes, or just click on your merged layer and drag it onto the Trash icon at the bottom of the Layers panel and then create a new one). Then lower the History Brush's Opacity (up in the Options Bar) to around 60%, paint over her again, and now you'll only bring back 60% of her original skin tone. Here's a little trick you might want to consider: paint over her skin tones at 60%, then go back up to the Options Bar, raise the Opacity back up to 100%, then paint over her uniform, which will bring back those original vibrant colors. It's a little more work, but I think you'll like the result.

STEP SIX: The second method is to paint over all of her with the History Brush at its default opacity of 100%, then just lower the Opacity of this layer to 60%, giving you the look you see here, which I think looks very natural with the desaturated surroundings. I wanted to give you both techniques and let you see which one you like the best for the particular photo you're working on.

SCOTT KELBY

STEP SEVEN: Here's a before/after using the second History Brush method. By the way, the reason her skin tone looks yellowish is because I put a gel over my off-camera flash to mimic the setting sun (I used a half-cut of CTO [color temperature orange] gel taped over the front of the flash).

STEP EIGHT: Here's a shot of the goalie's brother taken at the same shoot, but a little later, as the sun was going down. I used the exact same technique on him as I did with her (the second method).

Football Layout Turned Corporate

I actually saw this layout in a Snickers print ad for a contest promotion where you could win Super Bowl tickets. Anyway, although the ad featured players from the two teams in the Super Bowl that year, I thought this same type of sports-look layout would work great for other groups of people and other topics (like business managers, or delivery people, or "employee of the month" layouts, etc.). So, we're going to build that same look here from scratch, but we're going to apply it in a different way.

STEP ONE: Start by creating a new document that's 5x7" at a resolution of 240 ppi. Click on your Foreground color swatch and choose a light gray, then fill your Background layer with this light gray by pressing **Option-Delete (PC: Alt-Backspace)**. The graphic we're going to build in this document is 3 inches wide by 4 inches deep, and it will make your job a lot easier if you drag out some guides now. So, press **Command-R (PC: Ctrl-R)** to make your Rulers visible, then go up to the top ruler, click-and-hold on the ruler, drag down a horizontal guide, and place it 1" from the top. Then drag down another guide and place it at the 5" mark. Now drag a vertical guide from the left ruler out to the 1" mark, and then drag another to the 4" mark (so you have a tall rectangle made up of guides like you see here).

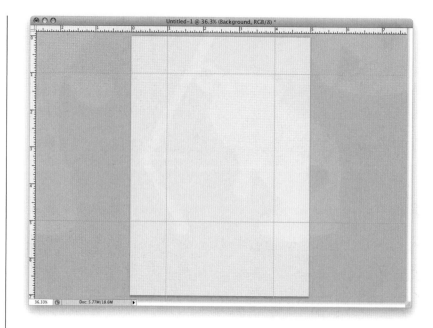

STEP TWO: Get the Polygonal Lasso tool (**L**; shown here), press-and-hold the Shift key, then use the tool to draw the shape you see here. By pressing-and-holding the Shift key, not only will it draw straight selections, but it will automatically give you exact 45° angles in the corners. If you make a mistake, just press the Delete (PC: Backspace) key and it will undo your last click of the Polygonal Lasso tool. When you get back to the point where you started, just click and it will complete the shape.

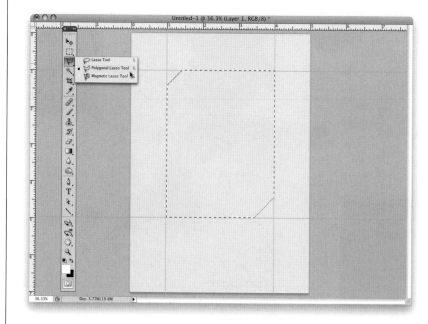

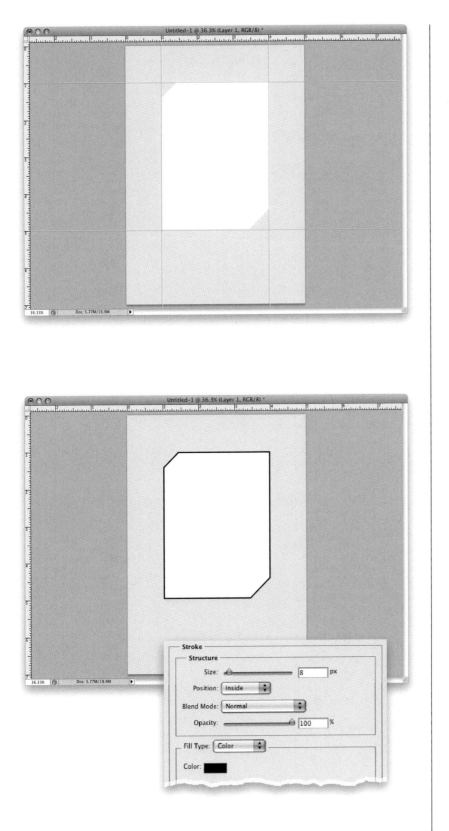

STEP THREE: Now go to the Layers panel and click on the Create a New Layer icon at the bottom of the panel to create a new blank layer. Press the letter **D**, then **X** on your keyboard to set your Foreground color to white, fill your selection with this white Foreground color (as seen here) using the same shortcut we used in Step One to fill the layer, and then press **Command-D (PC: Ctrl-D)** to Deselect (since we don't need the selection anymore). By the way—the reason we made the background light gray in Step One was so you could see the white shape stand out at this point. If not, it would be pretty tough to see a white-filled shape on a white background.

STEP FOUR: You don't need the guides any longer (after all, your shape is in place), so go under the View menu and choose Clear Guides. Now you're going to add a stroke around the shape using a layer style. Click on the Add a Layer Style icon at the bottom of the Layers panel, and choose Stroke from the pop-up menu. When the Layer Style dialog appears, set the stroke's Size to 8 px, set the Position to Inside (which makes the corners nice and sharp. If you leave it set to Outside, then the corners start to become rounded), then change the Color to black (all of this is shown here), and click OK to apply this black stroke around your white shape (as seen here).

Continued

STEP FIVE: Press-and-hold the Command (PC: Ctrl) key, then go to the Layers panel and click once directly on the top layer's thumbnail to put a selection around your shape. Now, you'll need to deselect just the top three-quarters of your selected shape, and to do that you press-and-hold the Option (PC: Alt) key, then get the Rectangular Marquee tool **(M)**, and click-and-drag out a square selection around the top three-quarters of your selected shape (as shown here).

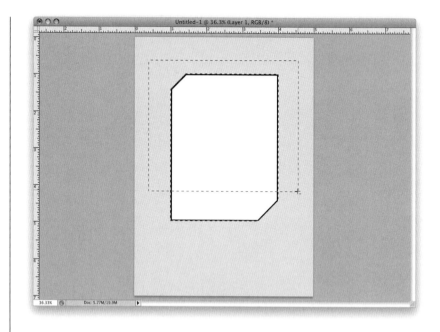

STEP SIX: Once you release the mouse button, it deselects the top three-quarters of your shape, leaving just the bottom quarter still selected (you can see it still selected here). Create another new blank layer, set your Foreground color to red, then fill that bottom-quarter selected area with red, as seen here. Now, you can deselect that bottom quarter.

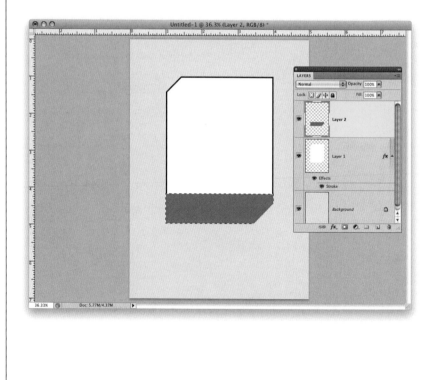

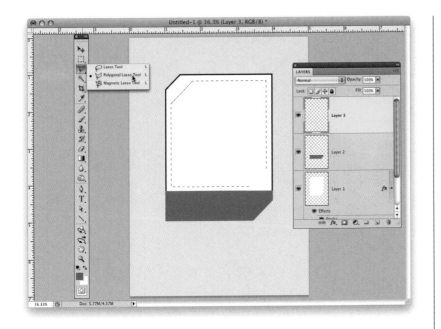

STEP SEVEN: Next, add one more new blank layer, get the Polygonal Lasso tool again, and now you're going to draw the shape that holds your photo. It's similar to the shape you drew earlier, but you're going to draw this shape inside your existing shape. So, press-and-hold the Shift key and use the Polygonal Lasso tool to draw the selection shape you see here (you don't really need to pull out guides to do this, but if you feel you need to, go for it).

STEP EIGHT: Once your selection is in place, click on your Foreground color swatch and set a light gray as your Foreground color, then fill your new selection shape with this light gray. Now, you can deselect.

Continued

STEP NINE: We have two more smaller shapes to draw before our basic cell is complete. Get the Rectangular Marquee tool again, press-and-hold the Shift key (so when you use the tool it makes perfectly square selections), then click-and-drag out a square selection at the bottom-left corner of the white area of your shape (as shown here).

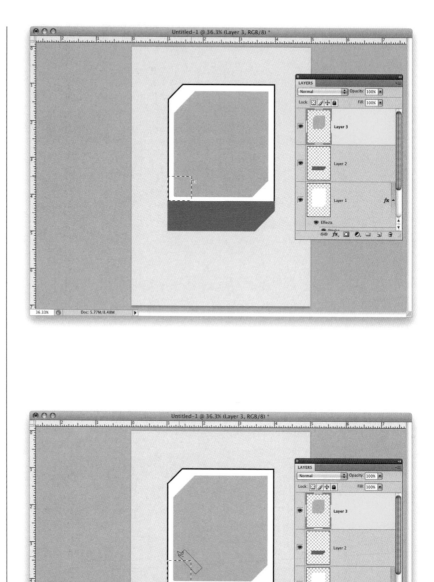

STEP 10: Now you need to cut off the top-right corner of your selection, and we're going to do this pretty much like how we removed the top of the main shape back in Step Five. Get the Polyg-onal Lasso tool, press-and-hold the Option (PC: Alt) key, so you're subtract-ing from the current selection, and then draw a line over the top-right corner of your square selection. You'll need to make a complete selection now, so just draw a little rectangle (like the one shown here), and when it's complete, it deletes the top-right corner, but leaves the rest of the selection in place.

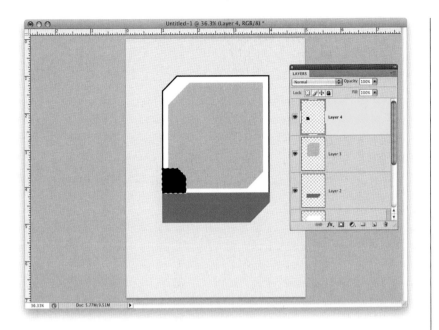

STEP 11: Once your selection is in place, create another new blank layer, then press **D** to set black as your Foreground color, and fill your selected area with black, as shown here. Now you can de-select. For our second (and final) shape, you'll need to go to the Layers panel, click on the Background layer, and create a new blank layer (which gives you a blank layer right below your original white shape).

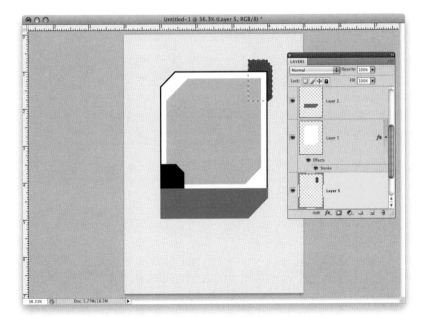

STEP 12: Take the Polygonal Lasso tool, press-and-hold the Shift key, and draw the shape you see here, which is another version of the two other shapes you've already drawn. Once the shape is in place, set your Foreground color to a dark gray, then fill your selected shape with your Foreground color, as seen here. Go ahead and deselect.

Continued

STEP 13: Now for a little special touch. Get the Rectangular Marquee tool and make a really thin rectangular selection (like the one you see here, where I zoomed way in so you could see it), then fill it with black, and deselect. I know, this is an awfully little thing, but it's all about the little things, right? Next, you'll need to make this dark gray layer and the white main shape layer into just one single layer. To do that, go to the Layers panel, click on the white shape layer, then press **Command-E (PC: Ctrl-E)**, which merges this white layer with the layer directly beneath it (the dark gray shape layer).

STEP 14: You're going to add a drop shadow to this newly merged layer, so click on the Add a Layer Style icon at the bottom of the Layers panel and choose Drop Shadow from the pop-up menu. When the Layer Style dialog appears, set the Angle to 39°, the Distance to 22 px, and the Size to 32 px (as seen here), then click OK to give you a soft drop shadow, set down and to the left, like you see here.

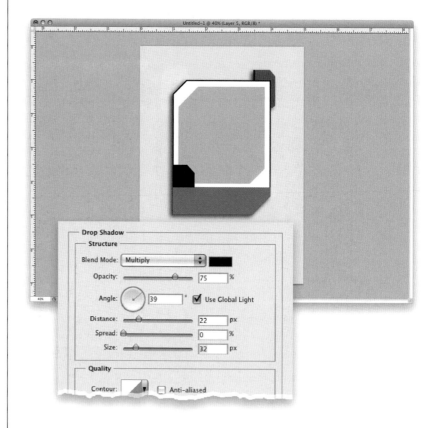

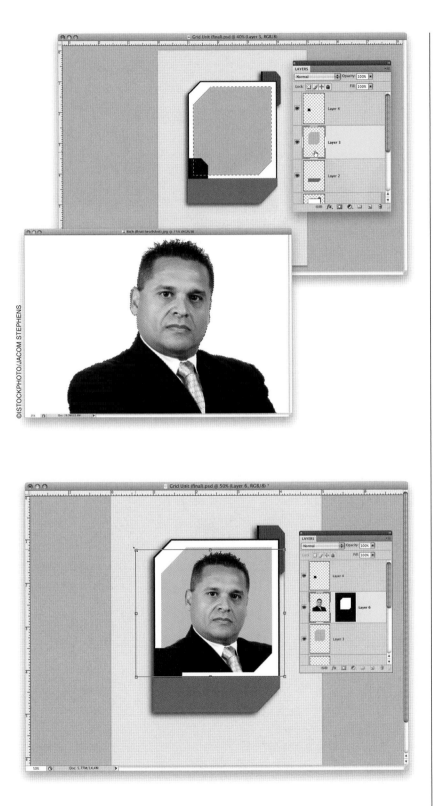

©ISTOCKPHOTO/JACOM STEPHENS

STEP 15: In this step, you're going to put a photo inside the gray shape you created inside the white shape. In the Layers panel, click on the gray shape layer, then press-and-hold the Command (PC: Ctrl) key and click on the layer's thumbnail to put a selection around the gray shape (as shown here). Now, open the photo you want inside the gray shape. To make it easy to select the subject, he was shot on a white seamless paper background (remember, you can download this same image to follow along with—the Web address for the book's downloads page is listed in the book's intro). Click the Magic Wand tool (press **Shift-W** to get it) once on the background to select it (you may have to Shift-click in one of the top corners to get the entire background selected), then press **Command-Shift-I (PC: Ctrl-Shift-I)** to Inverse the selection, so that instead of having the background selected, you have the subject selected. Press **Command-C (PC: Ctrl-C)** to Copy your subject into memory.

STEP 16: Switch back to the document we created, go under the Edit menu, and choose Paste Into to paste the photo you just copied into memory into your selected area. When your photo appears pasted inside that selection, you may need to use Free Transform to scale it to fit inside the box, and reposition it. So, press **Command-T (PC: Ctrl-T)** to bring up Free Transform, press-and-hold the Shift key to keep your resizing proportional, then grab a corner point and drag inward to scale the photo down to size or outward to scale it up. If you can't reach the Free Transform handles, press **Command-0 (zero; PC: Ctrl-0)** and the image window will resize so you can reach the handles. When you're done, just press **Return (PC: Enter)** to lock in your transformation.

Continued

STEP 17: It's time to add some text (like the person's name, a fictitious player number, and a two-letter title, as if they had a football position, like LB for Linebacker or QB for Quarterback, but in a corporate version of this look, it could be VP or CEO, GM, etc.), so grab the Horizontal Type tool **(T)** and make some up. The font I used here is Rockwell, but you can use any font you'd like (if you want Rockwell, I found it at www.fonts.com for $29). Once your type is in place, you'll need to do one thing that will help with the next step: Scroll down to the layer where your photo was pasted in. You'll see a thumbnail of the photo and, to the right of it, a black layer mask thumbnail. You need to click once directly between these two thumbnails, and a Link icon will appear, linking the mask with the photo (as shown here). You'll need to do this now, so you can resize this entire image later.

STEP 18: Press-and-hold the Command (PC: Ctrl) key, and in the Layers panel, click on every layer (except the Background layer) to select them (your selected layers will appear highlighted). Then, from the flyout menu at the top right of the Layers panel, choose New Group from Layers (as shown here). This puts all your layers into one folder (called a Group in layer-speak), which makes working with all these layers much easier (really, that's why you'd make a group in the first place—because once you start to have a lot of layers, things can become really cluttered and confusing. Imagine how crazy things would be on your computer if you didn't use folders to organize things, eh?).

STEP 19: Open a new document in the size you want your final document to be (in this case, I created an 8.5x11" letter-sized document at a resolution of 240 ppi). Go back to your original document and, in the Layers panel, click on the layer named "Group 1" and drag-and-drop it right onto your new document. Now you can resize the group of layers as if they were just one layer. Bring up Free Transform, press-and-hold the Shift key (to keep your resizing proportional), grab any corner point, and drag inward to shrink the size of the group (as shown here). Make it small enough so you can make a row of five of them across, then lock in your resizing.

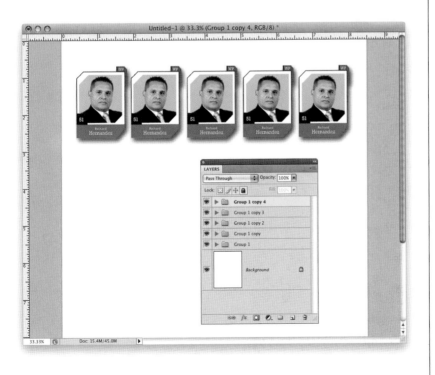

STEP 20: Get the Move tool **(V)**, press-and-hold **Option-Shift (PC: Alt-Shift)**, then click directly on the group itself out in the image area (not in the Layers panel). Now, drag to the right, and the entire group will be duplicated (you're basically dragging a copy. That's what holding the Option key does—when you hold it, it makes a copy [duplicate] of whatever you're dragging with the Move tool. The reason you're holding the Shift key is to make sure your duplicate stays perfectly aligned with the original). Drag yourself out four copies, until you have five across like you see here (if you look in the Layers panel, you'll see you now have five groups).

Continued

STEP 21: Make sure you still have the Move tool, then press-and-hold the Command (PC: Ctrl) key, go to the Layers panel, and click on the second and fourth layer groups from the top (as shown here). Press the Down Arrow key on your keyboard 10 times to move those two selected groups down a little from the rest (as seen here).

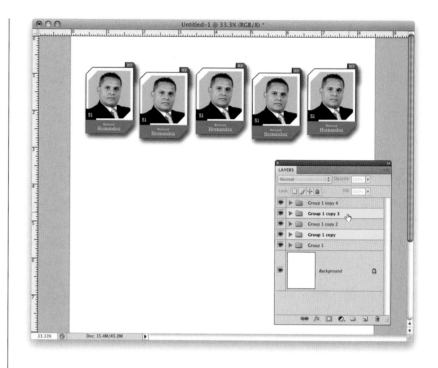

STEP 22: Now select all five groups in the Layers panel, then press-and-hold Option-Shift (PC: Alt-Shift), click on any one of the five groups in the image area, and drag straight downward to duplicate all five groups, creating a second row of five (as seen here). *Note:* If you're going to be photographing the people on your team, to get a more realistic "football" look, don't have them angle their shoulders (like a traditional portrait). Instead, have them pose more like a standard football player shot, with their shoulders flat, facing directly toward the camera.

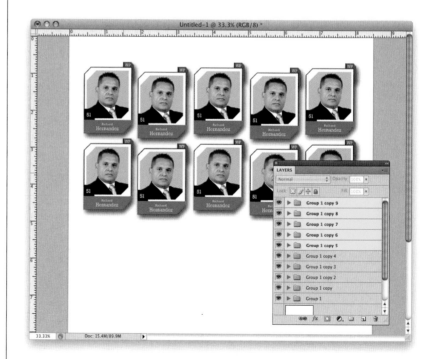

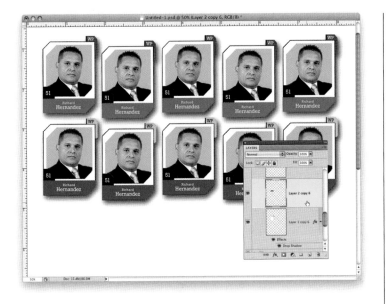

STEP 23: You can change the colors of the bottom row if you'd like, and you do that by going to one of the duplicate groups in the Layers panel, expanding the group by clicking on the little right-facing arrow beside the folder, and then scrolling down to the layer with the red bar. Choose a new Foreground color, and fill this bar with your new color (purple, in this case) by pressing **Option-Shift-Delete (PC: Alt-Shift-Backspace)**. Now, in the Layers panel, click on the white shape layer, then take the Magic Wand tool and click it on the dark gray area at the top right to select that area. Choose a contrasting Foreground color (I chose yellow), and fill your selected area with this new Foreground color. Finally, get the Horizontal Type tool, click on the layer for the type that appears on that upper tab, then highlight it and change the text color from white to black (click on the color swatch up in the Options Bar). Repeat this process for the other four cells on the bottom row.

STEP 24: Now you're going to add a background photo. In this case, we're going to use a football-on-the-field shot, in keeping with the theme (you can download this same background shot, if you'd like, from this book's downloads page, listed in the book's intro). Once you open the background photo, get the Move tool, and drag-and-drop that background photo onto your main document. Then, in the Layers panel, click-and-drag it so it appears just above the Background layer (that way it appears behind all the cells you created earlier).

Continued

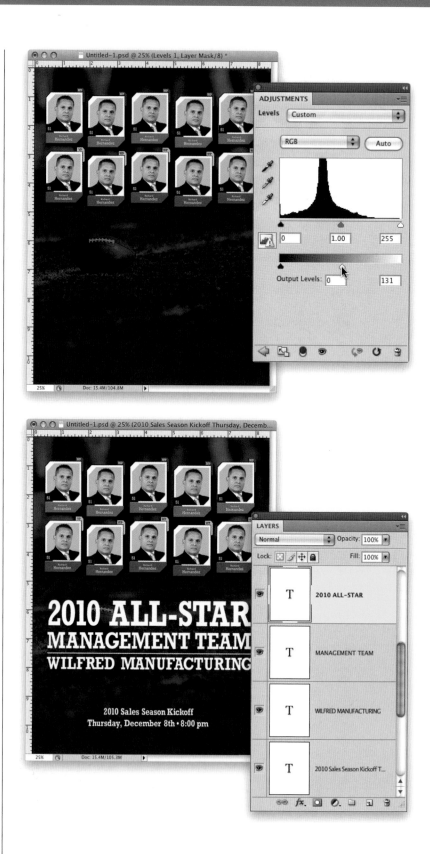

STEP 25: You're going to make an adjustment to that background photo, so it doesn't distract or compete with the cells you created. Start by removing all the color from the photo by pressing **Command-Shift-U (PC: Ctrl-Shift-U)**, which is the shortcut for Desaturate. Next, go to the Adjustments panel and click on the Levels icon (the second icon from the left in the top row). When the Levels options appear, drag the bottom-right Output Levels slider to the left (as shown here) to darken the overall image, which helps to make your cells stand out.

STEP 26: We're almost done. Now, you can add any text you'd like below the whole cell area. Here, I added a few lines of text with the Horizontal Type tool, using the same font that I used for the "players" names in each cell. The key to doing the stacked lines of type, and making it look good, is to not add space between the letters to make each line fit—instead you increase (or decrease) the size of the font until it's a perfect fit. It also helps to pull out vertical guides (from the rulers) before you start sizing your text—that makes it much easier to align each line of type. After the type is in place, get the Line tool (it's one of the Shape tools—press **Shift-U** until you have it), click on the Shape Layers icon at the left end of the Options Bar, and then set the Weight (also in the Options Bar) to 8 px. Make sure your Foreground color is set to white, then press-and-hold the Shift key, and draw a line separating the company name from the "MANAGEMENT TEAM" line.

STEP 27: Now that you've got the whole thing designed, it's time to swap out our original team member placeholder photo with the real members of your management team (or tag football league, or employees of the month, etc.). To do that, switch to the Move tool, press-and-hold the Command (PC: Ctrl) key and, right within your image, click once on the cell you want to edit, and that layer group will become selected in the Layers panel (that's an awfully handy shortcut). Now, expand that layer group, scroll down to the photo layer and drag it onto the Trash icon at the bottom of the Layers panel to delete it. Click on the gray shape layer to make it the active layer, then Command-click (PC: Ctrl-click) right on the layer's thumbnail to put a selection around that gray shape.

STEP 28: We're going to do what we did back in Steps 15–16, which is open the photo you want to appear in this next cell, put a selection around your subject, copy that selection into memory, then return to this main document, and choose Paste Into from the Edit menu. Then you'll use Free Transform to resize your subject to fit properly in the cell, and you'll go to the Layers panel to update the Type layers with your subject's name, player number, and two-or-three letter position. You'll do this for each of the remaining cells (hey, I didn't say this was a quick technique, but the good news is that as long as you save a copy with the layers intact, you can use this as a template for a quick update in the future).

Reflected Sky Logo Technique

I saw this technique in a logo for the company that created the video game *Project Gotham Racing*, and what caught my eye from the standard Web reflection look is that the reflection actually came from a photograph, and that really made it stand out from the rest. Although that reflection part is fairly simple, there's a bit of setup to get to the part of the logo where the reflection is added, so we get to learn an awful lot along the way (which is really what this book is all about, eh?).

STEP ONE: Create a new document by going under the File menu and choosing New. In the New dialog, choose Web from the Preset pop-up menu, under Size, choose 800x600, and click OK. Get the Rounded Rectangle tool from the Toolbox (shown here in the Shape tools, or press **Shift-U** until you have it), then go up to the Options Bar and click on the third icon from the left (so your shape is just made up of regular pixels, rather than being a Shape layer [the default] or a path [which is what the second icon gives you]). Also, you'll need to make the corners a little more rounded, so increase the Radius amount (shown circled in red here) to 15 pixels (the default setting is 10—the higher the number, the more rounded the corners become). Now, click on the Create a New Layer icon at the bottom of the Layers panel, press **D** to set black as your Foreground color, then click-and-drag out a wide rectangular shape, like the one you see here.

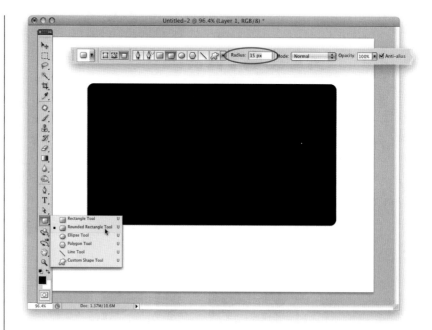

STEP TWO: Now you're going to create a gradient that goes from dark red to bright red to dark red again. The easiest way to do this is to edit an existing three-color gradient. Get the Gradient tool **(G)**, then go up to the Options Bar and click on the gradient thumbnail to bring up the Gradient Editor. Click on the eighth gradient in the top row (Orange, Yellow, Orange). To change the color of the gradient, just double-click on the little color stops under the gradient ramp in the middle of the dialog and the Color Picker appears, where you can choose your colors (so choose dark red on both ends, and a bright red for the middle stop).

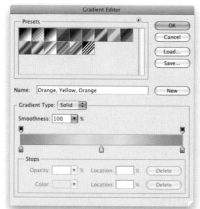

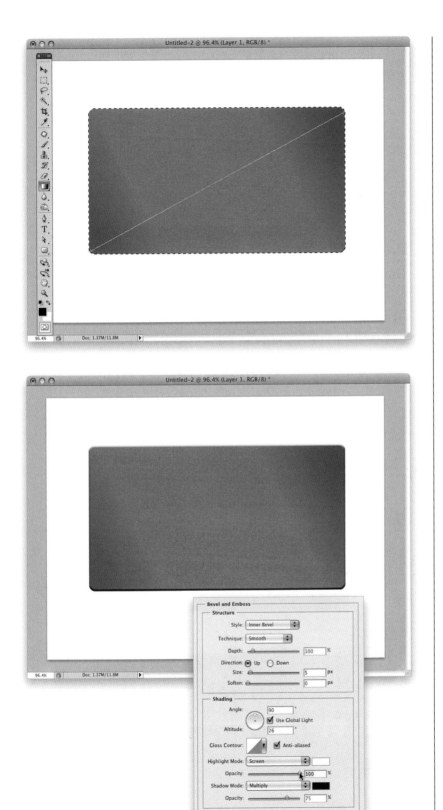

STEP THREE: Click OK once your gradient colors are in place. Now go to the Layers panel, press-and-hold the Command (PC: Ctrl) key and click directly on the thumbnail of the layer with your shape to put a selection around your shape (seen here). Then take the Gradient tool and click-and-drag it diagonally from the bottom-left corner to the top-right corner of your selected shape to apply this gradient over your shape (as I did here). Press **Command-D (PC: Ctrl-D)** to Deselect.

STEP FOUR: We need to add a slight bevel to the shape (mostly to get a highlight along the top of the shape), so click on the Add a Layer Style icon at the bottom of the Layers panel and choose Bevel and Emboss from the pop-up menu. When the Layer Style dialog appears, set the Depth to 100%. Then in the Shading section, set the Angle to 90° (so the highlights appear right across the top), the Altitude to 26°, then increase the Highlight Mode Opacity to 100% (as shown here) to really make that highlight bright.

Continued

STEP FIVE: Now you'll need to add a thin black stroke around the shape, so if you clicked OK, choose Stroke from the Add a Layer Style icon's pop-up menu (or if you still have the Layer Style dialog open, you can just click on Stroke in the list of layer styles on the left). In the Stroke options, increase the Size to 3 px (you can leave all the rest of the settings at their default), and click OK to apply a black stroke around the shape (seen here). *Note:* If you previously changed your stroke color, click on the color swatch and choose black in the Color Picker.

STEP SIX: Next, you'll need to select the bottom quarter of the shape, and there's a pretty cool trick for doing just that. Get the Rectangular Marquee tool **(M)** and draw a rectangular selection loosely around the bottom quarter of this shape (it will extend beyond the sides and bottom, but don't worry—that's what the trick is). Once your selection is in place, switch to the Move tool **(V)**, then press the Up Arrow key on your keyboard one time and it will automatically snap to the edges of your shape (as seen here). I know—that's a way cool tip. The reason it works is because your shape is on its own layer, and your selection has nowhere to go but to snap to the edges. Now, set your Foreground color to black, press **Option-Delete (PC: Alt-Backspace)** to fill this selection with black, then deselect.

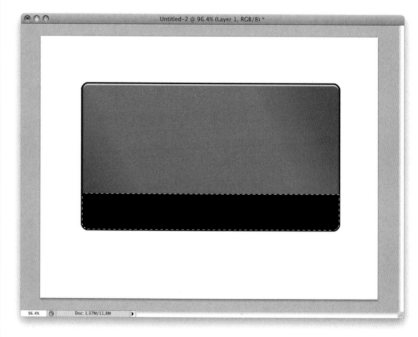

SCOTT KELBY

STEP SEVEN: Open a photo of an outdoor scene (you can download the photo shown below from the book's downloads page, mentioned in the intro of the book). With the Move tool, click on this photo and drag-and-drop it onto your main document, and position it like I have here—with the top of the photo extending off the top of the image area. *Note:* If you have Photoshop set up to use tabbed images, drag the image up to your red-and-black document's tab, hover there until the red-and-black image appears, then drag down over the red-and-black image and drop the photo onto it. If you don't have tabbed documents, but can't see both images, go under the Window menu, under Arrange, and choose Cascade.

STEP EIGHT: Click on the Create a New Layer icon at the bottom of the Layers panel to create a new blank layer, then get the Rounded Rectangle tool again, but this time drag out a wide, thin rectangle like the one you see here. Once you've drawn it, go to the Layers panel, press-and-hold the Command (PC: Ctrl) key, and click directly on this layer's thumbnail to put a selection around your thin wide shape. Now that your selection is in place, you really don't need that Shape layer any longer (you just needed the selection—not the shape), so you can drag that Shape layer onto the Trash icon at the bottom of the Layers panel to delete it.

Continued

STEP NINE: Since you deleted that Shape layer, you're now back on the photo layer (and your selection is still in place), so press **Command-Shift-I (PC: Ctrl-Shift-I)** to Inverse your selection, so everything is selected except the photo inside that thin, wide rectangle. Press the Delete (PC: Backspace) key to delete all parts of the photo surrounding that rectangle (as seen here). Now, you can deselect.

STEP 10: Next, you'll have the bottom of the photo fade into the background, and to do that, click on the Add Layer Mask icon at the bottom of the Layers panel (it's the third icon from the left, shown circled here in red). Now, get the Gradient tool, go up to the Options Bar and click on the down-facing arrow to the right of the gradient thumbnail to get the Gradient Picker, and choose the third gradient from the left in the top row (the Black, White gradient). Take the Gradient tool, click it just above the bottom of your photo, and drag upward to have your photo fade away at the bottom of the image (as seen here).

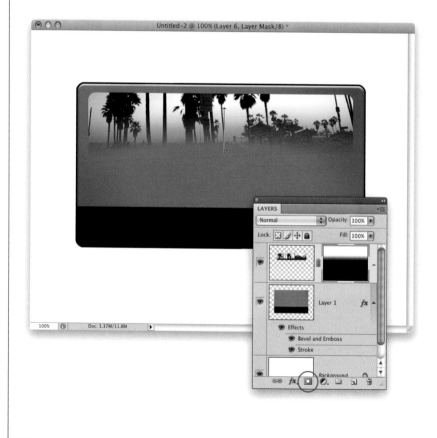

STEP 11: To really see the effect appear, you have two more simple changes to make: (1) go to the Layers panel and change the layer blend mode from Normal to Screen, which makes the photo lighter and somewhat see-through, and (2) lower the Opacity to 40%, where, at that point, it gets its reflective look (as seen here), almost like the reflection of the world outside on a window.

STEP 12: Now, click back on the red rectangle layer and choose Drop Shadow from the Add a Layer Style icon's pop-up menu at the bottom of the Layers panel. Set the Angle to 48°, increase the Distance to 13, the Size to 21, and click OK to add a drop shadow to the lower left. Lastly, add some text, using the Horizontal Type tool **(T)**, to finish things off (the text "CSR" is set in the font Satisfaction, which costs $15 from MyFonts.com, and the "Sports Fashion" text font is Eurostile Bold Extended).

Stacking Photos Collage

I saw this technique in an ad for HP printers, and although at first glance it looks like a bunch of photos thrown together, there actually is a layout and more organization than you might think. It starts with using the right number and type of photos, and then arranging them in a particular way. Here's how it's done:

STEP ONE: For this particular layout, you'll need 17 photos, and ideally they should all relate to each other in some way (so they might all be vacation photos, or family photos, or photos of flowers, etc.). So, start by putting your 17 photos in a folder. Then go under Photoshop's File menu and choose New. When the New dialog appears (seen here), choose a letter-sized page (8.5x11") at whatever resolution you want to use (I usually print to a color inkjet printer, so I'm using 240 ppi as my resolution), then click OK to create a new blank document.

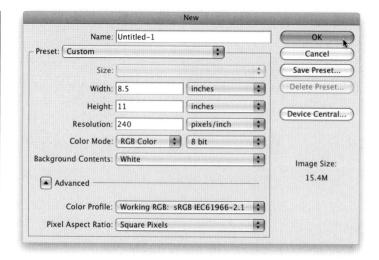

STEP TWO: Pick the image you want as the main focal point of your collage, open it, and use the Move tool **(V)** to drag it into your blank document. Now press **Command-T (PC: Ctrl-T)** to bring up Free Transform, so we can scale the image down in size—just press-and-hold the Shift key, grab a corner point, and drag inward (as shown here) until the image is about the size you see here. Press **Return (PC: Enter)** to lock in your transformation. *Note:* If, after dragging it onto the page, your image is larger than the borders of the page, you won't be able to reach the Free Transform handles. So, just press **Command-0 (zero; PC: Ctrl-0)**, and the window will resize so you can reach all the handles.

SCOTT KELBY

STEP THREE: The center image needs to be perfectly square (rather than the standard rectangular shape of digital camera images), so get the Rectangular Marquee tool **(M)**, press-and-hold the Shift key (which constrains your selection so it's perfectly square), and drag out a square selection over the most important area of the photo (as shown here).

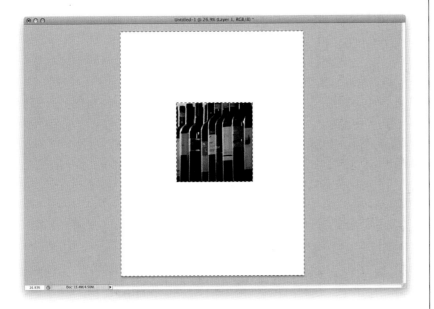

STEP FOUR: So, at this point you have a square selection in place, but we need to erase everything but that square selected area. To do that, press **Command-Shift-I (PC: Ctrl-Shift-I)**, which is the keyboard shortcut for inversing your selection, so now everything except that square is selected. Then, press the Delete (PC: Backspace) key, and everything but that square part of the photo is deleted (as seen here). Now press **Command-D (PC: Ctrl-D)** to Deselect your selection.

Continued

STEP FIVE: You're now going to drag four vertical photos into your layout, and use Free Transform to make them a bit smaller than your main image. Use the Move tool to position these with one on either side of the main image, and in the Layers panel, drag them below the main image (so they appear behind it), then back on your image, drag them so about one-third of the image is tucked behind that main image (as seen here). Place the other two vertical images above and below the main image, and leave a gap between each image and the main image (as shown here). *Note:* From now on, when you bring an image in, make sure you drag it below the main image in the Layers panel.

STEP SIX: Now add four horizontal images, crop them so they're square (using the same method you learned earlier), and position them in the four corners, as seen here. Again, be sure that these are stacked on lower layers, so all the photos we've imported so far appear behind the images already in place. If you have a photo that isn't behind the others, just go to the Layers panel and drag it below.

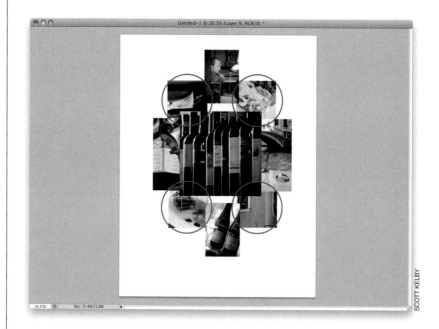

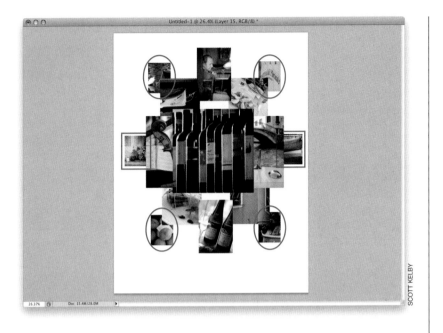

STEP SEVEN: Add four more vertical photos (if they're not vertical, you can crop them, or simply use the Rectangular Marquee tool to make a vertical selection and drag-and-drop the selection onto your document), and place them under the corners of the four square photos you added in the last step (as seen circled here). Then add two more vertical photos on either side (shown here inside the red boxes).

STEP EIGHT: Here, we're adding the last two photos (both vertical), and they go on the left and right sides at a very large size. You're going to put them side-by-side, with a small gap between them. After I added these last two photos, I decided I didn't like them where they were, so I used them to replace a couple of the smaller photos and added two new photos as the large ones. I added an extra capture below, with all the other layers hidden, so you can see how the new large photos are placed. Next, go to the Layers panel and click on the layer that has your main square center image (it should be the top layer in the stack of layers in the Layers panel, since it's in front of everything else).

Continued

STEP NINE: We're going to add what looks like a drop shadow behind all of your images, but because we need the shadow to be on more than one side of the image, instead of applying just a drop shadow, we're going to apply an outer glow, which puts a drop shadow effect on all sides of the image. Click on the Add a Layer Style icon at the bottom of the Layers panel and choose Outer Glow from the pop-up menu, which brings up the dialog you see here. Starting at the top of the dialog, change the Blend Mode pop-up menu to Normal (by default, it's set to Screen, which is about worthless for almost everything you'd ever want to do here. Why it's the default setting is an entirely different discussion—one where there's a lot of cussing. But I digress). Now lower the Opacity to 40%, then click on the color swatch and change the glow color from light yellow (don't ask) to black. Lastly, increase the Size (the softness of your shadow) to 10, then click OK to apply a soft all-around drop shadow to your main photo.

STEP 10: Here's what the Outer Glow layer style looks like applied to just the center front-most image. (You'll notice, I moved a few of the other images around and added a couple new ones, just to mix things up a little.) Now, if you're thinking that we have to do this for 16 layers, you're right, but there's a huge shortcut we can take. Control-click (PC: Right-click) on the layer we just applied the outer glow to, and a contextual menu will appear (seen here in the Layers panel). From this contextual menu, choose Copy Layer Style. This copies that Outer Glow layer style, with all the same settings you just applied.

SCOTT KELBY

STEP 11: In the Layers panel, click on the next layer down to select it. While pressing-and-holding the Command (PC: Ctrl) key, click on all the other layers in your document (but not the Background layer) to select them, too. Now, once all these other layers are selected, Control-click (PC: Right-click) on any one of those selected layers, and when the contextual menu appears, choose Paste Layer Style. Now that Outer Glow drop shadow layer style will be applied to all the other layers at once, as seen here (sweet short-cut!). These drop shadows are what adds separation and depth to the collage.

STEP 12: The last step, adding a color background, is totally optional, but if you want to do that, here's a tip that will help you choose a color that's guaranteed to work with your collage: Get the Eyedropper tool **(I)** from the Toolbox, then click on a prominent color in one of your images. In the example shown here, you can see I've clicked the Eyedropper tool on the pinkish color of the wall next to the green shuttered windows (it's shown circled here in red), which makes that color my new Foreground color. Now, just click on the Background layer and press **Option-Delete (PC: Alt-Backspace)** to fill your Background layer with that color (as seen here). You can try sampling different colors from different photos and refilling the Background layer to see which one looks the best. That's it!

Creating the "Tilt-Shift Toy Model Look"

This technique of taking a wide-angle or overhead photo and transforming it, so it looks like a tiny toy model, caught on like you can't believe. There are entire Flickr groups packed with people recreating this tilt-shift lens look, which really does make your photo's subject look like a tiny toy model. Luckily, it's one of the shortest, and easiest, techniques in the whole book.

STEP ONE: Open the photo you want to apply the effect to. The effect works best on photos where you've taken the photo from a high vantage point. The photo shown here (which you can download from the book's downloads page, mentioned in the book's intro) was an aerial photo taken from a heli-copter, but you don't need an aerial shot—a shot from a bridge, an overpass, from the window of a hotel, etc., will work fine. The reason you want this high viewing angle is that you want kind of the same viewing angle of a city that you would see of a toy model if you walked up on it.

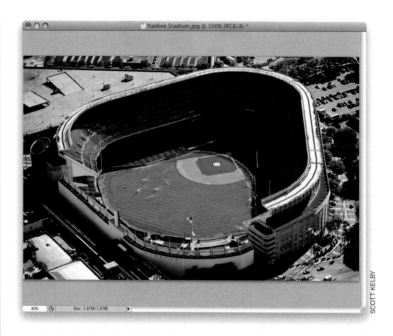

SCOTT KELBY

STEP TWO: Press the letter **Q** to enter Photoshop's Quick Mask mode, and then press **D** to reset your Foreground and Background colors to their defaults of black and white. Now, get the Gradient tool **(G)** and, up in the Options Bar, click on the Reflected Gradient icon (it's the fourth one from the left, shown circled here in red) and turn on the Reverse checkbox to the right. Take the Gradient tool, and click-and-drag it from the point you want to be in-focus downward (the farther you drag, the more that will be in focus, but drag farther than you'd think, because the in-focus area winds up being much smaller than you'd think). When you do this, you'll see a red mask appear (as seen here). The clear parts will be in focus, the red parts will be out of focus, but there will be a soft transition between the two.

STEP THREE: Press the letter Q again, to leave Quick Mask mode, and now you'll see a horizontal, rectangular selection across the center of your image going from side to side (that's the in-focus part). Now, go under the Filter menu, under Blur, and choose Lens Blur. When the dialog appears, under Depth Map, turn on the Invert checkbox, then in the Iris section, from the Shape pop-up menu, choose Hexagon (6), and for Radius, choose 35 (as shown here; the Radius controls how blurry your lens blur will be). Then in the Specular Highlights section, set the Brightness to 50.

STEP FOUR: When you click OK, the blurring is applied. Just press **Command-D (PC: Ctrl-D)** to Deselect, and now your image looks like a very small toy model (or architectural model), like the one shown here.

CHAPTER **2**

Studio 54

studio effects

This chapter is about creating Photoshop effects that look like you created them in a studio, but actually you could have created them in your basement while sitting around in your underwear. That's part of the magic of Photoshop—nobody knows what you're wearing. And although they might like to imagine you're doing all this from a trendy loft studio in Soho, chances are you're not. Now, that doesn't mean you're in your basement—you might be in your parents' basement, but if you're 35 or 40, you should probably have your own basement (and your own underwear, as well). But there are advantages to having your fake studio in your basement. One, of course, is overhead. When

you work in a basement, everything is overhead, because essentially you're underground, so now when you talk about your studio you can refer to it as your "underground studio," which sounds kind of like an "underground bunker," which reminds me of Archie Bunker from the hit 1970s TV show *All in the Family*, which was big back when the famous New York disco Studio 54 was big, but of course that was years before the movie of the same name, which was based on the disco, was released (it starred Mike Myers), which is actually what this chapter is named after. Like the way I pulled that together at the last minute? I know. It's a gift.

High-Tech Sports-Look Product Setup

I saw this effect in some TV ads for NFLshop.com (where you can buy real NFL jerseys and team gear), and they used the look in several places on the website as well, tying it back to the TV ads. The effect has you creating a high-tech looking grid floor that seems to fade off, with a dramatic lighting effect falling right where your product (or in this case, a logo) would be, with a soft drop shadow under it to enhance the look. Here's how it's done:

STEP ONE: Go under the File menu, choose New, and create a new document that has a resolution of at least 200 ppi (the one I'm creating here is 8 inches wide by 5 inches high at a resolution of 200 ppi).

STEP TWO: Press **D** to set your Foreground color to black, then press **Option-Delete (PC: Alt-Backspace)** to fill your Background layer with black. Create a new layer (click on the Create a New Layer icon at the bottom of the Layers panel), then click on the Foreground color swatch to bring up the Color Picker and change the color to a medium gray. Now, fill this layer with that gray color using the same shortcut you just learned (or you can go under the Edit menu, choose Fill, and from the Use pop-up menu, choose 50% Gray, then click OK).

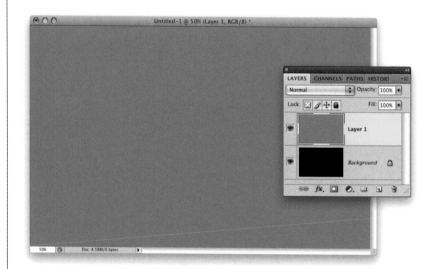

STEP THREE: Reset your Foreground color to black, and then to create the rows of dots we need, go under the Filter menu, under Sketch, and choose Halftone Pattern. When the dialog appears, set the Size to 6, the Contrast to 0, and then set the Pattern Type to Dot (as shown here). This creates rows of kinda blurry black and white dots (seen in the preview on the left side of the filter dialog).

STEP FOUR: Click OK, and you can see here how the pattern looks when applied to your layer.

Continued

STEP FIVE: To get rid of the blurriness, and make the dots nice and round, press **Command-L (PC: Ctrl-L)** to bring up the Levels dialog (seen here), then drag the shadows Input Levels slider (the black-filled triangle appearing under the left side of the histogram) to the right until the shadow amount reaches around 150 (you'll see the amount displayed in the field under where the slider used to be). Then drag the highlights Input Levels slider (the white triangle found on the far-right side) over to the left until it's about ½" from the shadows slider (to around 197). As you do this, the blurring goes away, and the dots become nice and uniformly round. Now, create a new layer, drag it beneath your dots layer, and then fill it with a medium gray (as seen here). *Note:* Moving the shadows and highlights sliders close together like this is what removes the blurring, but as you're dragging, you'll see that where you drag to also determines how large the dots are, and how much space there will be between them.

STEP SIX: In the Layers panel, click on your dots layer to make it the active layer. Now, go to the Channels panel (found under the Window menu), press-and-hold the Command (PC: Ctrl) key and click directly on the RGB channel's thumbnail (as seen here) to load that channel's luminosity as a selection (this puts a selection around all the white areas).

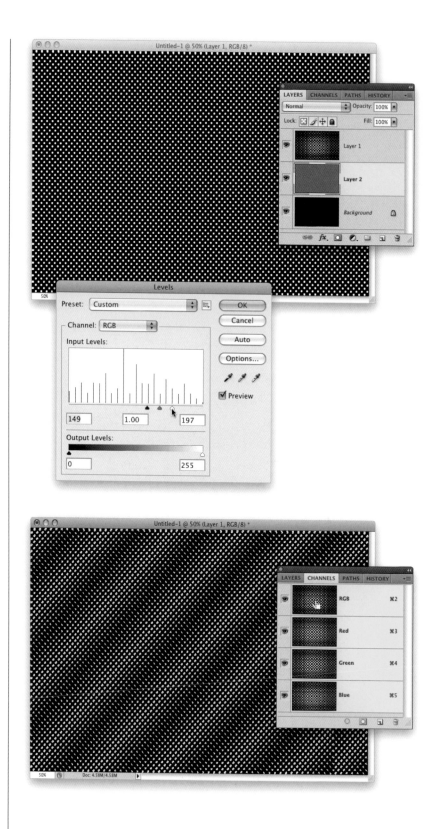

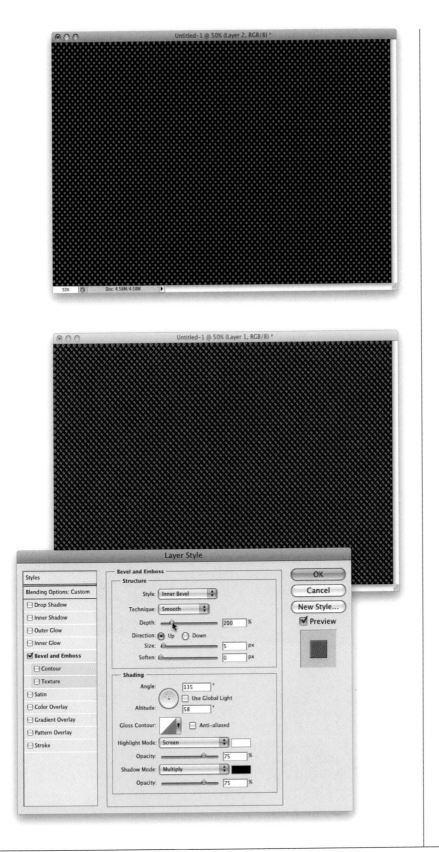

STEP SEVEN: We need the white dots to be transparent, so press the Delete (PC: Backspace) key to delete those white dots, then press **Command-D (PC: Ctrl-D)** to Deselect. Now, as you see here, you'll see gray dots where the white dots used to be (that's the gray from the layer below). Go ahead and switch back to the Layers panel.

STEP EIGHT: To give some depth to the dot pattern, you're going to add a bevel to the gray dots. Click on the Add a Layer Style icon at the bottom of the Layers panel and choose Bevel and Emboss from the pop-up menu. When the Layer Style dialog appears (seen here), increase your Depth amount to 200%. Then go down to the Shading section, turn off the Use Global Light checkbox, and in the Angle circle, drag the little crosshair closer to the center point (or just type in 135° for your Angle and 58° for Altitude). Changing the direction of the light like this helps make the effect stand out a bit more. Click OK to apply this bevel to your layer. Now that we have the colors right and the bevel added, you'll need to merge this dots layer permanently with the gray layer below it by pressing **Command-E (PC: Ctrl-E)**.

Continued

STEP NINE: Here's how the beveled dot pattern looks now. Press **Command-T (PC: Ctrl-T)** to bring up Free Transform, and then press **Command-0 (zero; PC: Ctrl-0)** to expand the image window slightly, so you can reach the Free Transform handles (as seen here). Note that there are only two layers—your black background and your dots layer—because you merged the dots layer with the gray layer in the last step.

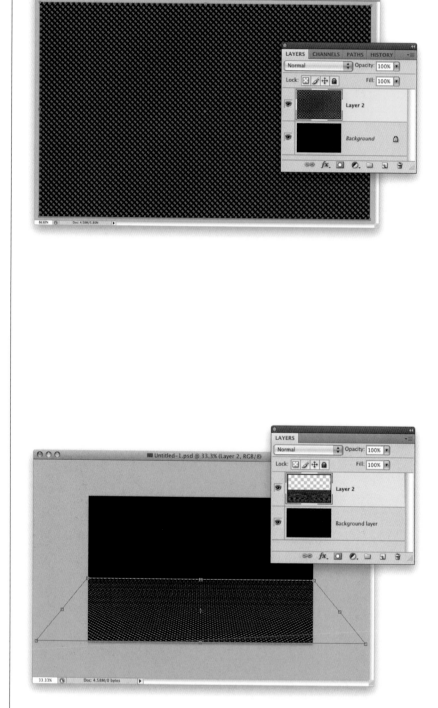

STEP 10: We need to flatten out this dot pattern, so it looks more like a slightly raised view of a tabletop, so although there is a Perspective function for Free Transform, instead we're going to do this manually using the Distort function (because the Perspective function can sometimes distort the dots in a funky way). Press-and-hold the **Command (PC: Ctrl) key**, grab the top-right corner point, and drag straight down about two-thirds of the way down the image. Grab the top-left corner point and do the same thing. Next, grab the bottom-right corner point and (while still pressing-and-holding the Command key) drag straight out to the right, then grab the bottom-left corner point and do the same thing. This gives you the perspective look you see here. Now, press **Return (PC: Enter)** to lock in your transformation.

STEP 11: We're going to use a layer mask and a solid-to-transparent gradient to fade the edges of our dot grid, so it looks like they fade off into black. To do that, get the Gradient tool **(G)**, then up in the Options Bar, click on the down-facing arrow to the right of the gradient thumbnail to open the Gradient Picker, and click on the second gradient (as shown here), which is the Foreground to Transparent gradient.

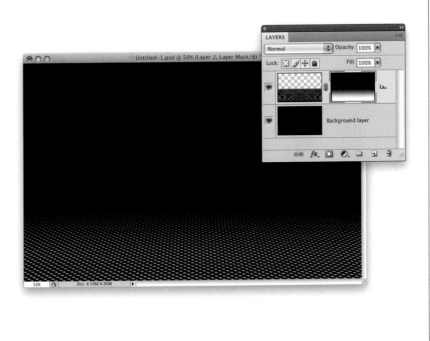

STEP 12: Go to the Layers panel, and click on the Add Layer Mask icon at the bottom of the panel (it's the third icon from the left). This should make your Foreground color white, so press **X** to switch it to black. Now go back to the image, click the Gradient tool near the top center of your dot grid, and then drag downward about an inch or so, and it fades away the top edge of your dot grid (as seen here).

Continued

STEP 13: Now, do the same thing for both sides to fade the edges away to black (as seen here).

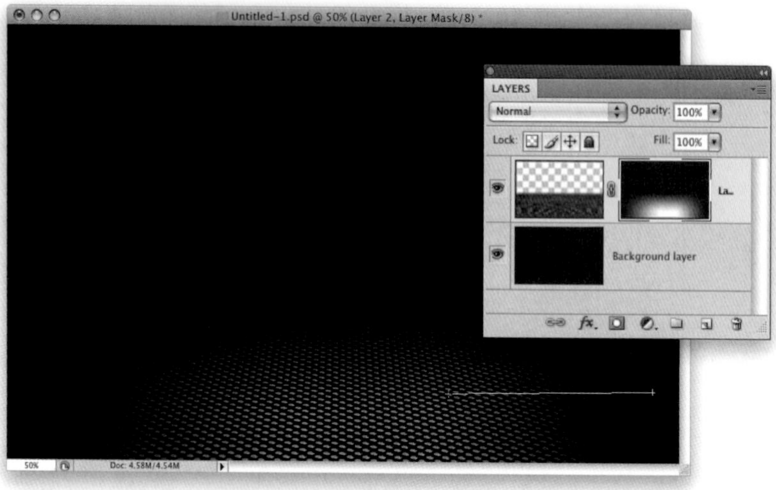

STEP 14: At this point, you've got fades on the top, left, and right, and you want a more subtle fade on the bottom (which will help to make it look more like there's a spotlight falling on your grid). So, go up to the Options Bar (up top) and lower the Opacity of the Gradient tool to 50%, then click-and-drag from the bottom of your image to around 1" inside your dot grid (as shown here) to subtly fade the bottom edge to black (as shown in the next step).

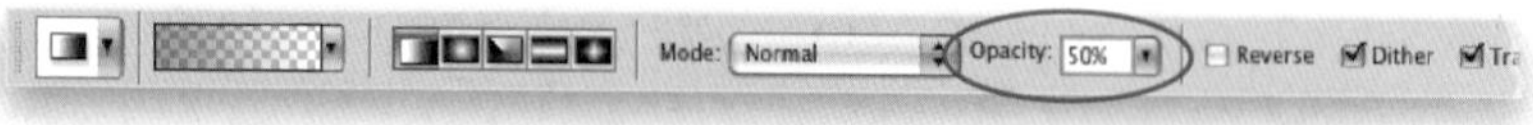

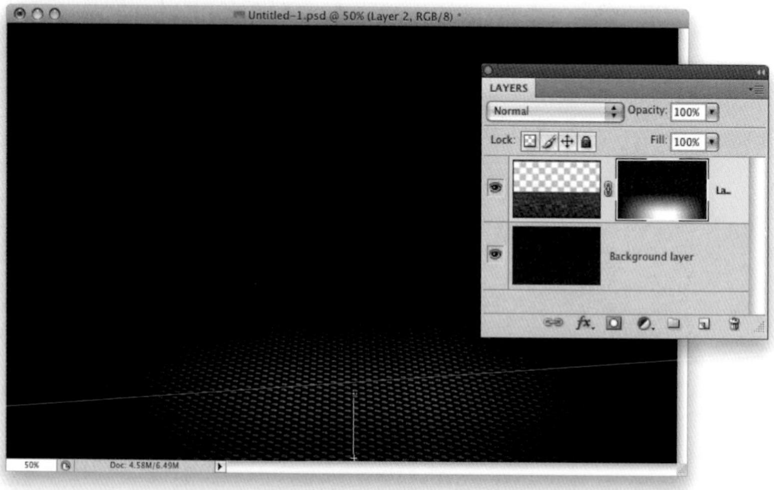

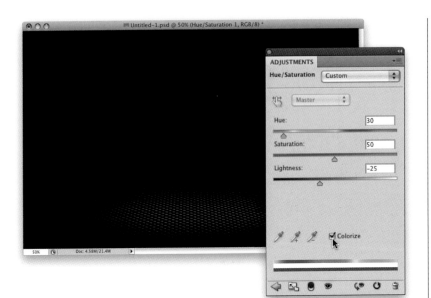

COREY BARKER

STEP 15: Now, let's add some color to the dot grid. In the Adjustments panel, click on the Hue/Saturation icon (in the second row, the second icon from the left), and when its options appear, turn on the Colorize checkbox (as shown here), then use the Hue slider to choose which color you'd like for your tint (the color you want for your dot grid). If the color seems too muted, increase the Saturation to around 50, and if it then seems too bright, drag the Lightness slider to the left.

STEP 16: Open the document with your logo (or a product shot), get the Move tool **(V)**, and click-and-drag just the logo itself over onto your main document (as seen here). If your logo has a solid color background area around it, you'll need to put a selection around just your logo (or product) first (try selecting the background with the Magic Wand tool [press **Shift-W** until you have it], then press **Command-Shift-I [PC: Ctrl-Shift-I]** to Inverse your selection), and then drag over just it alone—without the background. Now, you can position your logo (or product) over the brightest area of the grid (as seen here).

Continued

STEP 17: You're now going to add a drop shadow to your logo, but we can't easily use the built-in drop shadow, because it will want to put the shadow behind your logo, and not below it on the grid. So, to get the shadow to cast below the logo, we'll have to make one ourselves. Start by pressing **Command-J (PC: Ctrl-J)** to duplicate the layer. Then press **Option-Shift-Delete (PC: Alt-Shift-Backspace)** to fill your logo with black (this black-filled copy of your logo is what we're going to turn into your drop shadow). Next, bring up Free Transform again (as seen here).

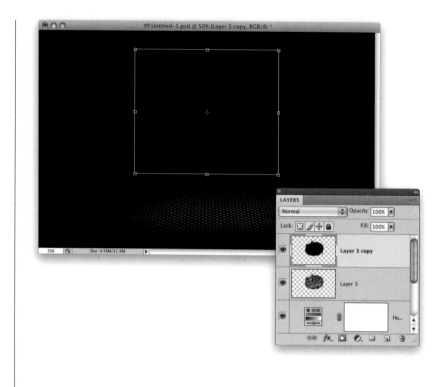

STEP 18: Press-and-hold the Shift key, and drag the black-filled logo straight down beneath your full-color logo. While still pressing-and-holding the Shift key, grab the top-center point, and drag it straight downward, squashing your black logo down until it's nearly flat (as seen here), then lock in your transformation.

STEP 19: To soften your shadow, go under the Filter menu, under Blur, and choose Gaussian Blur. When the Gaussian Blur dialog appears, enter 9 pixels (as shown here), then click OK to apply the blur, which softens all the edges.

STEP 20: Lastly, go to the Layers panel and lower the Opacity of this layer to around 50% to lighten the shadow, and to make it more transparent, so you see some of the dot grid through it (which helps the shadow look more realistic). That's it!

Adding Texture and Aging to a Photo

This technique caught my eye when a photo by photographer Laura Boston Thek was chosen as the Image of the Week on the member's portfolio website for the National Association of Photoshop Professionals (NAPP, for short). She had taken a vacation photo from her trip to Venice, Italy, and then applied a paper texture to the image, which gave it this historical, archival look, and I heard from a number of folks who wanted to know how this was done. Well, here's how it's done:

STEP ONE: First, open the photo you want to apply the effect to. As luck would have it, my family had taken a vacation trip to Venice, too, so I already had a source image to use (and you can download this same source image from the book's downloads page, listed in the book's intro).

STEP TWO: You'll need a paper texture image, like the one shown here. (You can download this same texture image from the book's downloads page, too, courtesy of our friends at iStockphoto.com.)

STEP THREE: Get the Move tool **(V)** and drag-and-drop this paper texture image over on top of your photo. (*Note:* If you press-and-hold the Shift key while you drag-and-drop, it will center the paper texture image over your photo, as you see here.) If you're using Photoshop CS4's tabbed windows feature, it's a bit clunkier. You'll click-and-drag the paper texture image itself up to the tab for your photo document and just pause there a moment. The photo document will appear, and you'll drag your cursor down to the center of your photo area, then release the mouse button, and your image will appear (I told you it was clunky and this is the main reason why I don't use the tabbed windows feature).

STEP FOUR: Chances are, your paper texture isn't going to be a perfect fit over your photo (look at the image back in Step Three, and you can see a gap on the left and right sides because the image isn't wide enough), so you're going to have to stretch it to fit. Of course, you could just go to Free Transform and stretch the sides (after all, it's just a background texture, right?), but it's just as easy to use CS4's Content-Aware Scale feature (which helps to keep the "stretched" look to a minimum). So, go under the Edit menu and choose Content-Aware Scale (as shown here). This brings up scaling points around the edges of your image. Just grab the right-center point and drag to the right to stretch your texture to fill that gap. Now, do the same thing on the left side (you could do the top and bottom if it needed it, too), and once your full image area is completely covered, press the **Return (PC: Enter)** key to lock in your transformation.

STEP FIVE: You're going to use a layer blend mode to blend this paper texture into the photo on the layer beneath it. Of course, the question is which layer blend mode will look best? Here's how to find out: Make sure you have the Move tool, then press **Shift-+** (the plus sign on your keyboard), and each time you press that, it will change your layer to the next blend mode in the menu. So in just a few seconds, you'll be able to run through all the blend modes and choose the one that looks best to you. In this case, after running through them all, I thought the Multiply mode looked best, so I stopped there on my second time through.

Continued

STEP SIX: The downside of using the Multiply layer blend mode is that it makes the image look much darker. One way to minimize the darkening is to lower the Opacity of this layer to around 50% (as shown here), which not only lightens the effect of Multiply, but also lowers the intensity of the texture, which I think in this case is a good thing. *Note:* When going through your layer blend modes, there are a few modes that will be the "most likely" ones you choose. They are: Multiply, Screen, Overlay, and Soft Light. You won't always choose those, because depending on the photo, you might go with something else, but my bet is that 99% of the time it'll be one of those four blend modes.

STEP SEVEN: If you really want this photo to have that "historical archival" look to it, the colors in the photo probably wouldn't be as bright and vibrant as the ones taken by today's digital cameras. So, to deal with that, first go to the Layers panel and click on the Background layer. Then go to the Adjustments panel and click on the Hue/Saturation icon (it's the second one from the left, in the center row). This brings up the Hue/Saturation options (seen here). Now, just drag the Saturation slider quite a bit over to the left (as shown circled here in red) to desaturate the color a bit and give it a more realistic look.

STEP EIGHT: Now that we've done all this, to me the photo looks a bit dark, but a quick Levels adjustment will fix that. Click on the top layer in your layer stack, then go to the Adjustments panel and click on the Levels icon (it's the second icon from the left in the top row). When its options appear, simply click on the white highlights slider (on the far-right side, just below the histogram) and drag it over to the left to around 215 (as shown here) to brighten the highlight areas, which makes the entire photo look brighter, and completes the effect (a before/after is shown below).

Before

After

Gritty High-Contrast Look for Portraits

This technique is incredibly popular right now, but before I show it to you, there's a critical part of it that happens before you get into Photoshop: the lighting has to be high contrast, too. The most common way to light your subject to get this effect is to put two flashes on either side and behind your subject, usually without a softbox or diffuser—just a reflector or bare bulb. These two lights will skim the sides of your subject, and create very bright highlights. Then you use one flash as your main light in front (on the left or right) with a softbox (or use a ringflash), so it's a bit softer. In short, if the lighting is high contrast, this effect will look good. If not, it won't.

STEP ONE: Here's the three-light setup I used for the shot we're going to use in this tutorial (it looks much more complicated than it is). There are three lights: (1) The main light is a flash mounted above the subject's head, with a beauty-dish attachment, although it's not necessary to have a beauty dish at all. (2) Behind him and to his right is a flash with a tall, thin softbox (called a strip bank), and (3) another flash with a strip bank is behind him and to his left. The two flash units behind him are aimed at his sides. The only problem with this setup is that since two of the flashes are aiming at the camera, you might get lens flare (which tends to wash out the color, among other things), so I placed two black flags (as seen in the photo) to block the flashes from hitting my lens, then I shot between them (as seen here in the setup shot).

BRAD MOORE

STEP TWO: You can download the image shown here if you don't have a photo with high-contrast lighting (the download address is in the book's intro). This is a RAW image, so when you double-click on it, it opens in Camera Raw. The image is underexposed, so drag the Exposure slider over to +1.65, then press-and-hold the Shift key, and you'll notice that the Open Image button at the bottom right has changed to Open Object (as seen here). Click that button to open your brightened image in Photoshop as a Smart Object.

SCOTT KELBY

STEP THREE: Once the image opens in Photoshop, you can tell it's a Smart Object layer by looking at the layer's thumbnail in the Layers panel. If it's a Smart Object, you'll see a little page icon in the bottom-right corner of the thumbnail (shown circled here in red). The advantage of opening it as a Smart Object is that we can go back into Camera Raw anytime and change our settings (which we're going to do in a minute, to a copy of the RAW file). We're going to duplicate the layer, but if we just drag it down to the Create a New Layer icon at the bottom of the Layers panel (or use the regular keyboard shortcut for duplicating a layer—Command-J [PC: Ctrl-J]), then this new layer will be tied to the original layer, and any changes we make to the duplicate will also be applied to the original. In this case, we need our two layers to be separate, and in the next step you'll learn how to break that connection.

STEP FOUR: Control-click (PC: Right-click) directly on an open area of your Smart Object layer (not on the thumbnail) and a contextual menu will appear. From this menu, choose New Smart Object via Copy (as shown here). This makes a copy of your Smart Object layer, but it breaks the connection to the original layer. Now we can edit this copy separately, and the changes we make to this layer will only affect this one layer (and not the original).

Continued

STEP FIVE: Now that you've got a copy of your Smart Object layer, double-click directly on that layer's thumbnail to bring up the Camera Raw window again (as seen here). Increase the Fill Light amount to 100 (which will make your photo look really washed out), then drag your Blacks slider to the right to around 29 to bring back some of the shadow area color and contrast. This makes the photo look pretty bad (as seen here), but it will get better soon. Don't click OK quite yet, though.

STEP SIX: You're going to make a few more edits, so first drag the Clarity slider (which controls midtone contrast) all the way to the right to 100, then drag the Saturation slider all the way to the left (to remove all the color from the photo. See? I told you we'd fix that color problem). Lastly, let's bring some more contrast to the shadow areas of this photo by dragging the Blacks slider a little farther to the right—over to around 33—to make the photo nice and contrasty, and then click OK to apply these changes to your copied layer.

STEP SEVEN: To blend this very contrasty black-and-white layer in with our original full-color Smart Object layer below it, go to the Layers panel and change the layer blend mode from Normal to Luminosity (as seen here).

STEP EIGHT: Here's how the photo looks with the blend mode changed to Luminosity. You can see how much more contrasty and edgy the photo looks with just this one change. (You can turn the visibility of this layer off and on to see a quick before and after—just click on the Eye icon to the left of the top layer's thumbnail, and then click on the spot where it used to be to make it visible again.)

Continued

STEP NINE: At this point, you'll have to make a decision: Do I want this effect applied just to my subject, or do I want it over the entire image? If I had shot this on location, I would normally apply it to the entire image, but since this was shot in a studio on a solid background, I'm going to apply the effect just to selected areas of my subject. To do that, press-and-hold the Option (PC: Alt) key and click on the Add Layer Mask icon at the bottom of the Layers panel (it's shown circled here in red). This hides your high-contrast layer behind a black mask (you can see the black mask appear to the right of your layer's thumbnail in the Layers panel).

STEP 10: Now, you can "paint" the contrasty look where you want it. Get the Brush tool **(B)**, click on the Brush thumbnail in the Options Bar, and choose a small, soft-edged brush from the Brush Picker, make sure your Foreground color is set to white, then start painting over the subject's clothes, the mic, his hat, his watch, his arms, and even his face, but try to avoid areas of his skin that should be smooth (like his cheeks). Remember, you're painting in contrast, so paint over areas of his skin you want to look really contrasty, and avoid the areas you'll want to look smooth (and avoid any areas with blemishes, spots, etc.). Here, I'm painting in contrast along the left side of his neck. I also painted over his beard, his eyes, his lips, nostrils, and along the edges of his face.

STEP 11: Once you're done painting in contrast on the top layer, press **Command-Option-Shift-E (PC: Ctrl-Alt-Shift-E)**, which creates a new layer that looks like a flattened version of your file. The advantage of this (over actually flattening the file) is that you keep your Smart Object layers intact, in case you need to go back and make other changes. Now, press **Shift-J** until you get the Healing Brush, so we can remove any blemishes, spots, etc., on his skin (the reason we do this is that, later, something we're going to do is going to greatly accentuate any visible blemishes, so we remove them now while it's still easy). Press-and-hold the Option (PC: Alt) key and click in a smooth area of skin. Then choose a brush size that is just slightly larger than the blemish you want to remove, move over the blemish and just click once, and the blemish is gone (as seen here).

STEP 12: One of the big secrets to this technique is to dodge and burn (brighten and darken) the highlights and shadows already in your photo. You're actually going to over-accentuate them, which gives the image a more three-dimensional, almost illustrated, look. I always start by burning (darkening) first, so get the Burn tool from the Toolbox (or press **Shift-O** until you have it). Go up to the Options Bar and, from the Range pop-up menu, choose Shadows, then lower the Opacity to 20% (as shown here).

Note: If this were any previous version of Photoshop, I would never recommend using the Dodge and Burn tools, because they were pretty awful, but in CS4, Adobe greatly improved the results you get from them, and now they actually work pretty darn well, so now we use them.

Continued

STEP 13: Now, before you begin dodging and burning, duplicate your top layer by pressing **Command-J (PC: Ctrl-J)**. Choose a medium-sized, soft-edged brush from the Brush Picker, then start painting over the dark (shadow) areas of your photo. In our example, I used the Zoom tool **(Z)** to zoom in so I would have a clearer view, then I started painting over his beard, the dark part of his left cheek, right under the center of his bottom lip, and any shadow areas of his face, his hat, and his neck. The goal is to make the dark shadow parts of this image even darker.

STEP 14: Here's how the photo looks after a minute of burning (notice how the shadows on his face look darker, and I'm even burning the parts of the wrinkles in his shirt, as seen here). If it seems like the changes you are making here are pretty subtle, try hiding this layer from view for a moment, and you'll see that it's having a bigger effect than it first seems.

STEP 15: Now get the Dodge tool (press **Shift-O**), go up to the Options Bar, and set the Range to Highlights (so it only affects the highlights), set the Opacity to no more than 20%, then start brightening the highlight areas of his face, hat, shirt, etc., by painting over them. Go through the entire image, and everywhere you see a highlight, paint over it to make it more apparent. Here, I've painted over the highlights on his cheeks, his hat, the wrinkles on his shirt, and the bright areas on his neck, the left side of his face, etc. Anywhere that's a little bright—make it brighter. Now, as you paint over these areas, some of them (like the areas on his face) are going to get an orange color. Don't worry, we'll deal with that next.

STEP 16: To get rid of the color problems caused by your dodging and burning, go to the Layers panel and change the Layer blend mode from Normal to Luminosity, and those edits now blend right in (compare this image with the one in Step 15 and you'll see what I mean. Compare the color of his cheeks).

Continued

STEP 17: Stop for just a moment and hide your top layer from view (click on the Eye icon), and you'll instantly see what a difference this dodging and burning makes (it has more effect than it feels like it's having, right?). Now, because you did all your dodging and burning on a copy of your top layer, you could make the layer visible again, then lower the Opacity of this layer, which would reduce the intensity of the effect (I didn't here, but I did want to let you know that an advantage of dodging and burning on a duplicate layer is that you have control over the effect after you've applied it, by lowering the Opacity setting).

STEP 18: Now you're going to add some really intense sharpening, and when you add this much sharpening, it really magnifies any skin blemishes or spots your subject has, which is why we were careful to remove them earlier with the Healing Brush tool. Okay, for our hyper-sharpening, first we're going to duplicate the top layer. Then, go under the Filter menu, under Other, and choose High Pass. When the dialog appears, increase the Radius to around 110 pixels (as shown here), and click OK.

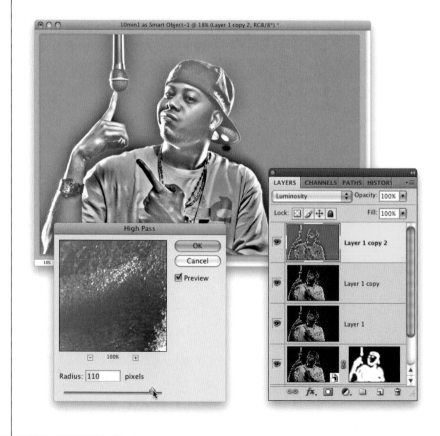

STEP 19: This turns the sharpened layer nearly gray (with outlines of color), so to get your sharpening to blend in with the rest of your image, you're going to change the layer blend mode of this layer from Normal to Soft Light (as shown here), and now the sharpening blends right in with your photo. Because the Soft Light blend mode is a mode that adds contrast, your image probably looks a bit too dark at this point. So, we'll use the trick we used earlier to have the sharpening only appear where we want it (and not over the soft blemish-removed areas of his skin, or along the outside edges of his shirt, the mic, or his face, because it might reveal a black glow, which sometimes appears when applying a lot of that High Pass filter sharpening).

STEP 20: Press-and-hold the Option (PC: Alt) key and click on the Add Layer Mask icon at the bottom of the Layers panel to hide your high-contrast layer behind a black mask (as seen here). Now get the Brush tool, choose a soft-edged brush, make sure your Foreground color is white, and paint over detail areas that you want to appear super-sharp and contrasty. I painted over the wrinkles in his shirt, over the inside area of the mic, over his ballcap, his shirt, his hands, his beard, his earring, his eyes, his eyebrows, and his lips—just the high-detail areas (and not the areas we want to stay soft).

Continued

STEP 21: Some of the adjustments and tweaks we've made up to this point have made the color in the photo very vibrant—and in almost every case, too red. So, go to the Adjustments panel and click on the Hue/Saturation icon (the second one from the left in the second row) to bring up the Hue/Saturation options (seen here). Choose Reds from the second pop-up menu from the top, and then lower the saturation a bit by dragging the Saturation slider to the left, which removes some of the red and gives your subject's skin somewhat of a desaturated look (as seen here).

STEP 22: One of the finishing touches most commonly seen with this look is to burn in (darken) the edges around your subject, so they appear almost in their own soft spotlight. To do that, press Command-Option-Shift-E (PC: Ctrl-Alt-Shift-E) again to merge all your layers into a new layer at the top of your layer stack. Then, duplicate the top layer, and change the layer blend mode of this duplicate layer to Multiply (as seen here) to make a much darker version of your photo. This is what we're going to use for our burned-in edges.

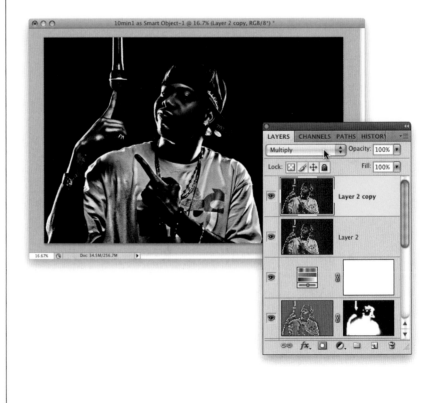

STEP 23: Lastly, click on the Add Layer Mask icon at the bottom of the Layers panel to add a standard layer mask to your layer. Now, get the Brush tool, and choose a huge, soft-edged brush (this brush should be so big that it's a little larger than your subject's head). Press **X** to switch your Foreground color to black, then take the Brush tool and just click once over your subject's face, and it deletes the darkening over that one area. It may take five, six, or a few more clicks to reveal the brighter version of your subject on the layer below, which leaves you with the effect you see below in the After photo. *Note:* In the After photo, I did do one extra thing: After looking at the final photo, I thought his eyes looked too dark, so I duplicated the top layer and changed the layer blend mode to Screen (which makes the image very bright). Then I Option-clicked (PC: Alt-clicked) on the Add Layer Mask icon to hide this brighter version behind a black mask, and painted in white over his eyes to lighten that area. That's it.

Before

After

CHAPTER 3

Commercial Break

commercial special effects

This chapter is about commercial effects you see used every day (I'm not talking about effects used in commercials, I'm talking more about effects you see used in commercial work, so they could be in anything from website design, to annual reports, to brochures, to magazine layouts). The name "Commercial Break" is actually from a song by the same name from a rapper named D12, from his album *D12 World*. I found the song by searching in Apple's iTunes Store, and I actually found two versions of the song: one marked Explicit and one marked Clean. I listened to the free 30-second preview of the explicit version, and sure enough— they were right. Now, I did notice a phrase in that version that I thought would be hard to make "clean," so then, just for fun, I played the clean version, and they muted a small part of that naughty phrase. About a syllable. However, I'm not sure how much that helped, because I can't imagine there's a single person alive today that would not immediately know what that phrase was. I would imagine that even Tibetan monks, who would listen to the clean version, would look at each other and say, "Dude, did he just say what I think he said?" And then the other Tibetan monk would look at him and say, "Don't call me dude!"

High-Tech Sports-Look Bio Page

I originally saw this layout on the NASCAR website and liked it right away. There's a lot more going on here than it appears at first, and although it takes a few minutes to go through this entire project, you'll learn a lot by doing it because it's got a little bit of everything in it. Plus, this is a very flexible layout that can be tweaked and used in lots of different ways—from websites to slide presentations. So, don't let all the steps fool you. There's nothing really hard here (in fact, it's all pretty easy), it just takes a few steps to build this puppy from the ground up.

STEP ONE: Press **Command-N (PC: Ctrl-N)** to open the New dialog and create a new document that's 12" wide by 8" high at a resolution of 72 ppi. Click on the Foreground color swatch, choose a dark gray from the Color Picker, and fill your Background layer with this gray by pressing **Option-Delete (PC: Alt-Backspace)**. Click on the Create a New Layer icon at the bottom of the Layers panel, and then take the Rectangular Marquee tool **(M)** and click-and-drag a rectangular selection that's almost as big as the entire image (leave a little bit of gray showing all around, like you see here). Now press the letter **D** to set your Foreground color to black, and fill this selection with black by again pressing Option-Delete (PC: Alt-Backspace), then Deselect by pressing **Command-D (PC: Ctrl-D)**.

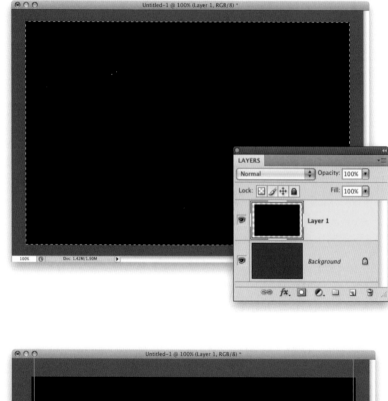

STEP TWO: Press **Command-R (PC: Ctrl-R)** to make Photoshop's rulers visible, press **V** to get the Move tool, then create a horizontal guide by clicking directly on the ruler at the top of the image window and dragging straight down near the bottom of the window. Then click-and-drag another guide down near the top of the window. Drag a vertical guide out from the left-side ruler and place it just to the inside right of the black rectangle, leaving a little gap. Do the same thing for the left side, so your guides look like the ones here (later, we'll put a photo in that space). *Note:* These guides are always available to help you line up things, so anytime you need one, just go to the rulers and click-and-drag one out. To remove a guide, click on it and drag it back to the ruler it came from.

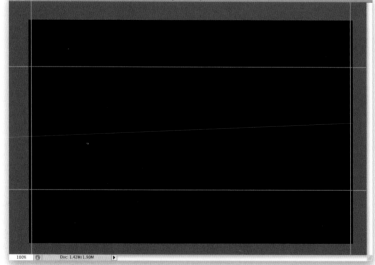

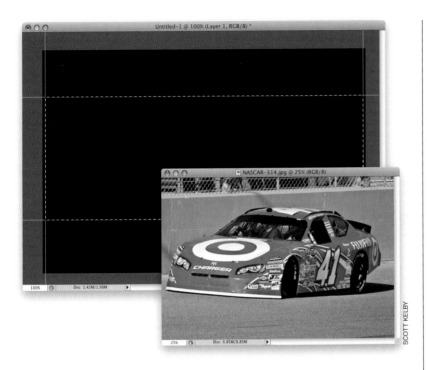

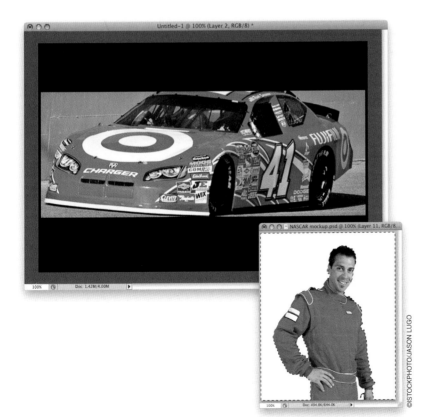

STEP THREE: Get the Rectangular Marquee tool again, and click-and-drag out a rectangle within your two horizontal and two vertical guides (like the one I've drawn here). Now open the photo of the race car. (*Note:* You can press **Command-R [PC: Ctrl-R]** to turn off the rulers.) Once it's open, press **Command-A (PC: Ctrl-A)** to put a selection around the entire image, and then press **Command-C (PC: Ctrl-C)** to copy that image into Photoshop's memory (you can close the race car photo). Now return to your main document and your selection will still be in place.

STEP FOUR: Go under the Edit menu and choose Paste Into, and the photo you copied into memory in the previous step will appear inside that selected area (and the selection will automatically deselect). If you don't like the position where the photo appears inside that rectangle, you can just take the Move tool and click-and-drag it up, down, left, right, etc., or use Free Transform (**Command-T [PC: Ctrl-T]**) to change the size. Don't worry, it will stay within that rectangular area while you reposition or resize it. Once it's positioned the way you like it, open this photo of a driver, as shown here. Get the Magic Wand tool (press **Shift-W** until you have it) and click it once on the white background area behind the driver to select it. Now press-and-hold the Shift key, and click in the white area inside his arm—this adds that area to the selection. Keep holding the Shift key, and click any other unselected white areas (next to his other arm, for example). Once it's all selected, press **Command-Shift-I (PC: Ctrl-Shift-I)** to Inverse your selection, so now the driver will be selected (rather than the background).

Continued

STEP FIVE: With the Move tool, click-and-hold on the driver, then drag-and-drop him right onto your main image. If he's too big (and he probably will be), bring up Free Transform, press-and-hold the Shift key, then click on a corner point, and drag inward to scale him down to size (press **Command-0 [zero; PC: Ctrl-0]** if you can't see the Free Transform handles). When the size looks about right, press **Return (PC: Enter)** to lock in your resizing. Now, since he was selected with the Magic Wand tool, you'll probably see a little bit of white "fringe" around his entire body, which looks pretty lame, so in the next step we'll have to deal with that.

STEP SIX: The quickest way to get rid of edge fringe like this is to go under the Layer menu, under Matting, and then choose Defringe (as shown here). This brings up the Defringe dialog, and by default it's going to remove 1 pixel of edge fringe. Just leave everything as it is, click OK, and that should do the trick in getting rid of that white fringe.

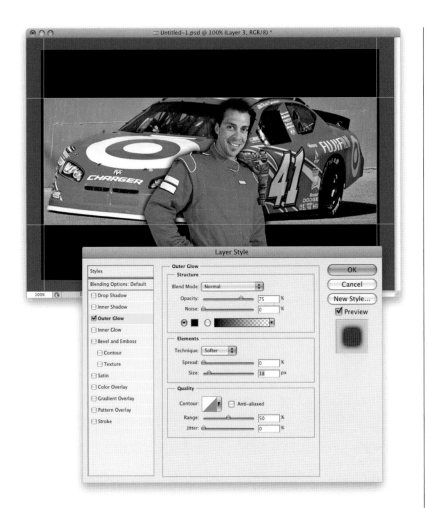

STEP SEVEN: Now we're going to add something like a drop shadow, but since we want the shadow to appear on all sides of him, we're going to add a black outer glow instead. Click on the Add a Layer Style icon at the bottom of the Layers panel and choose Outer Glow. When the Layer Style dialog appears, change the Blend Mode to Normal, then click on the yellow color swatch, change the glow color to black, and increase the Size to around 18 px (the size is really the softness of the glow, so the higher the amount, the softer and wider the glow). Now click OK, and you'll see the black drop-shadow-like glow behind your driver (as seen here).

STEP EIGHT: Later we're going to add some text up at the top, so let's create a gradient bar up there now. Create a new layer, then get the Rectangular Marquee tool and make a long, thin rectangular selection across the top, between the two side guides (as shown here). Get the Eyedropper tool **(I)** and click once on a bright red area of his clothes to set this as your Foreground color. Then press **X** to swap the Background and Foreground color swatches, and click the Eyedropper on a darker red area of his clothes (so now your Foreground color is set to dark red and your Background color is set to bright red). Get the Gradient tool **(G)**, click on the down-facing arrow next to the gradient thumbnail up in the Options Bar and choose the Foreground to Background gradient in the Gradient Picker, then click-and-drag your gradient from the top to the bottom of your selected area, so the dark red is at the top and bright red is at the bottom (like you see here). Don't deselect quite yet.

Continued

STEP NINE: You're going to create a checkered flag graphic that's going to go inside that selected gradient rectangle. Start by creating a new document that is 12" wide by 2" deep at 72 ppi. Get the Custom Shape tool from the Toolbox (or press **Shift-U** until you have it), and then go up to the Options Bar and click on the third icon from the left, shown circled here in red. This makes it so your shape will just be regular old pixels, rather than making it a path or a Shape layer. Then, click on the Shape thumbnail in the Options Bar to open the Shape Picker, and choose the Grid shape from the default shapes (as shown here).

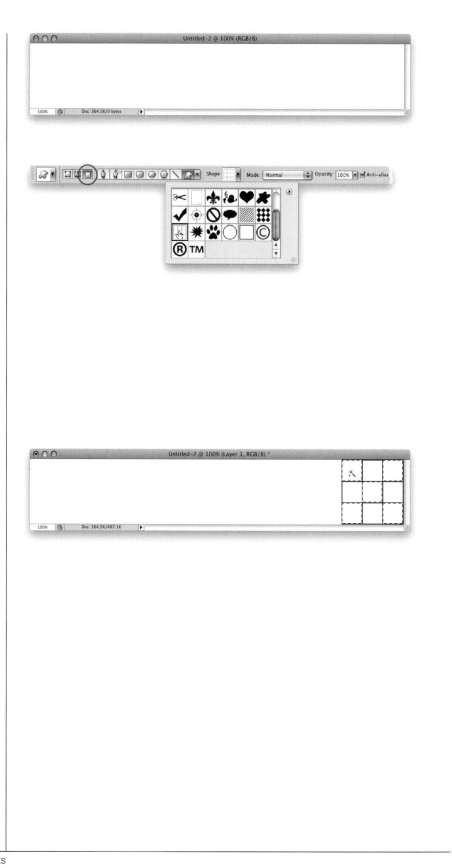

STEP 10: Now create a new blank layer, press **D** to set your Foreground and Background colors to the default black and white, and then take the Custom Shape tool and click-and-drag out a nine-square grid over on the far-right side of the document (as seen here). Once it's in place, switch to the Magic Wand tool and click in the top-right square to select it. Then make more selections by pressing-and-holding the Shift key and clicking in the bottom-right square, the center square, the bottom-left square, and finally the top-left square to select those five squares (as seen here, where they're all selected).

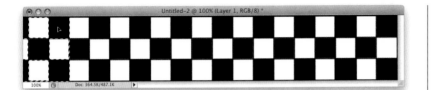

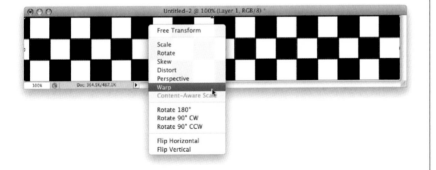

STEP 11: Fill those five squares with black (your Foreground color), which makes a checkerboard pattern. Now, don't deselect yet. Instead, Shift-click on the black strokes on each side of the checkerboard to add them to the selection. Get the Move tool, press-and-hold **Option-Shift (PC: Alt-Shift)**, click on the selected checkerboard, and then drag straight over to the left, and it makes a copy. Holding the Shift key will have this copy line up its squares with your original set (each checkerboard is three squares wide, right? But you'll have to line it up by moving over just two squares. You'll see why when you start to try this yourself). Keep dragging yourself copies (while pressing-and-holding Option-Shift), until they fill the document from side to side with a checkerboard pattern like you see here (yours may look a little different, depending on how you drew your original grid). When you get to the end, you can deselect.

STEP 12: Now you're going to bend this checkerboard, so it's tipping away from you and tilting a bit. Bring up Free Transform, and Control-click (PC: Right-click) anywhere inside your checkerboard. From the contextual menu that appears, choose Warp (as shown here).

Continued

STEP 13: Go up to the Options Bar and, from the Warp pop-up menu, choose Arc. In the Bend field, type in 10, then press the **Tab key** twice to jump over to the V (vertical) field, and enter 25 to give you the shape you see here. Now, lock in your warp.

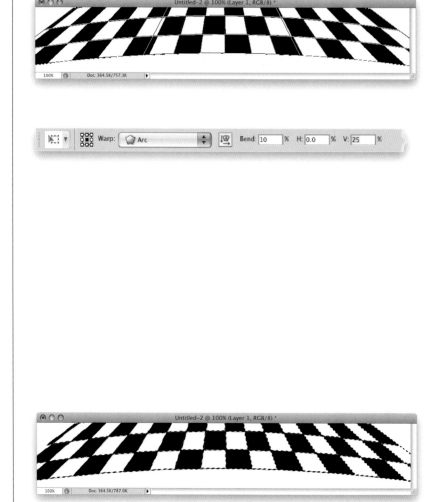

STEP 14: You'll need a selection around just your checkerboard, so go to the Layers panel, press-and-hold the Command (PC: Ctrl) key, and click once directly on the layer's thumbnail to put a selection around your checkerboard layer (as shown here). Copy this checkerboard into memory.

STEP 15: Switch back to your main document (your selection should still be in place), go under the Edit menu, and choose Paste Into to paste your checkerboard pattern into your selection (as shown here). Use the Move tool to reposition the checkerboard, if needed.

STEP 16: So that the checkerboard blends a little better with the red gradient background behind it, lower the Opacity of this layer to around 20% at the top of the Layers panel. Now we're going to add a reflection to the top of this red bar, so get the Rectangular Marquee tool and draw a long, thin rectangular selection across the top of the red gradient bar (as seen here).

Continued

STEP 17: Create a new blank layer, and then press the letter **X** to make white your Foreground color. Now get the Gradient tool, open the Gradient Picker, and click on the second gradient in the top row, which is the Foreground to Transparent gradient (and since your Foreground color is currently white, your gradient will go from white to transparent, as shown here). Take this tool, click just above the rectangular selection, and drag down to the bottom of it to add a gradient that is white at the top and quickly fades down to almost clear (if you wanted it to be completely white, then you'd start dragging downward near the bottom of the selection. By starting to drag outside the selection, it means that a little bit of white will appear at the top of the gradient, which in this case, we wanted). Now lower the Opacity of this layer to around 60%, so it's a bit more see-through.

STEP 18: You're going to be adding some text over the bottom half of the photo, behind your driver, so we're going to add a backscreen effect to do that. Start by going to the Layers panel and clicking on the background photo layer (Layer 2) to make it the active layer. Now create a new blank layer, then get the Rectangular Marquee tool, and click-and-drag a rectangle around the bottom half of the photo (as seen here). Set your Foreground color to black, then fill your rectangle with black (your Foreground color, as shown here), and deselect.

©ISTOCKPHOTO/SHARON MEREDITH

STEP 19: In the Layers panel, lower the Opacity of this solid black layer to around 60%, so that area is darker, but you can still see through to the race car on the background. Here, you can adjust one other thing: the position of the background photo. If it seems too distracting, go the Layers panel and click on the background photo layer again, then get the Move tool, and just click-and-drag it around a bit, so it looks better. It's a little thing, but they're all little things.

STEP 20: Now, open the photo of the other race car. Get the Magic Wand tool again and click it once on the white background. That selects most of the background, but not all the white background seen through the windows. It would take a long time to do this manually, which is why we're going to get Photoshop to help us out. Go under the Select menu and choose Similar (as shown here). What this does is puts a selection around all the other areas in your photo that are the same color as what you've already got selected. In this case, we had white selected, so it selects all the other white areas in the photo for us. (Pretty sweet—I know.) Now press **Command-Shift-I (PC: Ctrl-Shift-I)** to Inverse the selection, so you have the car selected instead of the background. *Note*: The race car has white highlights on its back window and numbers, so some of those small areas will probably get selected, too. If you are worried about them, just get the Lasso tool **(L)**, press-and-hold the Option (PC: Alt) key, draw a selection around those areas, and they'll be removed from your selection.

Continued

STEP 21: Get the Move tool and drag the selected race car over onto your main document, where it will probably be way too big. Bring up Free Transform, then press-and-hold the Shift key, grab a corner point, and drag inward to scale the car down in size. When it looks like the size shown here, lock in your transformation. Position the car to the right of the driver (as shown here).

STEP 22: Now you're going to make a copy of the race car layer, and turn that into a reflection, so press **Command-J (PC: Ctrl-J)** to duplicate the layer. Bring up Free Transform again, and then go under the Edit menu, under Transform, and choose Flip Vertical to flip this duplicate layer upside down (you'll see it upside down in the next step).

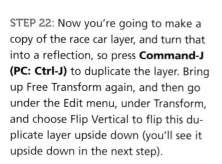

STEP 23: Press **Return (PC: Enter)** to lock in your Vertical Flip, then press-and-hold the Shift key, and with the Move tool, click-and-drag this flipped car straight down until the bottom of the wheels are touching (creating the mirror reflection you see here). Lower the Opacity of this layer to 30%. Now, the bottom of the upside-down car will be hanging off the bottom of your black square, so get the Rectangular Marquee tool and draw a rectangular selection around it (as shown here), and then press the Delete (PC: Backspace) key to remove that excess area, and deselect.

STEP 24: You're going to fade away the bottom of the driver in front (so he "fades to black"). In the Layers panel, click on the driver's layer (Layer 3) to make his layer active. Then click on the Add Layer Mask icon at the bottom of the panel (it's shown circled here in red). Make sure your Foreground color is set to black, then get the Gradient tool, click near the bottom of his leg, and then drag upward, and the bottom of the photo fades out (as shown in the next step).

Continued

STEP 25: Now we can start adding some text. To the right of the driver, using the Horizontal Type tool **(T)**, I added a block of text using the font Myriad Pro Bold (which comes with the Creative Suite and a bunch of other Adobe applications, so you probably already have it installed. If not, use Verdana or Helvetica). The font size is 12 points (but the Driver Details headline is 14 points). There's nothing fancy here—the categories are in all caps, and in gray, and the answers are in white. I used the same fonts to the left of the driver, just in different sizes and weight (the Phoenix type is 33 points Semibold, and the body copy is 12 points Semibold).

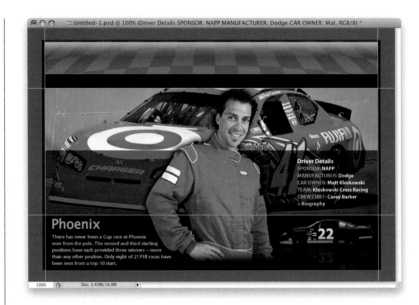

STEP 26: You'll add the driver's name in the top red gradient bar, and his race car number to the far right of it, so click on the top-most layer in the layer stack. The font I used is Myriad Pro Bold Italic at 54 points, but it didn't look to me like the white text stood out enough, so I created a hard black drop shadow behind it by: (a) duplicating the Type layer, (b) filling this duplicate text with black, and then (c) switching to the Move tool and pressing the Right Arrow key twice (to nudge the black text to the right), and then pressing the Down Arrow key twice (to nudge it two pixels down). Then I pressed **Command-[(Left Bracket key; PC: Ctrl-[)**, which moves this black duplicate layer behind the white layer, and since you offset it with the Arrow keys, it appears as a slight black drop shadow (as seen here). Just so you can see this better, I also did it for the number 41, but didn't move it behind the white type yet.

STEP 27: Here's how it looks once you use the keyboard shortcut to move that offset 41 behind the white type. Now, one last thing: To create a little depth, go to the Layers panel and click on the background photo layer (Layer 2), then create a new layer above it. We're going to add a thin inner shadow just above the photo to make it have more depth. To do that, get the Rectangular Marquee tool and draw a thin horizontal rectangle at the top of the background photo, from side to side (as seen here). With your Foreground color set to black, get the Brush tool **(B)**, and choose a small soft-edged brush from the Brush Picker (up in the Options Bar). Press-and-hold the Shift key, and click the Brush tool once on the top-left side of your rectangular selection. Then release the mouse button and, while still holding the Shift key down, move to the right side and click once on the top-right, and a straight line (a thin soft shadow) will appear between those two points. Lighten the effect by lowering the Opacity to 40% in the Layers panel (as seen here).

STEP 28: Go ahead and deselect. We're done at this point, so let's finally get rid of those guides we created earlier by going under the View menu and choosing Clear Guides (if you think you might need to make some adjustments, instead of choosing Clear Guides, press **Command-H [PC: Ctrl-H]**, which just hides the guides from view—it doesn't actually delete them. If you turn them back on, just don't forget to press Command-H again to hide them again when you're done). Here's the final image.

Continued

STEP 29: Here's a variation of the NASCAR page, but highlighting a cyclist instead of a driver. I changed the background photo to one of cyclists in a race, and added a bicycle in place of the small race car in the bottom right. Then, using the same fonts, I changed the text to match the cyclist.

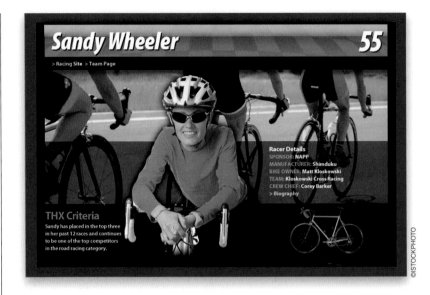

STEP 30: Just to show you how flexible this can be as a template, I also did a page changing it to a business layout. I substituted a businesswoman for the driver, a mobile phone for the small car in the bottom right, and a shot of some tall buildings for the background photo.

Line Burst Background Effect

Since circular line bursts are so popular as backgrounds these days, I knew I had to include it in the book. The example we're doing here I saw on a poster inside a Walt Disney World park bus when I was on vacation there with my family. It was for the ABC show *Good Morning America*, and it makes for a perfect project for learning about these line bursts (by the way, I have no idea what the official name of these things are, so I came up with "line burst." But believe me, I'm open to any better names, since "line burst" just doesn't have much oomph!).

STEP ONE: Create a new document that's 9x9" at a resolution of 72 ppi (we're using this low resolution for practice purposes only). Click on the Foreground color swatch in the Toolbox and set your Foreground color to blue (I used R: 29, G: 62, B: 174) and then fill your Background layer with that color by pressing **Option-Delete (PC: Alt-Backspace)**.

STEP TWO: Go to the Layers panel and create a new blank layer by clicking on the Create a New Layer icon at the bottom of the panel. Now, get the Rectangular Marquee tool **(M)** and create a tall, thin rectangular selection on the far-left side of the document (like the one you see here). You're going to fill this rectangular selection with a darker shade of blue, so set your Foreground color to R: 1, G: 21, B: 125, then fill the selected area with this new color by again pressing Option-Delete (PC: Alt-Backspace). Don't deselect yet.

Continued

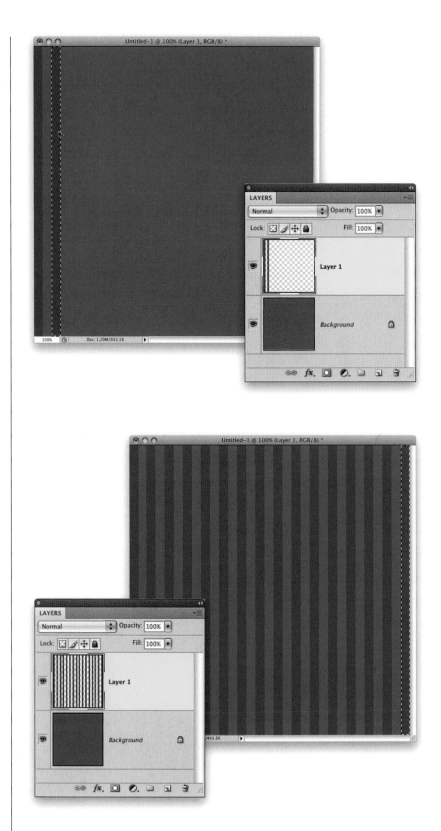

STEP THREE: Instead, press **Command-Option-T (PC: Ctrl-Alt-T)** to go into Free Transform and make a copy of your selected dark rectangle, then press-and-hold the Shift key (to keep things in a straight line), and drag the copy to the right. Leave approximately the width of one bar as the space between the two bars (as seen here). **Press Return (PC: Enter)** to lock in this duplication and move, but still don't deselect quite yet.

STEP FOUR: Now, press **Command-Option-Shift-T (PC: Ctrl-Alt-Shift-T)**, which is the keyboard shortcut that will create another bar that is spaced to the right exactly as you had spaced the second bar (think of it as "step-and-repeat"). Keep pressing that keyboard shortcut again and again until you have a row of perfectly spaced dark blue bars, like you see here. When you get to the last bar, you can finally deselect by pressing **Command-D (PC: Ctrl-D)**.

STEP FIVE: Now you're going to take the vertical bars and turn them into a circle of bars. So, go under the Filter menu, under Distort, and choose Polar Coordinates. The default setting for this filter is Rectangular to Polar, so all you have to do is make sure that's what's selected as your option, and then click OK.

STEP SIX: Here's how the rectangular bars look once you apply the Polar Coordinates filter to them. Now, for this particular layout we need the center of our circular bars to be a little lower than the center of our image area. So, switch to the Move tool **(V)**, click where the bars meet in the center of the image, and drag it downward, so the center is around 25% from the bottom of your document (as seen here). Of course, this leaves a huge gap at the top of your image, so we're just going to stretch it. Press **Command-T (PC: Ctrl-T)** to bring up Free Transform, click on the top-center handle point, and drag upward until your bars fill the entire image area, covering up that gap and aligning nicely with the edges of your document, as you see in the next step.

Continued

STEP SEVEN: Press the **Return (PC: Enter)** key to lock in your transformation, and you can see that now the center of your circular bars is in the lower part of the image (as shown here).

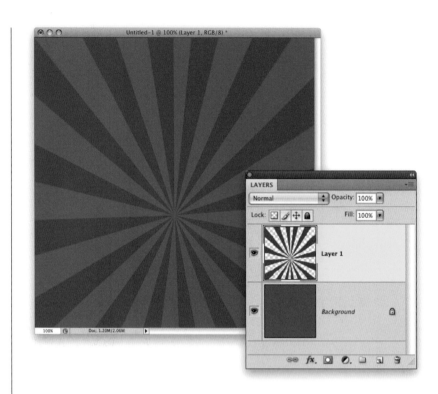

STEP EIGHT: Now, let's add some text. First, set your Foreground color to a dark yellow (I used R: 240, G: 170, B: 75). Get the Horizontal Type tool **(T)** and create your text (I used the font Futura Extra Bold, but you can use Helvetica Bold, or any really bold sans serif font). In Photoshop's Character panel (found under the Window menu), I set the font size to 72 and the tracking (the space between the letters) to –50, so the letters would be nice and close to each other. I also made the leading (the vertical space between the lines of text) nice and tight at a setting of 60 points. Lastly, I made the bottom word "ALBANIA" quite a bit larger than the other words (I set the font size to 115 points, which also caused me to increase the leading amount of "ALBANIA" to 94, because the tops and bottoms of the letters were touching).

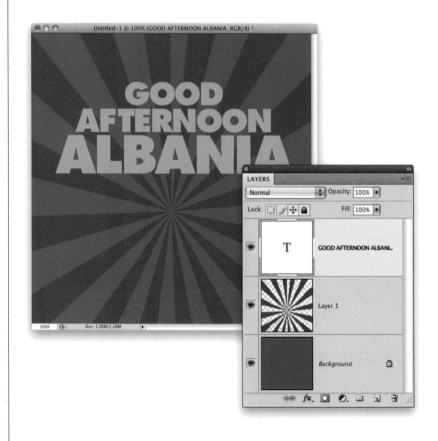

STEP NINE: We're going to add a little "swash" graphic under the text, so start by creating a new blank layer. Then get the Elliptical Marquee tool (press **Shift-M** until you have this round selection tool), and click-and-drag out a huge oval-shaped selection that extends right off the image area (you'll have to click on the bottom-right corner of your image window and drag it out, so you can see the gray area around your image). Make the oval similar to the one you see here (really, really big), and then fill your oval with your Foreground color (if you need to, press-and-hold the Spacebar to move your selection around while you're creating it). *Note:* On a Mac, while you're dragging out your oval, you'll see it extend off the sides like this, but in CS4, once you release the mouse button, your selection automatically becomes contained inside your document border (on a PC, your selection will not extend off the sides). That's okay, because you can't do anything out in that gray area anyway. I just wanted you to know, so you don't freak out. Hey, it could happen.

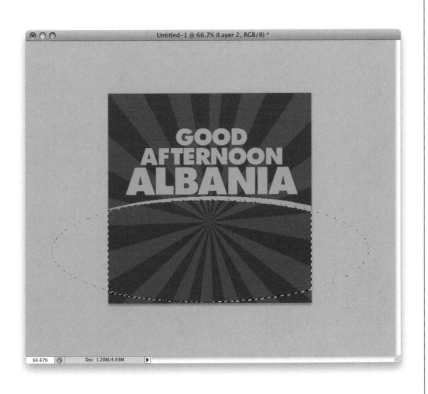

STEP 10: Go ahead and deselect the oval. Now you're going to create another huge oval-shaped selection just a little bit below the big oval that's already in place (like the one seen here). Leave just a little of the top of the original oval still visible, because once your new oval is in place, you're going to press the Delete (PC: Backspace) key to delete the rest of your big yellow oval, leaving just that curved sliver up at the top (as seen here). Now you can deselect again.

Continued

STEP 11: Next, you're going to cut a little chunk out of the far-right side of your yellow graphic sliver. This time, make a small, thin oval (like the one you see here) that cuts off the end of your sliver at an angle, then press the Delete (PC: Backspace) key to cut that area out (as seen here), and deselect.

STEP 12: Just one more little area to cut out, and then our little graphic sliver becomes a graphic swash (because a "swash" just sounds much better!). Draw another oval on the far-left side, just like the one you see here, so it cuts off the left side of the swash (see? Swash sounds better), then hit the Delete (PC: Backspace) key. Go ahead and deselect and you can see the final swash. There's still a couple more things to do, but at least you're done making ovals.

STEP 13: Now, you're going to add a gradient through your text that goes from your regular yellow on the left to an orange on the right. First, click on your Type layer in the Layers panel to make it active. Press the letter **X** to swap your Background and Foreground color swatches (at the bottom of the Toolbox), and then click on the Foreground color swatch to bring up the Color Picker. Choose a dark orange color (I chose R: 220, G: 110, B: 30), then click OK. Now, click on the Add a Layer Style icon at the bottom of the Layers panel, and choose Gradient Overlay. When the Layer Style dialog appears, click on the down-facing arrow to the right of the gradient to bring up the Gradient Picker. Click on the very first gradient (the Foreground to Background gradient) to use your Foreground (orange) and Background (yellow) colors as your gradient. Now, in the Gradient Overlay options in the Layer Style dialog (shown here), set the Angle to 180°, and drag the Scale slider down to 60%, so the gradient graduates from yellow on the left to orange on the right (as seen here), then click OK.

STEP 14: Let's apply that exact same gradient to our swash graphic. Press-and-hold the **Option (PC: Alt) key**, go to the Layers panel, click directly on the phrase "Gradient Overlay" beneath your Type layer, drag it up to your swash graphic layer, and release your mouse button (pressing-and-holding the Option key copies the layer style from one layer to another—you're basically dragging-and-dropping effects). Now, create a new layer. Near the bottom of your image area, with the Rectangular Marquee tool, make a large horizontal rectangular selection (like the one shown here), then fill it with your Foreground color and deselect (it actually doesn't really matter which color you fill it with, because in the next step, you're going to "drag-and-drop" that same gradient effect onto this bar.

Continued

STEP 15: Drag-and-drop a copy of the Gradient Overlay layer style from the swash layer to this rectangular bar layer to add the gradient (as seen here). Now you can press **D** to set your Foreground color to black, and use the Horizontal Type tool to add text for the website of the company (although I put my daily blog address as a subtle reminder to visit me there). Now let's add a logo below the swash, so create a new layer. Get the Elliptical Marquee tool again, press-and-hold the Shift key, so it creates a perfect circle, then click-and-drag out a circular selection below the center of the swash (press-and-hold the Spacebar to reposition it). Fill the circle with black (your Foreground color), and then add a white stroke around your black circle by clicking on the Add a Layer Style icon at the bottom of the Layers panel, and choosing Stroke from the pop-up menu. In the Stroke Fill Type section of the Layer Style dialog, just click on the Color swatch, change the color to white, click OK in the Color Picker, and then also in the Layer Style dialog. Now press **X** to make white your Foreground color, then add the CS4 text in the center of the black circle. (*Note:* I made the "4" a smaller font size, so it looked even.)

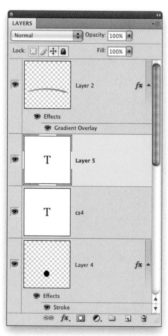

STEP 16: The final step is to darken the area behind the text and black circular logo, so it's not so hard to read over the center of the circular bars. Start by clicking on the circular bars layer (Layer 1) in the Layers panel, then create a new layer directly above it. Get the Eyedropper tool **(I)**, click on one of the darker blue bars to make it your Foreground color, then fill this new layer with this darker blue color. With the Elliptical Marquee tool, press-and-hold the Shift key and make a large circular selection where most of your text appears (as seen here). To soften the edges of your selection, go under the Select menu, choose Modify, and then choose Feather. When the dialog appears, enter 50 pixels and click OK. Now, press **Command-Shift-I (PC: Ctrl-Shift-I)** to Inverse your selection, then press Delete (PC: Backspace) to erase everything but that soft circle in the center, which completes the effect (seen here).

Sports Poster Backscreened Layout

Backscreening has always been popular (even before there was Photoshop), but in this case, we're taking things way beyond backscreening and recreating a poster I did for a local soccer league (the league president is one of my longtime friends). I did a photo shoot out at the field with some wonderful kids, and then took the images and created the poster you're about to create. Also, at the end of the project, I gave you an alternate layout, just so you can see how easy it is to customize a layout like this.

STEP ONE: Start by pressing **Command-N (PC: Ctrl-N)** to create a new document. Since we're just practicing, we can create a small, low-resolution document. The one we're creating here is 8" wide by 12" high at a resolution of 72 ppi. Now, click on the Foreground color swatch at the bottom of the Toolbox, and in the Color Picker, set it to a dark gray (I used R: 71, G: 71, B: 71), then fill your Background layer with this color by pressing **Option-Delete (PC: Alt-Backspace)**.

STEP TWO: Open the logo you want to add to your poster (you can download the sports logo you see here, if you'd like. Just go to **www.kelbytraining .com/books/CS4DD**). We need just the logo by itself, and not the white background it sits on, so get the Magic Wand tool (press **Shift-W** until you have it) and click it once on the white background to select it.

SCOTT KELBY

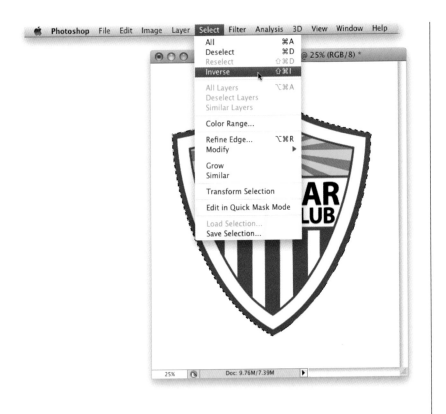

STEP THREE: At this point, the white background is selected, but that's exactly the opposite of what we need selected (which is the logo). So, go under the Select menu and choose Inverse (as shown here), and it inverses your selection, so now instead of the background being selected, the logo is selected (this is a pretty popular way to select any object on a solid background—you start by selecting the background, which is usually pretty easy, and then you inverse to select the object).

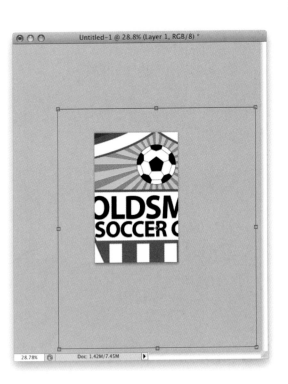

STEP FOUR: Now switch to the Move tool **(V)**, and click-and-drag the logo onto your gray background document (don't close this logo document quite yet, though, and keep your selection in place, too—you'll need this logo again in a few moments). When the logo appears in your new document, it's going to be pretty huge (as you can see here), but it's easy to resize. Press **Command-T (PC: Ctrl-T)** to bring up Free Transform. Because the logo is so much larger than the image area, you won't be able to reach the Free Transform handles until you press **Command-0 (zero; PC: Ctrl-0)**, which automatically resizes the window, so you can reach all four corner handles (as seen here). Just click on a corner handle and drag in to the size you want (press-and-hold the Shift key to keep it proportional).

Continued

STEP FIVE: Once you've got the size about where you want it, move your cursor outside the Free Transform bounding box, and click-and-drag in a circular motion to rotate your image (as seen here). When you're done, press **Return (PC: Enter)** to lock in your re-sizing and rotation.

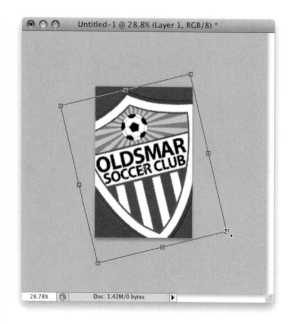

STEP SIX: To backscreen your logo, so it's just a subtle image in the back-ground, go to the Layers panel and lower the Opacity to around 5% (as seen here). You can see that the logo is still very visible, but now it's back-screened enough to where you can put text and photos above it without it dis-tracting from them.

STEP SEVEN: To make the logo appear even subtler, we're going to remove the color. You can try the Desaturate command (press Command-Shift-U [PC: Ctrl-Shift-U]), but I decided to manually desaturate the color using a Hue/Saturation adjustment layer, because when I used Desaturate, the stripes at the top of the logo disappeared. To use an adjustment layer, go to the Adjustments panel (found under the Window menu), click on the Hue/Saturation icon (the second icon from the left, in the second row), and then drag the Saturation slider all the way to the left (to –100, as shown here). This removes the color, but retains the stripes in the top of the logo. Why do two seemingly similar commands have such different results? I have no idea. However, there is another advantage to removing the color with an adjustment layer like this—we can delete the adjustment layer later if we change our minds (and we just might).

STEP EIGHT: Now open the color photo you want to appear above your gray backscreened background.

Continued

STEP NINE: Get the Move tool, and drag-and-drop this photo onto your poster document. When you do this, you'll find that the photo isn't quite wide enough to fill from side to side (there's a small gap on both sides). This is where CS4's Content-Aware Scale feature is worth its weight in gold, because it will let us stretch the edges of the photo, without distorting or stretching our soccer player. Go under the Edit menu and choose Content-Aware Scale. This puts Free Transform-like handle points around your image. Just drag the right-side point to the right until the gap is filled, then do the same to the left side, until the image fills the poster side to side (as shown here). Press **Return (PC: Enter)** to lock in your changes.

STEP 10: Remember earlier when I said not to deselect or close that logo document? That's because you need that logo again now. With the Move tool, click-and-drag that logo onto your document again, then use Free Transform to scale your logo down to the size you see here. Lock in your resizing, and then position the logo so it's centered under the photo (as seen here).

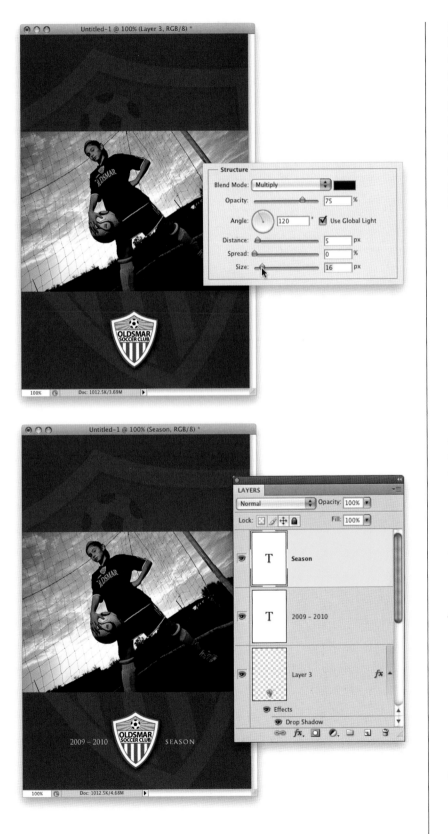

STEP 11: To create some separation between the logo and the background, we'll add a drop shadow. So, click on the Add a Layer Style icon at the bottom of the Layers panel, and choose Drop Shadow from the pop-up menu. When the Layer Style dialog appears, increase the Size amount to 16 (as shown here) to make the shadow softer, then click OK. This adds a soft drop shadow below and to the right of your logo (as seen here).

STEP 12: We're going to add some text on either side of the logo. I used the font Trajan Pro, which comes with the Creative Suite (so if you have the Creative Suite, it should already be installed in your Font pop-up menu). Press **D**, then **X** to set your Foreground color to white, get the Horizontal Type tool **(T)**, click it once in your document, and choose Trajan Pro from the Font pop-up menu up in the Options Bar. Set your font size to 16 points, type in "2009 – 2010" as your text, then click on the Move tool in the Toolbox and position the text on the left at about the center of the logo (as seen here). Press **Command-J (PC: Ctrl-J)** to duplicate this text layer, then press-and-hold the Shift key, and with the Move tool, drag this copy straight over to the right. Return to the Horizontal Type tool, highlight the duplicated text, and then type in "SEASON" (as seen here).

Continued

STEP 13: Let's add another line of type up top. With the Horizontal Type tool, type in "OLDSMAR SOCCER CLUB" in the font Helvetica Bold (or another font of your choice) at 13 points, and position it at the top center of the poster (as seen here). To make the type appear wider, I used Free Transform—bring up Free Transform, grab either the left or right center handle point, drag outward, and it stretches your type, which makes it wider and thicker, like the type you see here. When it looks good to you, lock in your stretching.

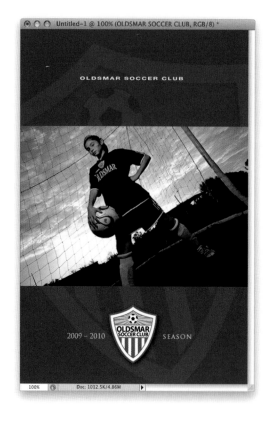

STEP 14: Now you're going to take an element from the logo (the soccer ball) and separate it, so you can use it in your poster. Switch back to the logo document (press **Command-D [PC: Ctrl-D]** to Deselect, if your selection is still in place around the logo). Get the Elliptical Marquee tool (press **Shift-M** until you have it), press-and-hold the Shift key, and click-and-drag out a circular selection around the soccer ball. This isn't as easy as it sounds, but you can use the trick I mentioned earlier to help you out: as you're dragging out your selection, press-and-hold the Spacebar—this will let you reposition the circle as you're dragging it out, and now it's simple to create a circular selection around the soccer ball (as seen here).

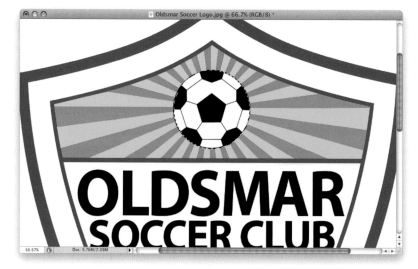

STEP 15: Get the Move tool, and click-and-drag your selected soccer ball over to your main document. Use Free Transform to shrink the size of your soccer ball down to the size you see here (be sure to press-and-hold the Shift key while resizing to keep it proportional), and position it so it's at the top center of your photo, with half the ball on the photo, and half on the poster background. This is a design trick that helps to unify the background and the photo (the overlapping soccer ball acts to visually tie them together). When it looks good, lock in your resizing.

STEP 16: Now let's put the same exact drop shadow on the soccer ball that we put on the logo. In the Layers panel, scroll down to the Logo layer (Layer 3), Control-click (PC: Right-click) on it, and from the contextual menu, choose Copy Layer Style. Then scroll back up to the small soccer ball layer, Control-click on that layer, and from the contextual menu, choose Paste Layer Style. This pastes the exact same drop shadow, with the same exact specs, onto this soccer ball (as seen here—notice the soccer ball now has a drop shadow, creating some depth above the photo). This completes our poster, but on the next page, I'm going to show you how easy it is to create a different look once you have these things already in place.

Continued

STEP 17: For our new look, click on the Eye icons next to each Type layer, along with the small soccer ball layer, then delete or hide the photo layer (by dragging the layer onto the Trash icon at the bottom of the Layers panel or by clicking on the Eye icon to the left of its layer), so all you have visible is the background, the backscreened large logo, and the small logo at the bottom. Now press D to set your Foreground and Background colors to their defaults of black and white.

STEP 18: In the Layers panel, click on the Background layer, press **Command-A (PC: Ctrl-A)** to select the entire background, then press the Delete (PC: Backspace) key to erase the gray background. Next, drag the Hue/Saturation layer that's directly above your backscreened layer onto the Trash icon to delete it. This brings back the color in your backscreened logo. Click on its layer and raise the Opacity to 15% to make the logo stand out a bit more. Now open a tall photo, and with the Move tool, drag it into your poster layout and position it like the one you see here. Click on the regular full-color logo layer, and use Free Transform to shrink the size of this smaller logo and position it below the center of the photo (as seen here).

SCOTT KELBY

STEP 19: Now, copy-and-paste the Drop Shadow layer style from the small logo layer to the new photo layer, using the technique you learned back in Step 16, to give you the look you see here. The last step is to add a white stroke around the photo, so click on the photo layer, then click on the Add a Layer Style icon at the bottom of the Layers panel and choose Stroke from the pop-up menu. When the dialog appears, change the stroke color to white (click on the black Color swatch and a Color Picker will appear), then click OK to apply a white stroke around your photo (you'll see the white stroke in the final image on the right below). Both of the final posters are shown below.

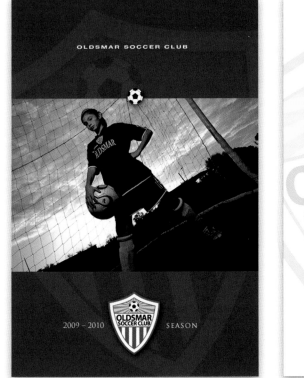

CHAPTER

4

W.C.

Dangerous Type

type effects

"Dangerous Type," named after the song by The Cars, is just about the perfect name for a chapter on creating type effects. Now, in all actuality, the really perfect name for a chapter on type effects would be "Type Effects," but I couldn't find a movie, TV show, band, or song named "Type Effects," however I was able to find a song named "The Darker Type" (by the band The Dying Effect, from their album "Bleed the Night"), which is what I was going to use, but when I heard the 30-second online preview of the "death metal" song, I realized that I could actually understand more of the words from any song by French pop musician Maxime Le Forestier, than I could from "The Darker Type," despite my complete inability to speak French, with the possible exception of the phrase, "J'ai une urgence de salle de bains," which I memorized just in case (which loosely translated means, "It's urgent that you call Sally Jessy Raphael, or actor Conrad Bain"). Anyway, I have to tell you—you don't want to play "The Darker Type" when you're alone with the lights out, because it's really scary sounding (which is surprising for the tender love song it sounds like it is). So, I went with "Dangerous Type," mostly because none of the lyrics made me want to bludgeon myself, which I think is a real plus.

Halftone Pattern Type Look

This look was made popular by a very slick series of TV and Web ads for Ford's F-150 truck. While the type effect itself is pretty simple, what makes the project a lot of fun (and a great learning experience) is going through all the steps you need to create the whole look of the ad from scratch, which is what we're going to do here. This particular look is incredibly popular right now (the overall grungy look, not just the type effect), so learning this look will probably come in even more handy than the type trick. Here's how it's done:

STEP ONE: Open the photo you want to apply this type effect to (you can download the photo shown here from the book's downloads page, mentioned in the book's intro). Now duplicate the Background layer (as seen here in the Layers panel) by pressing **Command-J (PC: Ctrl-J).**

©ISTOCKPHOTO/ROBERT PABICH

STEP TWO: Go under the Filter menu, under Artistic, and choose Cutout. This filter will give us a posterized look to our image (a look using only a few colors), without it looking as harsh as it would if we actually posterized the image. When the dialog appears, at the top right, choose 5 for Number of Levels (as shown here), set the Edge Simplicity to 0, the Edge Fidelity to 2, then click OK to apply this effect to the photo. As you can see here in the preview on the left side of the dialog, there's a cool effect on the photo, but we lost all the detail in the truck (and if you're doing this for a truck manufacturer or truck dealer, they're not going to want you to mess with the truck. That's why we duplicated the layer when we started—so we can go back and get parts of the original untouched image if we need it (and as it turns out, we need it).

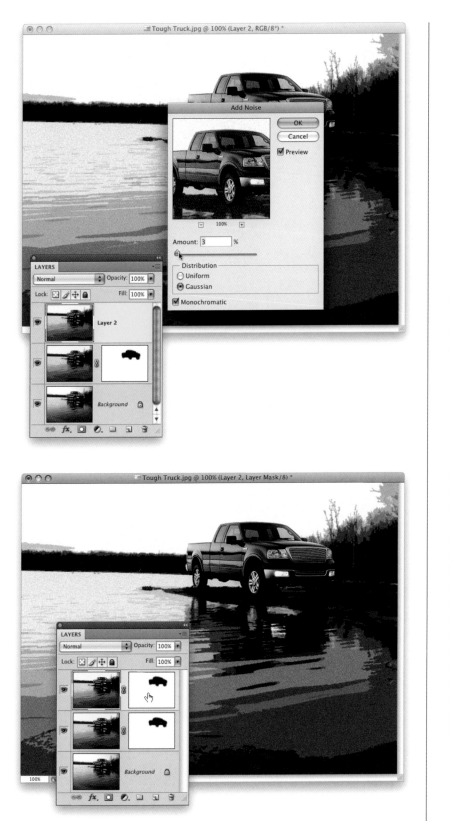

STEP THREE: Go to the Layers panel and click on the Add Layer Mask icon at the bottom of the panel. Press **X** to set your Foreground color to black, get the Brush tool **(B)**, choose a medium-sized, soft-edged brush (from the Brush Picker up in the Options Bar), and paint over the truck. As you do, the original untouched truck (from the layer below) is revealed, and now all our detail is back. Press **Command-Option-Shift-E (PC: Ctrl-Alt-Shift-E)** to make a new layer that looks like a flattened version of your file (doing this leaves all the other layers intact, in case we have to go back and make a change later). Now let's add some noise to grunge things up a bit. Go under the Filter menu, under Noise, and choose Add Noise. When the dialog appears (shown here), set your Amount at 3%, choose Gaussian as the Distribution (it looks better), and turn on the Monochromatic checkbox (so your noise doesn't look like little red, green, and blue dots). Click OK.

STEP FOUR: Now, to keep the truck looking good, you don't want noise all over it, but that's an easy fix. Go to the Layers panel and press-and-hold the **Option (PC: Alt) key**. Don't change layers, but click directly on the layer mask thumbnail in the center layer (the one where you painted back in the truck), and just drag-and-drop that layer mask onto the top layer in the stack (your noise layer). Pressing-and-holding the Option key copies the layer mask from one layer to another, and since your mask was of the truck, the noise is instantly removed from just the truck. (I know, copying masks is sa-weet!)

Continued

STEP FIVE: Now we're going to grunge things up even more. Open the paper texture file (shown here below) you downloaded from the book's downloads webpage (it's the same one we used in the "Adding Texture and Aging to a Photo" project in Chapter 2). Get the Move tool **(V)**, and just drag-and-drop that paper texture photo right onto your truck photo. Of course, this will just cover your truck photo, so at the top of the Layers panel, change the blend mode of this layer to Multiply (so it blends in and darkens the whole photo at the same time) and, since it's too dark, lower the Opacity of this layer to 45% (shown here). Okay, time for another one of those merged layers on top (like we did in Step Three), so press Command-Option-Shift-E (PC: Ctrl-Alt-Shift-E).

STEP SIX: Let's add some edge darkening by going under the Filter menu, under Distort, and choosing Lens Correction. When the dialog appears, first turn off the annoying Show Grid checkbox (yes, that's its official name—annoying Show Grid checkbox) at the bottom of the dialog. Now that you can actually see what's going on (don't get me started), go to the Vignette section on the right side of the dialog, and for Amount, enter –63 (that controls how dark your corners get), for Midpoint, choose 40 (that controls how far the edge darkening extends in toward the center of your photo), then click OK to darken the edges around your photo (as seen here).

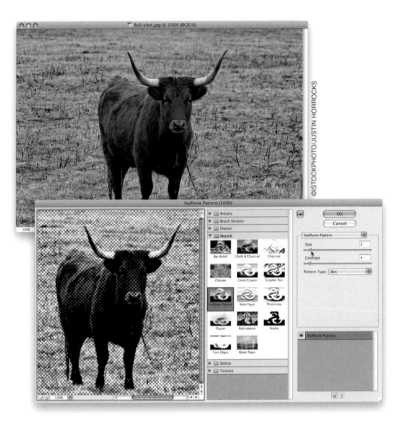

STEP SEVEN: Now open the photo of a bull (think: "Strong like a bull"), and then go under the Filter menu, under Sketch, and choose Halftone Pattern. When the dialog appears, at the top right, set the Size to 2, the Contrast to 4, make sure the Pattern Type is set to Dot, and click OK to give you the effect you see here in the preview on the left side of the dialog (a grayscale image with lots of repeating dots).

STEP EIGHT: With the Move tool, click-and-drag that gray-dotty bull over onto your main image, and position him over to the far left (like you see here). You're probably noticing that on your screen, he doesn't exactly "blend in," so change the layer blend mode for this layer to Soft Light, then lower the Opacity to around 60% to give you the effect you see here. Now, you can still see hard edges along the right side and top of the bull photo, but don't worry—you'll fix that in the next step.

Continued

STEP NINE: Go to the Layers panel and click on the Add Layer Mask icon at the bottom of the panel. With your Foreground color set to black, get the Brush tool **(B)**, and choose a really huge, soft-edged brush from the Brush Picker in the Options Bar (notice the size of my brush here). Just paint over those hard outside edges and, in seconds, they are gone, blending in nicely with the rest of the photo. The key is to start far away from the edges, and move slowly in as you paint short strokes up and down. You'll see your edges start to fade away as you get close to them. Now it's time (finally!) to add the text effect we came here for in the first place. We'll look at some tips on how to design with type, as well.

STEP 10: Start by getting the Horizontal Type tool **(T)** and choose a bold sans serif font. I used Helvetica Black, and in the Character panel (found under the Window menu), I set the Tracking (the space between the letters) to a negative amount, so that the letters are very close together—the top line of type is 6 points with the Tracking set to –80, which is very tight—and I chose a light brown for the text color by clicking on the Color swatch in the Character panel. Type in the line, "It's not just another truck." We're going to be using just one font for everything we do here, so it's quickest to just duplicate that first line of type, highlight it, and type in your new text. To do that, get the Move tool, then duplicate your Type layer, and click-and-drag that duplicate type straight downward, so it's beneath your original type. In the Layers panel, double-click directly on the duplicate text layer's thumbnail to highlight its text, then change its color to a dark gray. Now, you can just type "IT'S THE," like you see here, make it slightly larger (between 7 and 8 points), get back the Move tool, and position it so the left side is aligned with the top line of text (as seen here).

STEP 11: We want the lines of type below this to line up, so press **Command-R (PC: Ctrl-R)** to make the Rulers visible, then click on the left-side ruler and pull out a vertical guide, aligning it with the left side of your type. Pull out another vertical guide and align it with the right side of the word "THE" (as seen here). Now duplicate the IT'S THE layer, click-and-drag it downward, highlight the text, and type in the word "ALL," which needs to fill the area between the two guides. To do that, switch back to the Move tool, press **Command-T (PC: Ctrl-T)** to bring up Free Transform, press-and-hold the Shift key, click on the bottom-right corner handle, and drag outward until the text scales up to fill in that space. Reposition it as needed, then press **Return (PC: Enter)** to lock in your resizing. Do the same thing again, but change the text to read "NEW" (seen in the next step).

STEP 12: Now you're going to add "'09," but before you do, create two horizontal guides (click-and-drag them out from the top ruler), and position them as you see here, because the "'09" has to be exactly as tall as the lines "ALL" and "NEW." Duplicate the word "NEW," click-and-drag it to the right, highlight it, change the color to a dark yellow (I used R: 217, G: 168, B: 76), and then type in "'09." Use Free Transform to resize it, so it fits within the two horizontal grid lines. *Note:* To create the backwards apostrophe, press the Apostrophe key twice, then delete the first one. Also, I shrank the apostrophe, so it fit inside the "L" in the word "ALL." Then I did a baseline shift to move it upward by highlighting the apostrophe, then pressing **Option-Shift-Up Arrow key (PC: Alt-Shift-Up Arrow key)** a few times. Duplicate the word "NEW" again, reposition it, highlight it, and change it to "SERIES." Use Free Transform to scale it up until it reaches the end of the "9" (everything has to line up to something in type design).

Continued

STEP 13: You're going to start to apply the effect to the text. (*Note:* I've turned off the Rulers **[Command-R; PC: Ctrl-R]** and removed the guides [by choosing Clear Guides from the View menu] because we no longer need them.) First, click on the top layer in your layer stack and create a new blank layer at the top by clicking on the Create a New Layer icon at the bottom of the Layers panel. **Command-Shift-click (PC: Ctrl-Shift-click)** directly on the thumbnail for your top Type layer (the '09 layer, as shown here) to put a selection around the type on that layer. Then go to the next layer down (keep holding down those keys) and click on its thumbnail. It will add the word on that layer to your selection. Keep doing that (and keep holding those two keys down) for the rest of your Type layers, until there's a selection around all the Type layers you created (as seen here). By the way, what's making this work like this is the Shift key—when you hold it down, along with the Command key, it tells Photoshop to add the next thing you click on, so as you keep clicking on Type layer thumbnails, it keeps adding that layer to your selection already in place.

STEP 14: Click on the Foreground color swatch and set your Foreground color to a medium gray. Make sure you still have that new top layer selected in the Layers panel, and press **Option-Delete (PC: Alt-Backspace)** to fill the type selection with gray (as seen here). Don't deselect quite yet.

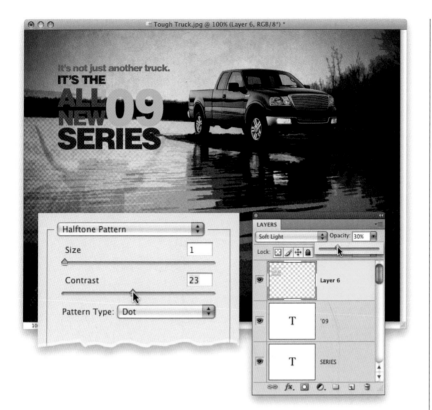

STEP 15: Go under the Filter menu, under Sketch, and choose Halftone Pattern. When the dialog appears, for Size, choose 1, for Contrast, choose 23 (as shown here), set your Pattern Type to Dot, then click OK. This puts a tight dot pattern over your type that looks pretty cool (I know it's hard to see here in the book, but you'll see it on your screen big time!). Now you can Deselect by pressing **Command-D (PC: Ctrl-D)**. To have your dots layer blend in with your type on the layer below it, go to the Layers panel and change the layer blend mode to Soft Light, and lower the Opacity to 30% (as shown here). Now, it nicely blends over the type, and most of the original color is still there.

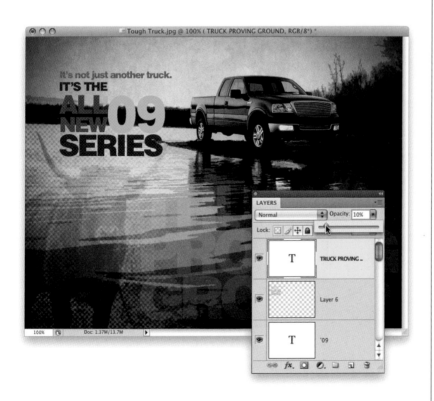

STEP 16: Let's add some really huge type, just for looks. Duplicate your "SERIES" Type layer, then click-and-drag the duplicate layer above your gray dots layer. Highlight the text on the layer, change the color to white, and type "TRUCK PROVING GROUND" (one word on each line). Use the same font and make it really huge. I made mine 38 points at –100 tracking. I also made the Leading (the vertical space between the lines of text) really tight, too—in the Character panel, I set the Leading to 28. Now, get the Move tool and move this type over to the lower right of the image and then lower the layer Opacity of this Type layer to 10% (as shown here), so the text is just barely there.

Continued

STEP 17: You're going to build another block of text, but these words are going to line up differently. Duplicate one of your Type layers (like the "SERIES" layer) and click-and-drag it up to the top of the layer stack. Highlight it, type "THE MOST," and then move it over to the right with the Move tool. Repeat this to create new Type layers for "EFFICIENT," "OF THE," "BIG," and finally "TRUCKS." Highlight the "EFFICIENT" text and change the color to that same yellow color you used on the '09 text. Do the same thing for "TRUCKS." Next, change the color of "THE MOST," "OF THE," and "BIG" to white. Now, you just have to resize them and then align them. If you look at the type here, you'll see that the first three lines ("THE MOST," "EFFICIENT," and "OF THE") are all aligned along the right, and they line up with the right side of the letter "R" in "TRUCKS." The word "BIG" is as tall as "EFFICIENT" and "OF THE" combined, and it's aligned with the letters "UC" below it. Again, everything has to line up with something, but that's actually good, because now it's no longer a guessing game, right? Now you know, "Oh, this should line up with these other letters."

STEP 18: Now it's time to put a selection around all those new Type layers, so we can add our text effect to them. Create a new blank layer at the top of your layer stack. Command-Shift-click (PC: Ctrl-Shift-click) directly on the thumbnails for all your new Type layers to put a selection around them (as shown here). Once all of them are selected, set your Foreground color to a medium gray, and fill your selection with this color. Don't deselect yet.

STEP 19: Press **Command-F (PC: Ctrl-F)** to apply the Halftone Pattern filter, using the exact same settings you used a few moments ago when applying the filter to the type at the top left (that keyboard shortcut does just that—it repeats your last filter using the same settings). Now, at this point, it's covering your type, but you want it to blend in. Last time, we changed the layer blend mode to Soft Light, but this time we're going to choose Multiply instead, because our text is white and yellow, rather than dark gray, brown, and yellow, so in this case, Multiply looks better (by the way, I didn't just magically know that. When I chose Soft Light it looked bad, so I went through some of the other blend modes until I found one that looked good— Multiply). This makes the text color look a little funky, and the effect appears too intense, but we'll fix both of those in the next step. Now you can deselect.

STEP 20: To finish this project off, all you have to do is lower the Opacity of this layer to 30%, which brings back the color, and makes the text effect not appear too intense. Here's the final image with that last tweak.

Fracturing Your Type

I saw this technique most recently in the movie poster for the movie *Fracture*, starring Anthony Hopkins and Ryan Gosling (fracturemovie.com). This technique has been used in a number of different ways, but besides just learning the technique, there are a few other interesting little techniques to learn along the way (plus, you've got to love a technique you can wrap up in just two pages).

STEP ONE: Start by pressing **Command-N (PC: Ctrl-N)** to create a new document (I made mine 800x600 pixels at a resolution of 72 ppi). Press **D** to set your Foreground color to black, then press **Option-Delete (PC: Alt-Backspace)** to fill your Background layer with black. Get the Horizontal Type tool **(T)** and create your text (I used the font Trajan Pro, which comes with the Creative Suite, in white at 135 points). Click on your Foreground color swatch and choose a light gray in the Color Picker, then click on the Add a Layer Style icon at the bottom of the Layers panel and choose Gradient Overlay. When the Layer Style dialog appears, click on the down-facing arrow to the right of the gradient thumbnail to bring up the Gradient Picker. Choose the first gradient, which is the Foreground to Background gradient (your gradient will go from white at the top to light gray at the bottom, as shown here), and click OK.

STEP TWO: Here you're going to add a little bit of a bevel, with some red in its shadow areas. Click on the Add a Layer Style icon at the bottom of the Layers panel and choose Bevel and Emboss from the pop-up menu. When the dialog appears, change the Style to Emboss, then at the bottom of the dialog, next to Shadow Mode, click on the black color swatch. When the Color Picker appears, choose a bright red as your color, click OK, then lower the Opacity of the bevel's shadow to 50% (as shown here), so the red doesn't stand out too much. Click OK to apply the subtle bevel effect you see here.

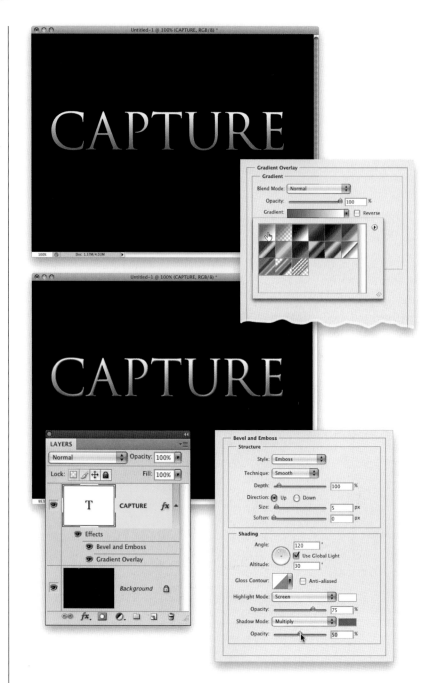

STEP THREE: Now, we have two issues to deal with: (1) to be able to cut through the type on the Type layer, we're going to have to convert it from editable type to regular pixels (like any other object in Photoshop), and (2) when we cut the text, the bevel and gradient layer styles will change. Here's how we get around both: Go to the Layers panel and click on the Background layer. Then create a new blank layer above it by clicking on the Create a New Layer icon at the bottom of the Layers panel. Now click on your Type layer, then press **Command-E (PC: Ctrl-E)**, which merges your Type layer with the new blank layer. This rasterizes your type and applies the bevel permanently. Problem solved. Now take the Polygonal Lasso tool (press **Shift-L** until you have it) and draw a selection over the top of the last three letters (like you see here).

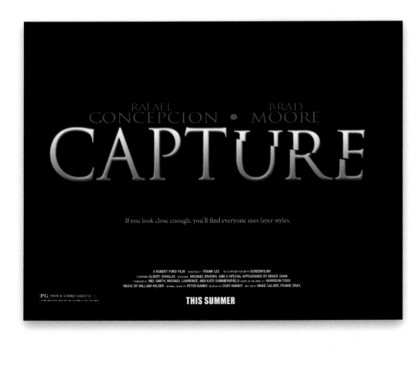

STEP FOUR: Get the Move tool **(V)** and press the Right Arrow key on your keyboard a few times, and it automatically selects the letters within the selection and moves them to the right to create the effect you see here. There is one more thing they did in the actual movie title: while the broken letters were still selected, they used Free Transform **(Command-T [PC: Ctrl-T])** to shrink those letters down a little bit, and then they nudged them back up a few pixels (using the Up Arrow key on their keyboard). You can now press **Command-D (PC: Ctrl-D)** to Deselect. The actors' names up top are in the same font (Trajan Pro), but in the Character panel (found under the Window menu), I increased the Horizontal Scaling to 130% to stretch the letters a bit. The tagline below the movie title is in the font Minion Pro (which also comes with the Adobe Creative Suite).

PlayStation Type Trick

I actually saw this technique at the end of a TV ad for a game built for Sony's PlayStation 3 game console, and I thought two things: (1) hey, that is pretty cool, and (2) I'll bet I can figure that one out. As it turned out, it was easier than I thought. Here's how it's done:

STEP ONE: Press **Command-N (PC: Ctrl-N)** to create a new blank document (I made mine 800x600 pixels at a resolution of 72 ppi). Press **D** to set your Foreground color to black, then press **Option-Delete (PC: Alt-Backspace)** to fill your Background layer with black. Next, add a new blank layer above your black Background layer by clicking on the Create a New Layer icon at the bottom of the Layers panel. Get the Polygonal Lasso tool (press **Shift-L** until you have it) and draw a long, thin diamond shape like the one you see here (this tool draws straight line selections, so it takes just five clicks to create this diamond shape).

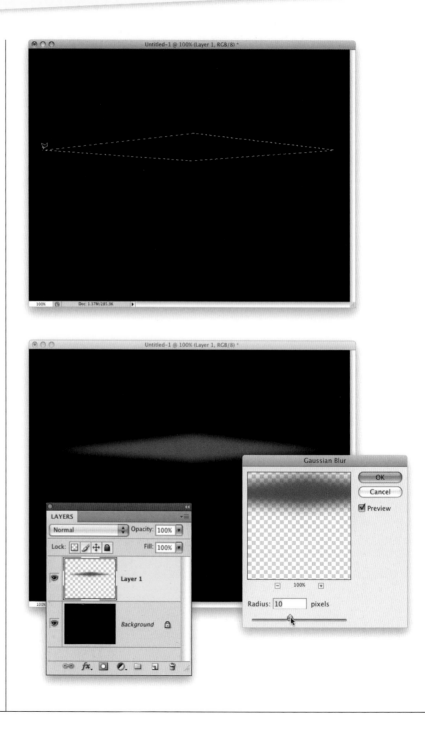

STEP TWO: Now click on the Foreground color swatch and set your Foreground color to a purple in the Color Picker (I used R: 98, G: 95, B: 166), then fill your selection with this purple color by pressing **Option-Delete (PC: Alt-Backspace)**. Deselect by pressing **Command-D (PC: Ctrl-D)**. Next, go under the Filter menu, under Blur, and choose Gaussian Blur. For your Radius, enter 10 pixels (as shown here), then click OK to soften the diamond shape.

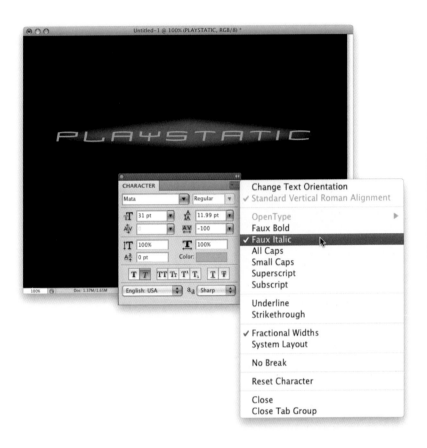

STEP THREE: This time, set your Foreground color to a medium gray, then get the Horizontal Type tool **(T)**. Click inside your image area, then type in your text. (I used the font Mata, which, besides having a version of it used for PlayStation, is the same typeface used for the movie *Spiderman*, which automatically makes it cool. At least to my son.) Also, the PlayStation version is in italic, and while I don't have an italic version of the font Mata, you can actually have Photoshop "fake it." Select your text, then go to the Character panel (found under the Window menu), click on the down-facing arrow at the top right, and from the flyout menu, chose Faux Italic to create a fake italic version of the font. Now, with the Move tool **(V)** position this text in the center of your blurry purple diamond (yes, that's its official name, but you can call it BPD).

STEP FOUR: Make a duplicate of this Type layer by pressing **Command-J (PC: Ctrl-J)**. Now press **Command-T (PC: Ctrl-T)** to bring up Free Transform, then Control-click (PC: Right-click) inside your image and choose Flip Vertical from the contextual menu, which flips your duplicate layer's text upside down. Press-and-hold the Shift key and click-and-drag the upside down text straight down until the bases of the two Type layers line up, creating a mirror reflection like you see here. Press **Return (PC: Enter)** to commit the transformation.

Continued

STEP FIVE: At the top of the Layers panel, lower the Opacity of this duplicate layer to 40% to help it stand out from the original Type layer above it. Now, click on the Add Layer Mask icon at the bottom of the Layers panel. With your Foreground and Background colors set to their layer mask defaults of white and black, take the Gradient tool **(G)**, choose the Foreground to Background gradient in the Options Bar, and click-and-drag from the top of your flipped type layer down to almost the bottom of the type to make it fade away (as seen here).

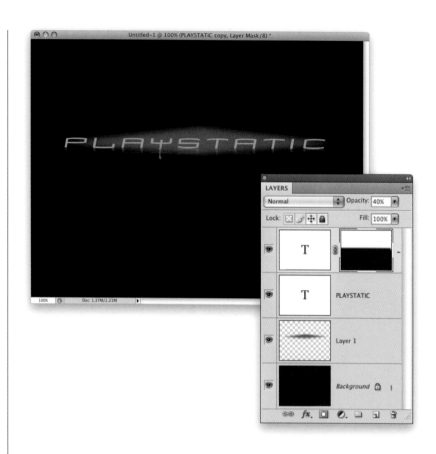

STEP SIX: In the Layers panel, click on the diamond shape layer (Layer 1), then get the Rectangular Marquee tool **(M)**, and click-and-drag a rectangular selection right along the baseline where the text meets, to down below the bottom of the diamond (in other words, select the bottom half of the diamond), and then press Delete (PC: Backspace). This leaves only the top of the diamond visible behind the regular text—not the reflected text (as seen here), which kind of gives you that "planet rising" effect. Now you can deselect, because we have to tweak a few things to finish this puppy off.

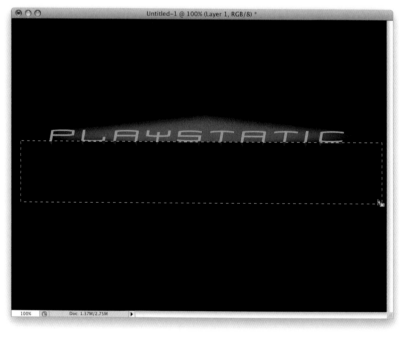

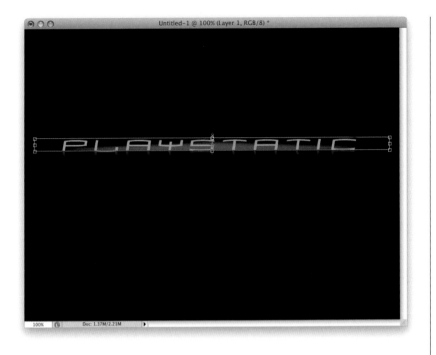

STEP SEVEN: The glow looks a little too high (we want it fully contained behind the letters—not sticking out the top), so bring up Free Transform again. Click on the top-center handle and drag straight downward to squash your glow a bit, so it isn't quite as high as the letters (like you see here), and then lock in your changes.

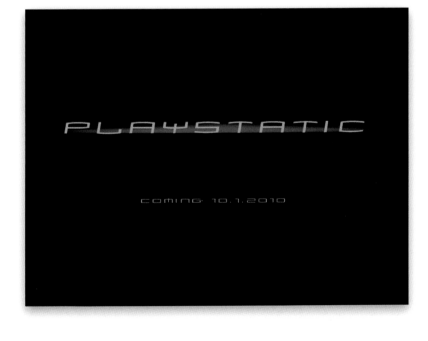

STEP EIGHT: When I looked at the final image (shown here), I thought the re-flection was a little too pronounced, so I went back to the reflected-type layer and lowered the Opacity from 40% down to 20%, for the look you see here, which is a bit more subtle. Also, I added the line of text near the bottom using the same typeface, but I went to the Character panel and turned off Faux Italic. By the way, that's a good thing, because the one "gotcha!" about using Faux Italic is that it doesn't automatically turn itself off. It'll stay on, faux italicizing every typeface until you remember to go turn it off. Now, does this make any sense to work like that? (I'm not a good guy to ask, because my answer may contain words not fit to print.)

Making Passport Stamp Design Elements

A lot of people use Apple's iPhoto to create their photo books, because it comes with such cool built-in templates, making the process really simple with great results (I use it for all my vacation photo books). In an older version of iPhoto, Apple had templates with little passport stamps on the pages, and they really had a nice look, but sadly, those templates have been replaced. Be that as it may, the passport stamp idea was really cool, and if you learn how to create those passport stamps, you can apply them anywhere. The trick is making them not look "too neat," because passport stamps are notoriously smudgy.

STEP ONE: Start by pressing **Command-N (PC: Ctrl-N)** to create a new document (I created a document here that's 800x600 pixels at a resolution of 72 ppi), and then create a new blank layer by clicking on the Create a New Layer icon at the bottom of the Layers panel. Next, get the Ellipse tool (press **Shift-U** until you have it), go up the Options Bar and click on the second icon from the left (so the tool creates a path, rather than pixels or a Shape layer), and then click-and-drag out an oval like the one you see here. Now click on your Foreground color swatch and choose a dark bluish gray color (I used R: 72, G: 80, B: 101).

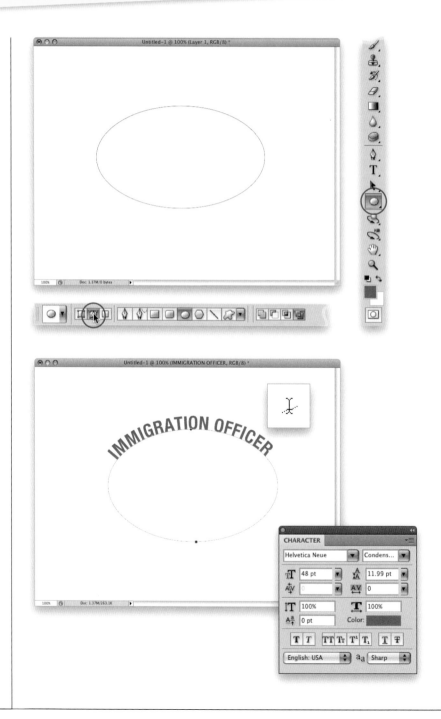

STEP TWO: Now you're going to create some text and have it follow along that oval-shaped path you just created. Get the Horizontal Type tool **(T)**, then go up to the Options Bar and click on the Center Text icon (it's two icons to the left of the color swatch). I chose Helvetica Neue Condensed Bold for my type, but you can use any sans serif bold condensed font. Now move your Type cursor right over the top part of the path and you'll see your cursor change into the one you see inset here. Just click and start typing the words "IMMIGRATION OFFICER," and it will wrap along the top of your oval (as seen here).

STEP THREE: Press **Command-J (PC: Ctrl-J)** to duplicate this layer, then switch to the Path Selection tool (**A**; the black-filled arrow just below the Horizontal Type tool in the Toolbox). Move your cursor over the curved text at the top, and it will change into a double-sided arrow. That's your indicator that you can now click-and-drag your copied text around the oval, so… do it—click-and-drag to the left until the duplicate of your of text rotates all the way down to the bottom of the oval (as shown here).

STEP FOUR: Go to the Layers panel, and double-click directly on the "T" thumbnail for this duplicate Type layer. This highlights the type at the bottom of your oval. Now, type in the city you want your passport stamp to be from (in this case, I typed in "PORTOFINO, ITALY"). If you look at the position of the text at the bottom of the oval in the previous step, you'll see it sits inside the path (the bottom of the type is resting on the path), but here it's moved down so the tops of the letters are touching the path instead (which is what you actually want). To make this happen, highlight your new text, and just press **Option-Shift-Down Arrow key (PC: Alt-Shift-Down Arrow key)**. Keep pressing that shortcut a few times until your text moves downward into the position shown here. This is the keyboard shortcut for Baseline Shift and what you're doing is shifting the type below its original baseline.

Continued

STEP FIVE: Create a new blank layer, then get the Elliptical Marquee tool (press **Shift-M** until you have it) and draw a large oval-shaped selection that's a little larger than your text-on-a-path (by the way, when you do this, the path you created back in Step One will be hidden from view). Once your selection is in place, go under the Edit menu and choose Stroke. When the Stroke dialog appears, set 8 px as your Width, for your Location, choose Center, and click OK to put a stroke around your oval-shaped selection.

STEP SIX: You're going to make another oval selection inside your text area (like the one you see here), and then you'll add an 8-pixel stroke to this selection, as well. Press **Command-D (PC: Ctrl-D)** to Deselect.

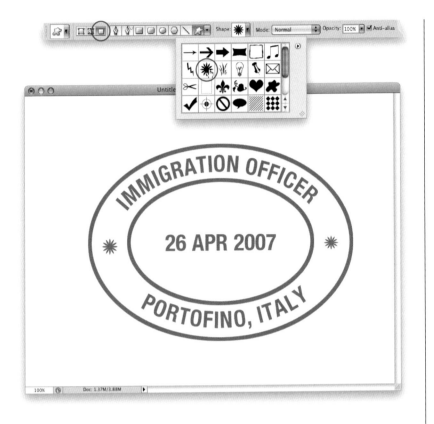

STEP SEVEN: Go back to the Horizontal Type tool and create a line of text in the center with the date of your trip (as shown here). Add another blank layer, and then get the Custom Shape tool (press **Shift-U** until you have it). Go up to the Options Bar, and click on the third icon from the left (so the shapes it draws are made of pixels, rather than a path). Then click on the Shape thumbnail and, from the Shape Picker, choose the Flower 5 starburst shape, and add one on either side of the oval (like you see here). They seem to add these little ornaments and shapes, like stars, or little airplanes, or other little do-dads, to these stamps, and since you're creating your own, you can pretty much choose any shape you'd like.

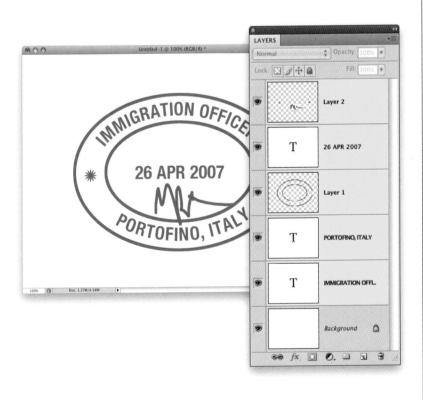

STEP EIGHT: While you're still on this same layer, grab the Brush tool **(B)**, choose a very small brush tip, and scribble out the signature of your pretend Immigration Officer (all passport stamps don't have a signature, but we're going to add one here). Once the scribbly signature is in place, you'll need to select all these layers and merge them into one single layer. Go to the Layers panel, press-and-hold the Shift key, and click on each of the Type and oval layers until they're all selected (as seen here, where all those layers are highlighted in the Layers panel).

Continued

STEP NINE: Now, press **Command-E (PC: Ctrl-E)** to merge all the selected layers into one single layer, and then you can apply some effects that will make the stamp look more realistic. One attribute that is pretty common among passport stamps is that they're kind of smudged a bit. You can get a similar look by going under the Filter menu, under Noise, and choosing Median. When the Median filter dialog appears, choose a Radius of 3 or 4 (see which looks better to you, based on which font you used), and then click OK.

STEP 10: Duplicate your stamp layer, then change the layer blend mode of this layer to Dissolve (as shown here). This makes the edges of your stamp a bit frayed, and helps make the stamp look more realistic. Merge this layer with the one beneath it. Now you can set this document aside, as we're going to build a page for your photos, and stamps, to sit on, and just for fun, we'll build a background that's pretty much like one of the page backgrounds Apple used to use in their photo book travel templates (the ones I talked about in this project's intro).

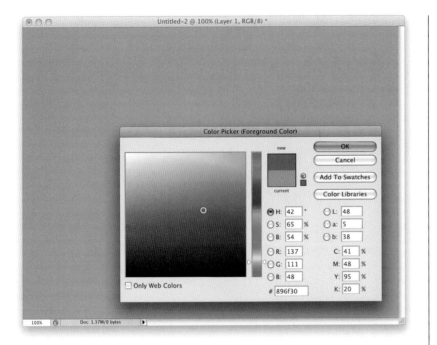

STEP 11: Create a new document that's 800x600 pixels at 72 ppi. Set your Foreground color to a light brown color (I used R: 196, G: 159, B: 68), then press **Option-Delete (PC: Alt-Backspace)** to fill your Background layer with this color. Now add a new blank layer, then click back on your Foreground color swatch and choose a darker shade of your brown color (as shown here, where I chose R: 137, G: 111, B: 48).

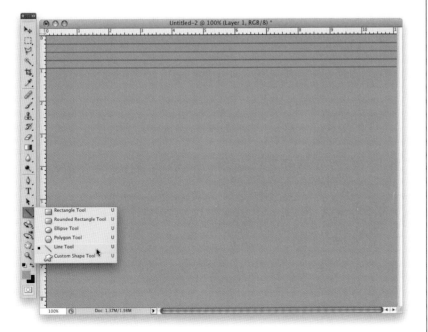

STEP 12: Press **Command-R (PC: Ctrl-R)** to make your Rulers visible, then get the Line tool from the Toolbox (as shown here, or just press **Shift-U** until you have it), press-and-hold the Shift key, and draw a series of straight horizontal lines, each ¼" down. Here I've drawn four lines, but you'll need to continue this all the way down the page. You can either draw all the lines, or once you've drawn those four lines, you can duplicate the layer, get the Move tool **(V)**, and then click-and-drag it down to add four more lines. Just keep repeating this again and again, until you've filled the image (if that sounds confusing, then just draw all the lines. It doesn't take long at all).

Continued

STEP 13: The lines stand out a bit too much, so once you're done, go to the Layers panel and lower the Opacity of this layer to 30% (as shown here). Here's what the image looks like after you've filled the layer with these lines and lowered the opacity. Okay, now go open the photos you want to appear on this page (I'm using two photos for this particular layout, and they're shown here). *Note:* You can turn off the Rulers now.

STEP 14: Get the Move tool and drag-and-drop one of those photos onto your background image. Once it appears, press **Command-T (PC: Ctrl-T)** to bring up Free Transform, press-and-hold the Shift key, grab a corner point, and click-and-drag inward to scale the photo down to size if needed, so it fits better on the page (as seen here). While Free Transform is still in place, move your cursor outside the Free Transform bounding box, and your cursor changes into a two-headed arrow. Click-and-drag in a counterclockwise motion to rotate your photo (as shown here), and then press **Return (PC: Enter)** to lock in your rotation.

STEP 15: To add a white photo border effect to your image, click on the Add a Layer Style icon at the bottom of the Layers panel and choose Stroke from the pop-up menu. When the dialog appears (shown below left), increase the Size of your stroke to 12 px, click on the black Color swatch and change your stroke color to white, then from the Position pop-up menu, choose Inside (so your stroke doesn't have rounded corners). Now, in the Styles section on the left side of the dialog, click on Drop Shadow. In the Drop Shadow options (shown below right), raise the Size to 13 to increase the softness of the drop shadow, then click OK to apply both the Stroke and Drop Shadow effects to your photo (as seen here).

STEP 16: Bring in your second photo and, in the Layers panel, click-and-drag it beneath your first photo. Now resize it to fit, and rotate this photo in the opposite direction (as seen here). To get the exact same Stroke and Drop Shadow effects applied to this new image, just press-and-hold the **Option (PC: Alt) key** and, in the Layers panel, click-and-hold directly on the word "Effects." Drag-and-drop this word directly onto the second photo's layer, and it copies the effects from that first layer and applies the same settings to the second layer (as seen here).

Continued

STEP 17: Head back to your passport stamp document. You're going to distress the stamp a little bit more before we apply it to your main page. In the Layers panel, click on the Add Layer Mask icon at the bottom of the panel. Now, press **X** to make black your Foreground color, and then get the Brush tool **(B)**. From the Brush Picker in the Options Bar, scroll down to the last row of brushes, and choose the Wet Sponge brush (it's second from the left in the bottom row). Click-and-drag the Master Diameter slider over to around 300 pixels. Then move your cursor out over the image, and just click once or twice on different parts of the stamp to age and distress it a little (a pretty common look for real passport stamps).

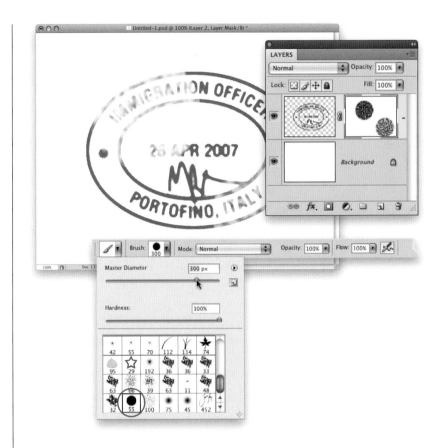

STEP 18: Now get the Move tool and drag-and-drop your passport stamp onto your main image document. When it appears in your main document, use Free Transform to resize and position it, then go to the Layers panel and click-and-drag its layer down in the layer stack, so your passport stamp appears behind the other photo layers (as seen here). Lower the Opacity of this layer (like you see here) to help it blend into the background a little.

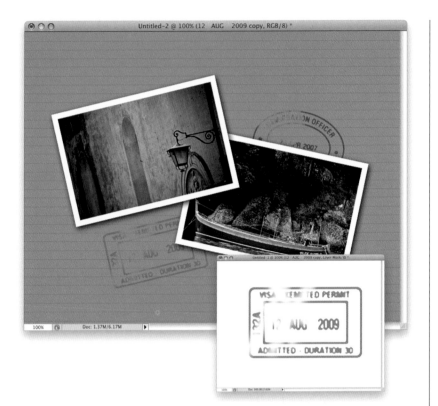

STEP 19: You now know the formula for creating other passport stamps (I used the exact same formula you just learned to create another stamp, which is shown here below). This one was easier because there's no circular type on a path, and because it's mostly text. Start by getting the Rounded Rectangle Tool (press **Shift-U** until you have it) and, up in the Options Bar, choose 20 as your corner Radius (the higher the number, the more rounded your corners will become). Then you do all the same things you just learned, but this time, finish it off using a round soft-edged brush.

STEP 20: Here's the final image with a couple of photos, a couple of passport stamps, and the background you created from scratch.

Creating Custom Type Designs

Photoshop lets you do something that I've found surprises a lot of people—it lets you create custom letterforms by tweaking an existing font. This is very popular in logo design. So, in this project, you're going to learn how to give yourself an advantage by delivering a custom look for your client that can't be duplicated by just typing in a name with a typeface. If you've never worked with paths before, don't let it freak you out, because what you're going to do is so simple anyone will be able to do it (plus, if you're a creative type—and if you're reading this book, my guess is you are—then this will open a new world of creating with type that's actually a lot of fun).

STEP ONE: Press **Command-N (PC: Ctrl-N)** to create a new document (mine is 800x600 pixels at a resolution of 72 ppi). Click on the Foreground color swatch and choose a medium gray, then get the Horizontal Type tool **(T)**, and choose the font Bickham Script Pro from up in the Options Bar or in the Character panel (found under the Window menu). (*Note:* If you upgraded to CS4 from Photoshop CS3, you already have this font installed. If you started with CS4, then it's not there because Adobe no longer includes this font, and you can download the paths to this font from this book's downloads page—this will make more sense in a moment.) Set the font size to 295 points, and type the word "pointe" in all lowercase letters.

STEP TWO: Now you're going to create some text above and below the word "pointe." In the Layers panel, click on the Background layer, then choose the font Trajan Pro (it comes installed with Photoshop) at a size of 30 points. Click on your document (you may have to click to the side of "pointe" since that font is so large), type in "THE LOFTS AT," then move your cursor away from your type until you get an arrow, and click-and-drag to position it nice and snug above the word "pointe." You can already see the first problem we have to deal with—the dot of the letter "i" is colliding with the word "LOFTS." We'll fix that, but first we need to add another line of text (in the next step).

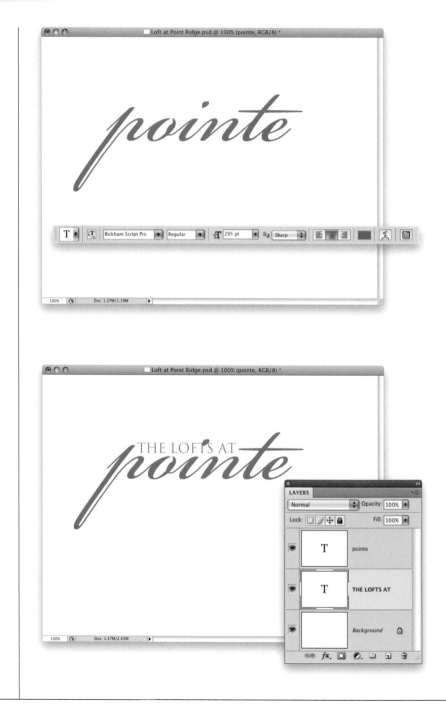

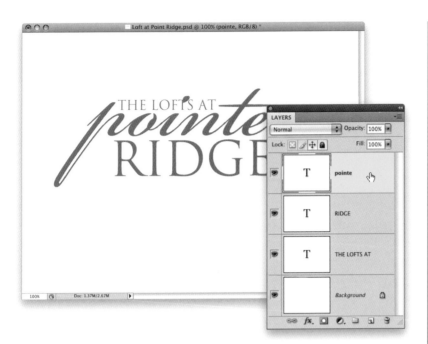

STEP THREE: With the Horizontal Type tool, click on the far-right side of your document, and type "RIDGE" in the same Trajan Pro font, but at a size of 108 points. Again, move your cursor away from the text until it becomes an arrow, then click-and-drag to position it just below the word "pointe" (as seen here). By the way, those two lines of text should line up on the left—the left side of the letter "T" in "THE," and the left side of the "R" in "RIDGE" should both be lined up with each other, like you see here. Okay, all our text is now in place, and it's time to start customizing. In the Layers panel, click on the "pointe" layer (as seen here) to make it the active layer.

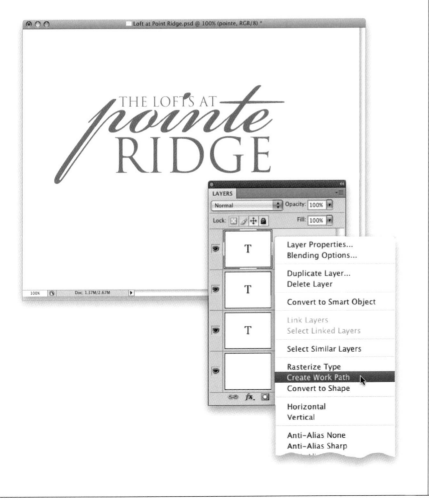

STEP FOUR: Control-click (PC: Right-click) directly on the "pointe" layer to bring up a contextual menu of options. From this menu, choose Create Work Path (as shown here). This puts a perfect path around your letters, as if you had drawn them from scratch using the Pen tool. The reason you're doing this is because now that this type has become a path, you can create your own custom letters (clients always love it when you tell them the font has been customized just for them).

Continued

STEP FIVE: Now that you have a path in place, you no longer need that "pointe" Type layer, so click-and-drag it onto the Trash icon at the bottom of the Layers panel to delete it. Next, add a new blank layer by clicking on the Create a New Layer icon at the bottom of the panel. Now we can get to editing our path. The tool we use for this is the Direct Selection tool, and it appears nested with the Path Selection tool, directly below the Type tools in the Toolbox (as shown here—it's the hollow arrow, not the black one), so go ahead and get that tool now.

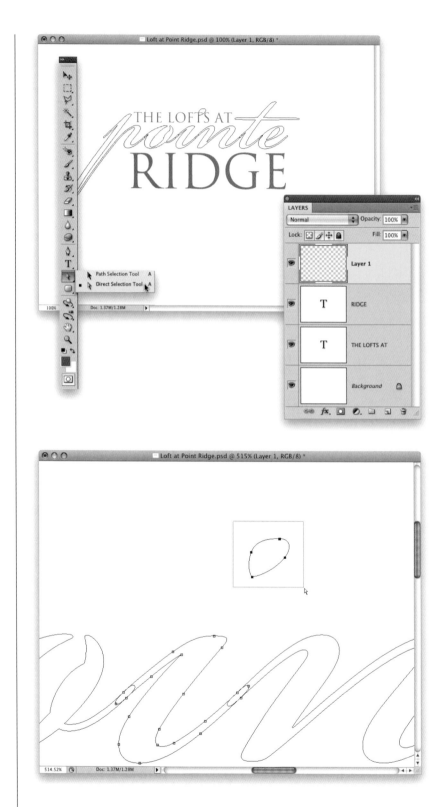

STEP SIX: First, let's hide the "THE LOFTS AT" Type layer, so it doesn't distract us while we're making our edits. Click on the Eye icon to the left of that layer in the Layers panel and that layer will be hidden from view. Now, let's start editing. I used the Zoom tool (**Z**; it looks like a magnifying glass) to zoom in really tight on the dot over the "i." Take the Direct Selection tool and click-and-drag out a square selection around the dot (as seen here) to select the four points that make up this dot. While it might look like you've selected other points in the word, don't worry, as long as your selection is just around that dot, that's the only part that will be affected by your next edit.

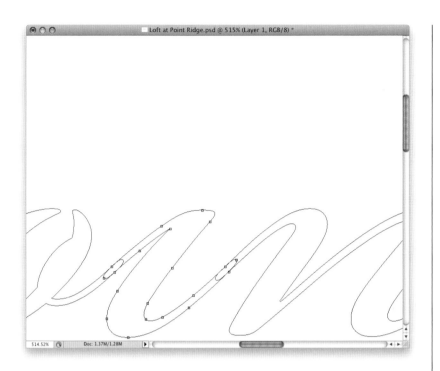

STEP SEVEN: Press the Delete (PC: Backspace) key and your selected dot is gone. Problem solved. Of course, that's not the main reason we converted to paths. We really did it to create our own custom versions of some of the letters, but while we're here, we might as well fix stuff, eh?

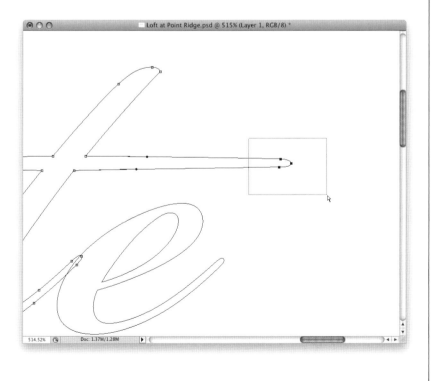

STEP EIGHT: Now, while still zoomed in, let's scroll over to the right end of the letter "t" in "pointe." We're going to extend the far-right side of the crossbar quite a bit, and you do that by clicking-and-dragging out another square selection around the end of the crossbar on the "t" (as shown here). This selects the three points that make up that end of the bar.

Continued

STEP NINE: Click on the path itself, right near the end (I clicked on the bottom—you can see my little arrow cursor on the far-right side of the crossbar), then just drag to the right (as shown here), and that part of the letter extends. Press-and-hold the Shift key as you drag to keep it straight, because you want to keep as much of the original shape as possible—you just want that one piece to be longer. Now, just click off the path (click anywhere else but the path). That's it—you've customized your first letter (wild cheers ensue!). Of course, you're not done yet (the crowd groans). By the way, you can make your "THE LOFTS AT" layer visible again—just go to the Layers panel and click where the Eye icon used to be.

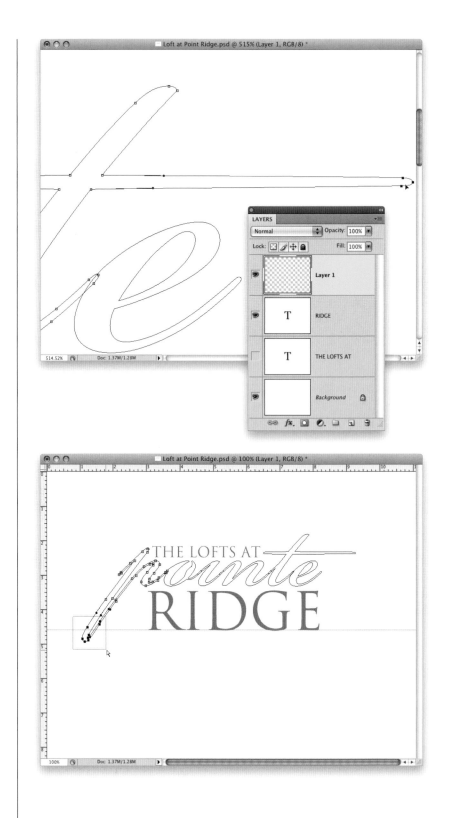

STEP 10: Press **Command-R (PC: Ctrl-R)** to make Photoshop's Rulers visible (seen here). Now, click directly inside the top ruler, drag down a guide, and position it right along the bottom of the word "RIDGE." See how the bottom of the "p" extends below the guide, which marks the baseline of where the word "RIDGE" sits? We want that lower part of the "p" (called the descender in typography circles) to be no lower than that guide. So, with the Direct Selection tool, drag out a square selection around the bottom of that descender (as shown here) to select the points in that area.

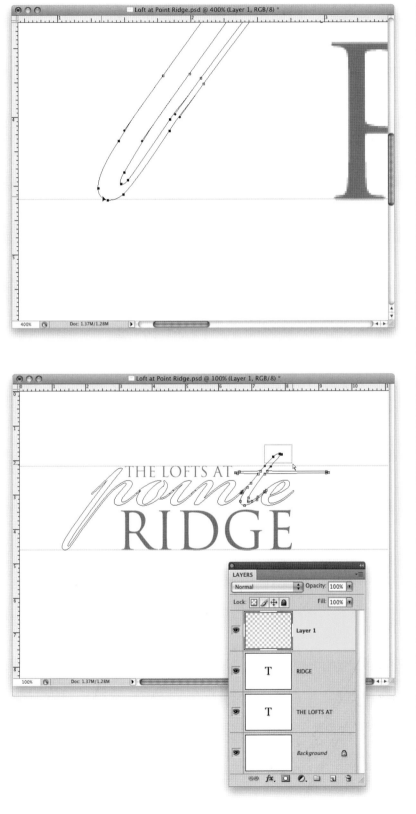

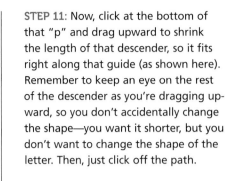

STEP 11: Now, click at the bottom of that "p" and drag upward to shrink the length of that descender, so it fits right along that guide (as shown here). Remember to keep an eye on the rest of the descender as you're dragging upward, so you don't accidentally change the shape—you want it shorter, but you don't want to change the shape of the letter. Then, just click off the path.

STEP 12: Click-and-drag another horizontal guide down from the top ruler and place it along the top of the words "THE LOFTS AT" (as seen here). You can probably guess what's next—that's right, we want to shrink the top of the "t" (called the ascender), so it fits within that guide. With the Direct Selection tool, put a rectangular selection around that part of the letter (as shown here) to highlight the points that control that part of the letter.

Continued

STEP 13: Switch to the Zoom tool again, and zoom in tight, so you can really see what's going on. Then go back to the Direct Selection tool **(A)**, grab the top of the ascender and carefully drag it in toward the rest of the letter, until it's right around that guide (as shown here), and then click anywhere off the path.

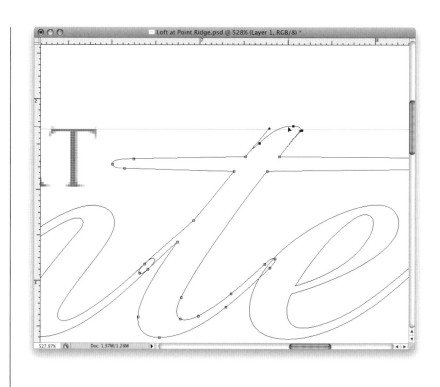

STEP 14: At this point, all your letter editing is done, so now it's time to turn those paths into a selection, which you do by pressing **Command-Return (PC: Ctrl-Enter)**. You can see here, the path has been turned into a selection. Also, you can press **Command-R (PC: Ctrl-R)** to turn off the Rulers and, from the View menu, choose Clear Guides to remove the guides.

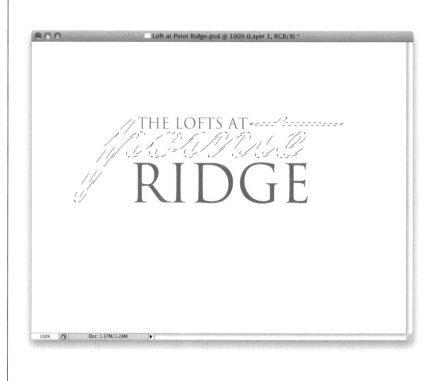

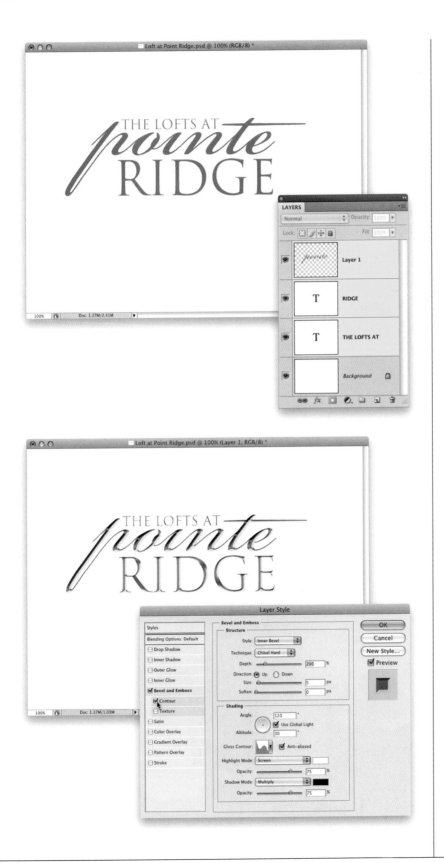

STEP 15: With your selection in place, press **Option-Delete (PC: Alt-Backspace)** to fill it with your gray Foreground color (as seen here), then you can Deselect by pressing **Command-D (PC: Ctrl-D)**. Next, we need all three of these layers with type to become just one layer, so go to the Layers panel, press-and-hold the Shift key, and click on the two other Type layers, so that all three of your layers with type are high-lighted (as seen here). Now, just press **Command-E (PC: Ctrl-E)** to merge them into one layer.

STEP 16: Now that your type is all on one layer, let's add an effect to finish things off (of course, this step is totally optional, but since this is a special effects book at heart, let's add a special effect). Click on the Add a Layer Style icon at the bottom of the Layers panel, and choose Bevel and Emboss from the pop-up menu. When the Layer Style dialog appears, from the Technique pop-up menu (in the Structure section, near the top), choose Chisel Hard. Increase the Depth to 200%, then down in the Shading section, turn on the Anti-Aliased checkbox (so the edges of the effect are smoother), and click on the down-facing arrow next to Gloss Contour to bring up the Gloss Contour Picker. Click on the Rolling Slope–Descending icon (the fourth icon from the left, in the second row) to add a metallic, chiseled look to your type (as seen here). To give it a little more "oomph," go to the Styles section on the left side of the dialog, and under Bevel and Emboss, turn on the Contour checkbox (as seen here), and then click OK to apply this effect.

Continued

STEP 17: Our effect is essentially done at this point, but we might as well put it into action. Open the photo you see here (you can download it from the book's downloads page, or you can open a photo of your own). Get the Move tool **(V)**, click on your Type layer, and drag-and-drop it onto your photo. It'll probably be too big, so press **Command-T (PC: Ctrl-T)** to bring up Free Transform, press-and-hold the Shift key, grab a corner point, and drag inward (as shown here) to scale the text down in size, then reposition it over the center of the image, and press **Return (PC: Enter)** to commit your transformation.

STEP 18: Here's the final image, with the customized letterforms, and the special effect, scaled down to size and positioned.

CHAPTER

5

Reflections of Passion

reflection effects

This may be my all-time favorite chapter title, because this is the type of title that publishers of computer books go wild over, because when people search for the word "passion" (which they sometimes do), this chapter will come up. Now, what they're hoping for is that someone who was looking for scenes of passion, but came across this chapter instead, might think to themselves, "Ya know, this isn't as intriguing as the passion I was looking for, but the reflection effects used in this chapter are so compelling that I'm going to rush out to the bookstore and buy this right now!" Laugh if you will, but this has actually been documented to happen at least 2.1 times in the history of book publishing. Anyway, if it's a saucy title, it helps sell books, so they're happy. Anyway, the title (which is just too perfect for a chapter on reflection effects) actually comes from a Yanni song. Now, you're probably thinking one of three things: (1) whatever happened to Yanni, or (2) who is Yanni, or (3) I am Yanni. In answer to (1), I'll tell you where he is: he's sitting around making up names for songs that are packed with smoldering passion. For example, other songs on his album included (I'm not making this up) "Secret Vows," "A Word in Private," "First Touch," and "Breakaway Underwear." (Okay, I made that last one up, but I had you there for minute, didn't I?)

The Basic Reflection Effect

Although you're going to see versions of this technique throughout this chapter (and even in other chapters), I thought we'd better get it out of the way right up front. Now, because I wanted this to be learned (and used) in a real world fashion, I went ahead and took the technique a little further, adding some other effects to it to finish it off (plus I didn't think you'd mind learning a few extra techniques).

STEP ONE: Press **Command-N (PC: Ctrl-N)** to create a new document that is 800x600 pixels at a resolution of 72 ppi. Click on the Foreground color swatch and choose a color in the Color Picker (I chose R: 163, G: 138, B: 90), then fill your Background layer with that color by pressing **Option-Delete (PC: Alt-Backspace)**. Now, you'll need to drag the object you want to create the reflection for onto this background. Here, we're using a screen capture of my blog (which you can download from the book's downloads page), or you can take a screen capture yourself of any webpage you'd like to practice with. To do this, press **Command-Shift-4** on a Mac, and click-and-drag a selection around the webpage. This creates a file called "Picture 1" on your desktop. On a PC, press **Alt-Print Screen**, then go into Photoshop and create a new document that is the size of the clipboard, and press **Command-V (PC: Ctrl-V)** to Paste the screen capture into the new document.

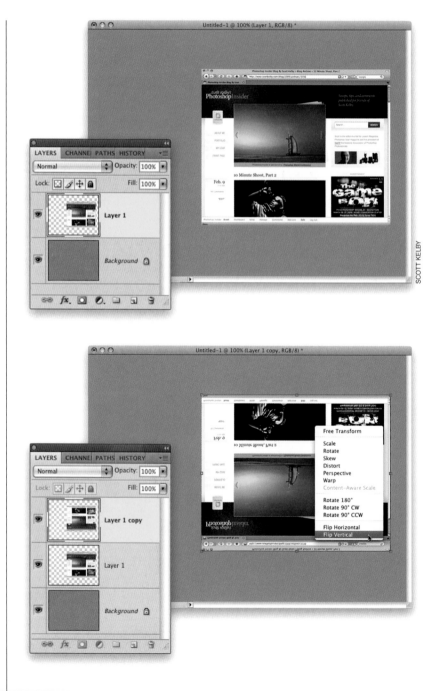

SCOTT KELBY

STEP TWO: Press **Command-J (PC: Ctrl-J)** to duplicate your webpage layer, then press **Command-T (PC: Ctrl-T)** to bring up Free Transform. Next, Control-click (PC: Right-click) inside your webpage and a contextual menu will appear. From that menu, choose Flip Vertical (as shown here) to flip this duplicate layer upside down. Press **Return (PC: Enter)** to lock in your change.

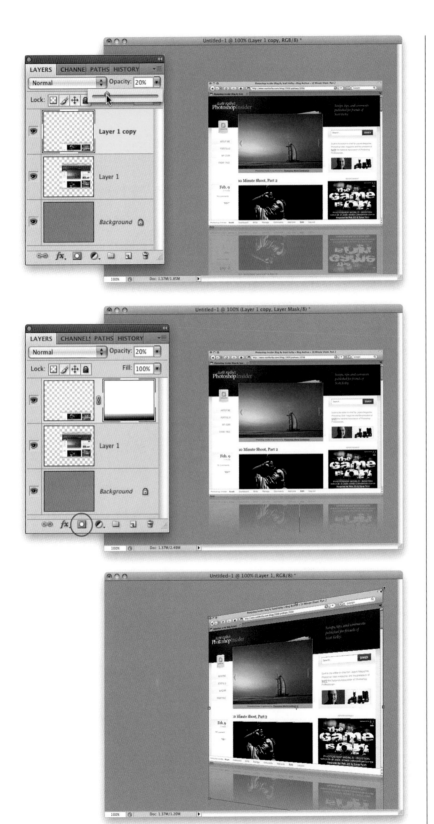

STEP THREE: Get the Move tool **(V)**, press-and-hold the Shift key (to keep things lined up), and click-and-drag straight downward until the top of the flipped webpage meets the bottom of the original (as shown here). Then, to create the reflection look, lower the layer's Opacity (in the Layers panel) to 20%.

STEP FOUR: The most popular look for reflections now is to have them "fade away" at the bottom. So, click on the Add Layer Mask icon at the bottom of the Layers panel (it's circled here in red), then get the Gradient tool **(G)**, click on the down-facing arrow next to the gradient thumbnail in the Options Bar, and choose the Foreground to Background gradient (in the top left). Now, click-and-drag from the top of the reflection downward, and stop just short of the bottom of the image window (as shown here) to fade away the bottom of the reflection. Press **Command-E (PC: Ctrl-E)** to merge these two layers into one single layer. (*Note:* That's the shortcut for Merge Down, which merges the layer you're on into the layer directly below it.)

STEP FIVE: Let's add another popular effect to our webpage—the perspective effect. Bring up Free Transform again. Although you could choose Perspective from the contextual menu you saw in Step Two, you'll save yourself some work by using the keyboard shortcut instead, because you're going to do two different transformations: (1) adding the perspective effect, and then (2) thinning up the image to remove the stretched look you get from adding perspective. The keyboard shortcut is to press-and-hold **Command-Option-Shift (PC: Ctrl-Alt-Shift)**, then grab the top-right corner point and drag upward (as shown here). As you do, it creates a perspective effect, expanding the right side (top and bottom). Don't lock in your changes yet.

Continued

STEP SIX: While Free Transform is still active, release those keys, then grab the left-center point and drag inward (to the right, as shown here) to remove the stretched look perspective gives to your object. Now you can lock in your two transformations.

STEP SEVEN: A popular little trick to give your object a slight 3D depth effect is to duplicate the layer, fill it with black (or a dark gray, or a color sampled from the page) and offset it a bit behind the page (like you see here). You do that by duplicating the layer, then pressing **D** to set your Foreground color to black (or choose a color from your webpage using the Eyedropper tool **[I]**—just click it on a color on your page, and that color becomes your Foreground color). Now, to fill that duplicate page with this color, press **Option-Shift-Delete (PC: Alt-Shift-Backspace)**. In the Layers panel, drag that layer behind your webpage layer, get the Move tool, and press the Right Arrow key on your keyboard a few times to offset this copy from the original, which gives you the slight 3D effect you see here. Don't offset it too far, or it will be obvious it's just a copy of the page.

STEP EIGHT: At this point, you can add some text—I used the font Myriad Pro, which comes installed with Photoshop CS4. I set the font size at 28 points. I also went to the Character panel and tightened the space between the letters by entering –40 in the Tracking field (it's shown circled here in red) and set the Leading field (above the Tracking field) to a little less than the font size. Next, create a pill-shaped button on a new layer using the Rounded Rectangle tool (press **Shift-U** until you have it) set to Fill Pixels, with the Radius (roundness) setting set at 40 up in the Options Bar. Then, choose Inner Glow from the Add a Layer Style icon's pop-up menu. When the dialog appears, choose black as your glow color, and set the Blend Mode pop-up menu to Normal to add a slight shadow inside the pill shape. While you're there, click on Drop Shadow in the Styles section on the left side, and in the Drop Shadow options, lower the Opacity slider to 30% to create a soft shadow behind the pill shape. Lastly, I added the glassy reflection technique you'll learn on page 148. The final image here shows how the page looks if you simply change the background color to black (and your 3D thick layer to medium gray). I also added a white stroke around the pill-shaped button by choosing Stroke from the Add a Layer Style icon's pop-up menu, and changing the Color to white.

Letter or Shape Double-Gradient Reflection

Apple has become such a part of popular culture that their design elements have become a part of popular design (luckily, their stuff looks really cool). A few years back, everybody was designing everything with a "gel" look, so gel buttons and bars were found on nearly every website and ad (and you still see them here and there), but Apple's reflected look has taken the place of the gel look, and in this particular project, we're going to use two different gradients on two different layers to recreate the reflected look Apple used on their Mac OS X Leopard product box (but of course, we're applying it to different letters).

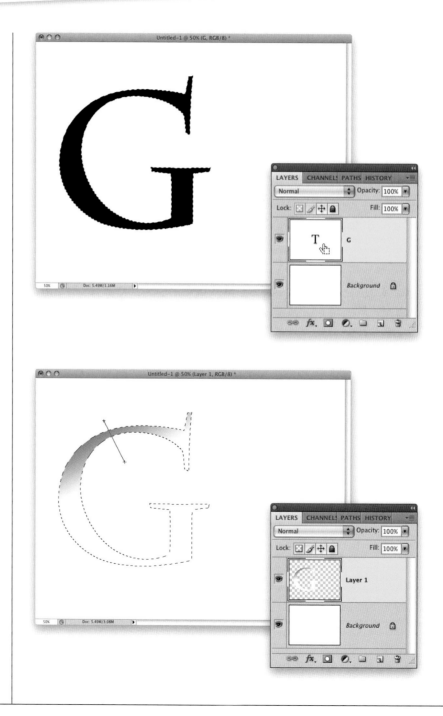

STEP ONE: Start by creating a new document that is 8x6" at a resolution of 200 ppi. (This technique works best if you start with a higher resolution, and then scale the image or shape down if you want to use it onscreen or on the Web.) Press **D** to set your Foreground color to black, then get the Horizontal Type tool **(T)** and type in the letter "G" using the font Charlemagne Std Bold (it comes installed with Photoshop CS4). We need to put a selection around your letter, so go to the Layers panel and Command-click (PC: Ctrl-click) directly on the thumbnail of your Type layer, and it puts a selection around your letter (as seen here). Now that your selection is in place, you don't need the Type layer any longer, so drag it onto the Trash icon at the bottom of the Layers panel.

STEP TWO: Create a new blank layer by clicking on the Create a New Layer icon at the bottom of the Layers panel. Make sure your Foreground and Background colors are the default black and white. Now, click on the Foreground color swatch and choose a medium gray color in the Color Picker. Get the Gradient tool **(G)**, click on the down-facing arrow to the right of the gradient thumbnail in the Options Bar, and choose the Foreground to Background gradient. Then, click-and-drag through your selection starting above and to the left of your selected letter, and dragging down through it at the angle you see here. This fills the top quarter with gray, and the rest of the letter with white (as seen in the Layers panel). Don't deselect yet.

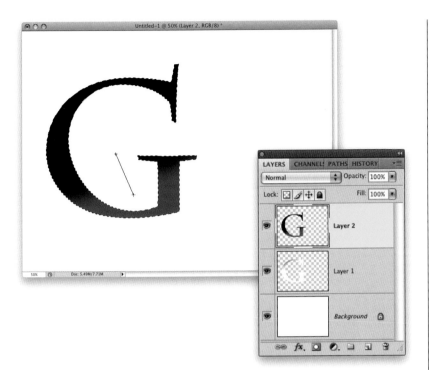

STEP THREE: Add another blank layer. Now you're going to create a new gradient—one that goes from black to dark gray. Start by setting your Foreground color to black, then click on the Background color swatch and choose a dark gray in the Color Picker. Take the Gradient tool and click-and-drag from around the center of the letter downward about an inch and a half (as shown here). This puts black in the top three-quarters of the letter and dark gray in the bottom quarter. Now, press **Command-D (PC: Ctrl-D)** to Deselect.

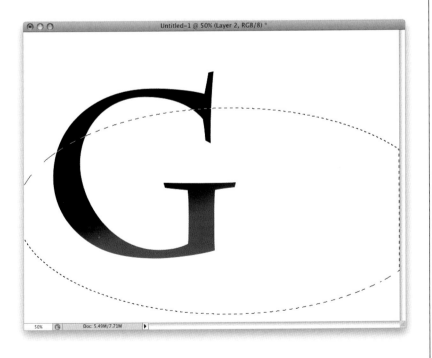

STEP FOUR: Get the Elliptical Marquee tool (press **Shift-M** until you have it) and click-and-drag out a huge oval-shaped selection, like the one you see here. What we're going to do with this is use it to cut a hole out of the top gradient, revealing the bottom gradient, which creates the reflected look (by the way, we're doing this on a letter, but it works the same way on an object or shape).

Continued

STEP FIVE: To get just the right angle, you're going to have to rotate this oval-shaped selection. To do that, go under the Select menu and choose Transform Selection. This puts Free Transform handles around your oval selection, and it works just like Free Transform, so move your cursor outside the bounding box and your cursor changes into a two-headed arrow (as seen here). To rotate the oval, just click-and-drag in a counter-clockwise direction until your oval looks like the one you see here. If you need to reposition your oval, just move your cursor inside the bounding box and you can click-and-drag it where you want it. When it looks good to you, press **Return (PC: Enter)** to lock in your rotation.

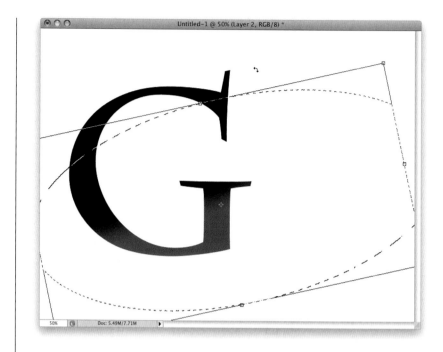

STEP SIX: Press **Command-Shift-I (PC: Ctrl-Shift-I)** to Inverse the selection, so rather than having the bottom of the letter selected, now you have the top. Just press Delete (PC: Backspace), and it deletes the top of the top layer, to reveal the gradient on the layer below it (as seen here). Now you can deselect.

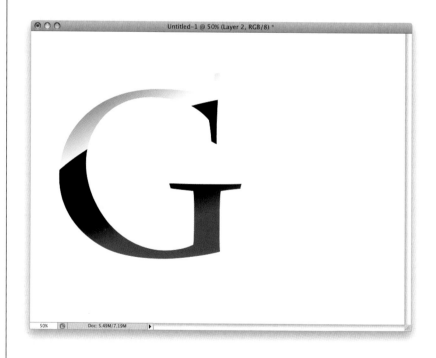

STEP SEVEN: We need both layers merged into one, so press **Command-E (PC: Ctrl-E)** to merge these two layers (well, it actually merges the top layer with the one directly beneath it, but the result is the same). You're now going to add a metallic stroke around the outside of your letter, so click on the Add a Layer Style icon at the bottom of the Layers panel and choose Stroke from the pop-up menu. When the Layer Style dialog appears, increase the Size to 5, then for Fill Type, choose Gradient. We want to use a special metallic gradient, so click on the gradient thumbnail to bring up the Gradient Editor, then click on the little right-facing arrow at the top right of the Presets section (it's shown circled here in red), and from the list of gradient presets that appears, choose Metals. When the warning dialog appears, choose Append, and then the metallic gradients will appear at the bottom of the presets. Click on the gradient that goes from gray to white to gray to white to gray (the Silver gradient, as shown here).

STEP EIGHT: In the Styles section on the left side of the Layer Style dialog, click on Bevel and Emboss. When those options appear, from the Style pop-up menu, choose Stroke Emboss. Go down to Gloss Contour, turn on the checkbox for Anti-Aliased, then click on the down-facing arrow to the right of the graph thumbnail to bring up the Gloss Contour Picker (seen here), and choose the Ring-Double contour (the third contour in the second row, as shown here). This adds a metallic effect to the metallic gradient you added as a stroke. Now, click OK to apply these effects to your letter. At this point, you're done with this letter, but if you wanted to do an additional letter, you'd pretty much follow the same steps (which we'll do on the next page, with one small exception).

Continued

STEP NINE: Get the Horizontal Type tool again, and type in "9." Press-and-hold the Command (PC: Ctrl) key and click on the layer's thumbnail to put a selection around the number. Now you can delete that Type layer, then add a new blank layer (sound familiar?). You've already got black and gray set up as your Foreground and Background colors, so you can save yourself a step by creating the second gradient first. However, since you used that metallic gradient in the Stroke layer style, once you get the Gradient tool, you'll have to go up to the Options Bar, click on the down-facing arrow to the right of the gradient thumbnail to get the Gradient Picker, and choose the first gradient (which is the Foreground to Background gradient). Then take the Gradient tool and click-and-drag it through the number starting above the middle of the number and dragging downward diagonally (like you see here). Don't deselect yet.

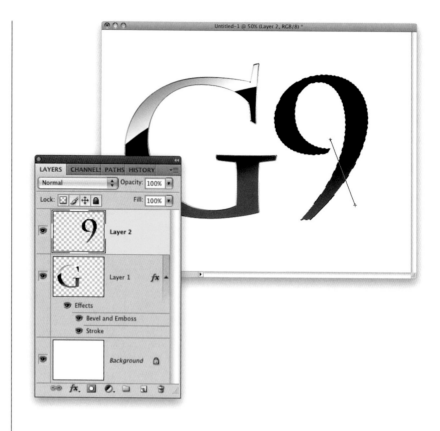

STEP 10: Now, hide that layer you just filled with a gradient from view by clicking on the Eye icon to the left of the layer. Press-and-hold the Command (PC: Ctrl) key while clicking on the Create a New Layer icon at the bottom of the Layers panel. This creates a new layer directly below your current layer (the hidden layer). Your selection should still be in place, so now you can create your other gradient, which was medium gray to white. Click-and-drag your gradient through the number (as shown here) to put gray at the top of the number, and white filling the rest. Now you can deselect, and you can make your top layer visible again (by clicking where the Eye icon used to be).

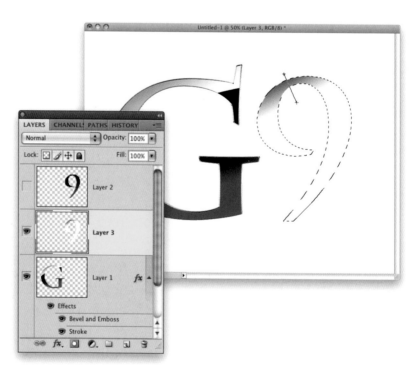

STEP 11: You're going to make the large oval again, then use Transform Selection to rotate the oval a bit, inverse the selection (as seen here), then click back on the top layer to make it active. Press the Delete (PC: Backspace) key to cut out the top of the number, revealing the gradient on the layer below it, and deselect. Merge these two layers together and we'll now add the same Stroke and Bevel and Emboss layer styles to the number that we added to the letter. Press-and-hold the **Option (PC: Alt) key**, click on the word "Effects" beneath the "G" layer, then just drag-and-drop it onto the "9" layer, and merge the "9" layer with the "G" layer.

STEP 12: Now that everything's on one layer, you can drag-and-drop this layer onto a different background (you can download the background you see here from the book's downloads page, listed in the intro of the book). The background is only 72 ppi and your letter and number are 200 ppi, so when they appear in your document, they'll be pretty huge, so press **Command-T (PC: Ctrl-T)** to bring up Free Transform. Press-and-hold the Shift key, grab a corner point, and drag inward to scale the text down to size. If you can't see the corner points, press **Command-0 (zero; PC: Ctrl-0)** to expand your image. (*Note*: One advantage to merging those layers before we moved them over to this other document is that it locks in the size of the stroke and bevel layer style effects we applied to them. If we left those "live," when you shrank them down, the effects would stay at their same size and strength, so they'd look kind of weird. The way around it is to go under the Layer menu, under Layer Style, and choose Scale Effects. This brings up a dialog with a slider, so you can scale the effects themselves down in size, until they look right, but of course, we didn't have to do that here because we merged down.)

Glassy Bar Reflection Trick

Last year, apparently, an international law was passed which stipulated that any and all buttons, banners, and bars on the Web, on TV, and basically on anything with a screen, must look glassy. Luckily, getting this look is one of the easiest techniques in the whole book. Here's how it's done:

STEP ONE: Create a new document (the one here is 800x600 pixels at a resolution of 72 ppi). Click on the Create a New Layer icon at the bottom of the Layers panel to add a new layer, and then get the Rectangular Marquee tool **(M)**. Press-and-hold the Shift key, then click-and-drag out a square selection in the center of the document (like you see here). Press **D** to set your Foreground color to black, then fill this selection with black (your Foreground color) by pressing **Option-Delete (PC: Alt-Backspace)**. Press **Command-D (PC: Ctrl-D)** to Deselect.

STEP TWO: Press **Command-J (PC: Ctrl-J)** to duplicate the layer, then press **Command-I (PC: Ctrl-I)** to Invert the layer (which switches your black square to a white square). The problem is you can't see a white square on a white background, so lower the Opacity of this layer to around 90%, just so you can at least see the outline of the shape (which you'll need for the next step).

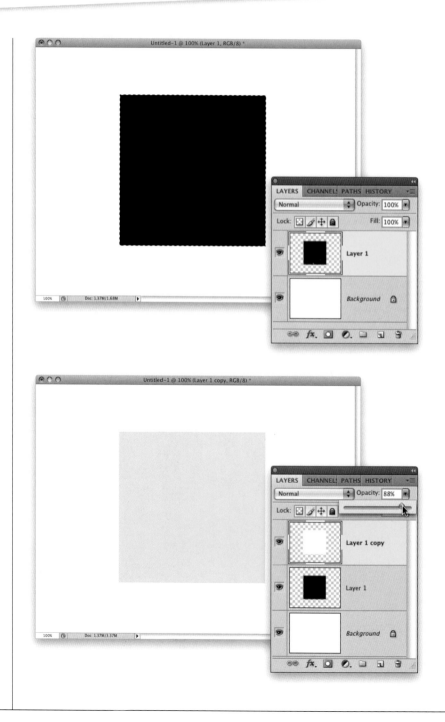

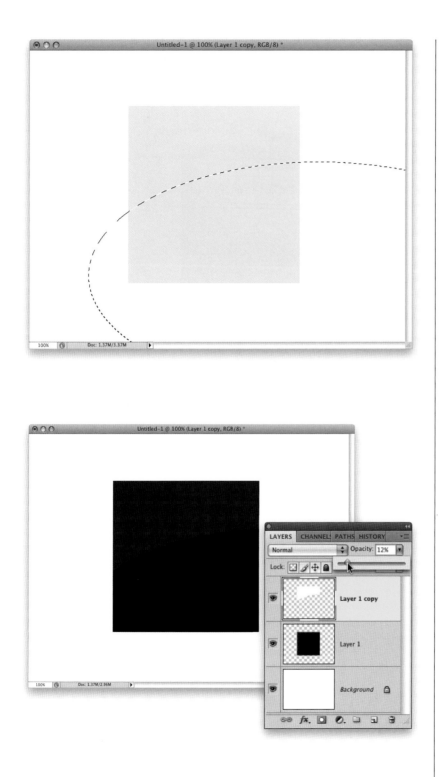

STEP THREE: Get the Elliptical Marquee tool (press **Shift-M**) and click-and-drag out a huge oval-shaped selection—so big that it extends off the image area (as shown here)—and position it so that it overlaps the center of the square (just press-and-hold the Spacebar while you're creating it to positon it).

STEP FOUR: Press the Delete (PC: Backspace) key to knock out the selected area from your white square, and deselect. Now, simply lower the Opacity setting of this white layer down to around 11% or 12% to give it that glassy look. In the next few steps, we'll add some text, a shape, and a variation.

Continued

STEP FIVE: Just for looks, we'll finish off our logo with a shape and some text. First, create a new layer, then get the Custom Shape tool from the Toolbox (it's two tools down from the Type tool—click-and-hold on it and all the shape tools will appear, then choose the bottom one). Now, go up to the Options Bar and click on the currently selected shape's thumbnail to bring up the Shape Picker (shown here). Click on the little right-facing arrow at the top-right corner of the Shape Picker, and from the flyout menu that appears, choose Nature, then click the Append button to add these shapes. Click on the stylized sun shape (as shown here), and then in the Options Bar, click on the third icon from the left (so your shape is made up of just pixels, and not a path).

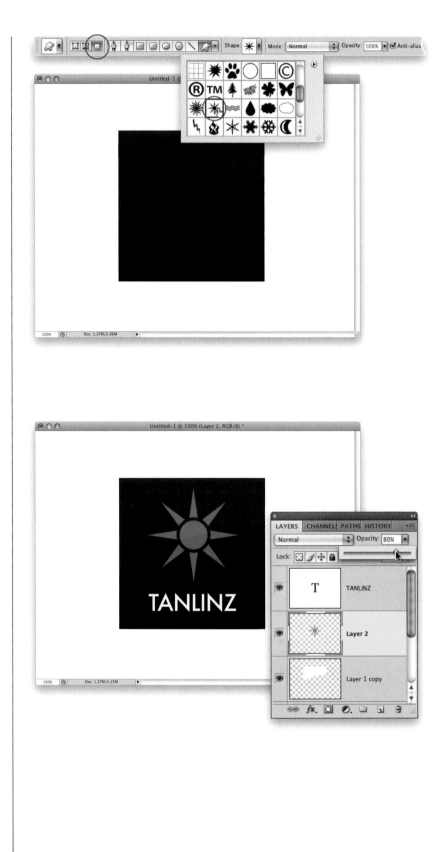

STEP SIX: Click on your Foreground color swatch and set your Foreground color to orange (I used R: 228, G: 66, B: 36), then click-and-drag out your shape and position it just above the center (as shown here). If you want the reflection to appear to pass over your shape, then just lower the Opacity of your Shape layer to 80% (as shown here). Now press **D**, then **X** to set white as your Foreground color, grab the Horizontal Type tool **(T)** and create your text (as shown here). I used the font Futura Medium at a point size of 55.

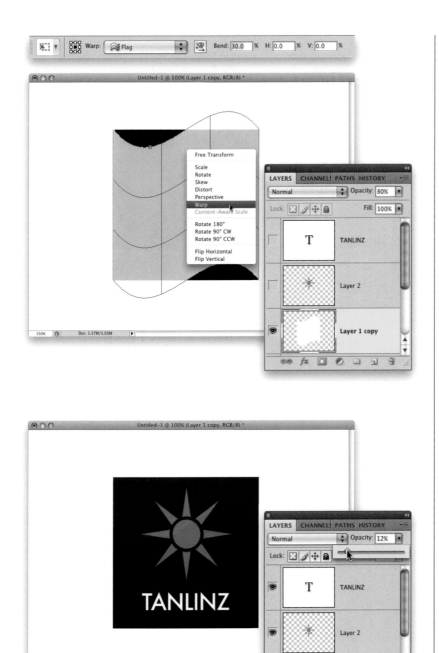

STEP SEVEN: Another popular variation for creating this look is to have more of a wave to your reflection. To do this, first hide your Type and Shape layers from view by clicking on the Eye icons to the left of each layer's thumbnail in the Layers panel. Then, go to your reflection layer and delete it by dragging it onto the Trash icon at the bottom of the Layers panel. Now, click on your black square layer and duplicate it again, then Invert it to white again. Lower the Opacity of this layer to 80%, then press **Command-T (PC: Ctrl-T)** to bring up Free Transform. Next, Control-click (PC: Right-click) inside your bounding box and, from the contextual menu that appears, choose Warp (as shown here). Go up to the Options Bar and, from the Warp pop-up menu, choose Flag, then lower the Bend amount to 30% to give you the shape you see here.

STEP EIGHT: Press **Return (PC: Enter)** to lock in your transformation, then get the Move tool **(V)**, press-and-hold the Shift key to keep the layer aligned, and click-and-drag straight upward until only the bottom third of your flag shape is showing. Lower the Opacity of this layer to around 10% or 12%, then make your Type and Shape layers visible again by clicking where the Eye icons used to be. Also, to crop off the extra area of white above the top of your logo, go to the Layers panel, press-and-hold the Command (PC: Ctrl) key, and click directly on the black square layer's thumbnail (don't change layers, just load that black layer as a selection—your active layer should still be the white flag shape layer). Now, press **Command-Shift-I (PC: Ctrl-Shift-I)** to Inverse your selection, then press Delete (PC: Backspace) to delete any leftover areas above your logo, and go ahead and deselect.

Creating Reflective Studio Backgrounds From Scratch

Here's another twist on the reflection effect, and Sony has used this one for a while now for their electronics products. The first place I noticed it was in the backlit ads you see in airports, but it's been used in everything from their print ads to their website (www.sonystyle.com). The product reflection is only a small part of this project, but I think this one is cool because you get to use a lot of different parts of Photoshop, and the final effect looks great, but is deceivingly simple (which is a good thing).

STEP ONE: Press **Command-N (PC: Ctrl-N)** to create a new blank document (I made mine 800x600 pixels at a resolution of 72 ppi). Press **D** to set your Foreground color to black, then press **Option-Delete (PC: Alt-Backspace)** to fill your Background layer with black. Next, get the Elliptical Marquee tool from the Toolbox (or press **Shift-M** until you have it), press-and-hold the Shift key (to constrain your selection to a perfect circle), and click-and-drag out a large circular selection like the one you see here. Now, press **X** to make white your Foreground color, then fill this circle selection with white using the same keyboard shortcut you used to fill your layer with black.

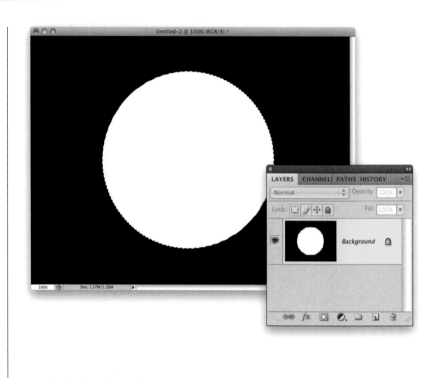

STEP TWO: You can Deselect by pressing **Command-D (PC: Ctrl-D)**. Next, go under the Filter menu, under Blur, and choose Gaussian Blur. For your Radius, enter 100 pixels (as shown here), then click OK to greatly soften the circle on the Background layer.

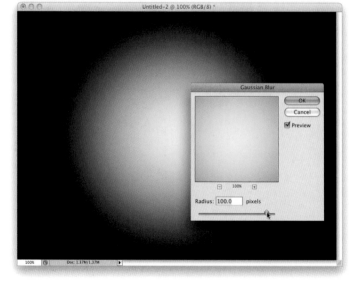

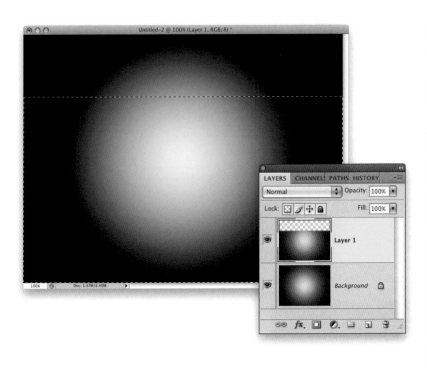

STEP THREE: Get the Rectangular Marquee tool from the Toolbox (or press **Shift-M** until you have it) and put a selection around the bottom three-quarters of your Background layer (as shown here). Press **Command-J (PC: Ctrl-J)** to put your selected area up on its own separate layer (if you look in the Layers panel here, you'll see that layer).

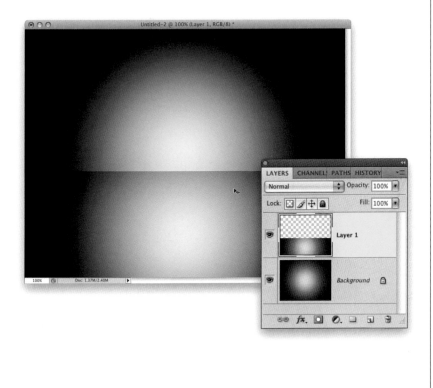

STEP FOUR: Get the Move tool **(V)**, press-and-hold the Shift key and click-and-drag straight downward (as shown here), so the top of this dragged layer is about an inch below the center of the image. This creates the "table" for your product to sit on.

Continued

STEP FIVE: Let's darken the table a bit, so it looks more separate from the background, by pressing **Command-L (PC: Ctrl-L)** to bring up Levels. Drag the center (midtones) Input Levels slider to the right (as shown here) to darken the midtones, which in turn darkens the fake table. Click OK. Then, press **Command-E (PC: Ctrl E)** to merge your table layer down into your Background layer.

STEP SIX: Now, let's add some color. Choose Solid Color from the Create New Adjustment Layer icon's pop-up menu at the bottom of the Layers panel. When the Color Picker appears, choose a blue color (I chose R: 18, G: 73, B: 112), and then click OK. This puts a solid color over your entire image, so you'll need to change the layer's blend mode from Normal to Color, which brings the color into your background (as seen here). The blue may be pretty punchy, so lower the layer's Opacity a bit to around 60% (as shown here).

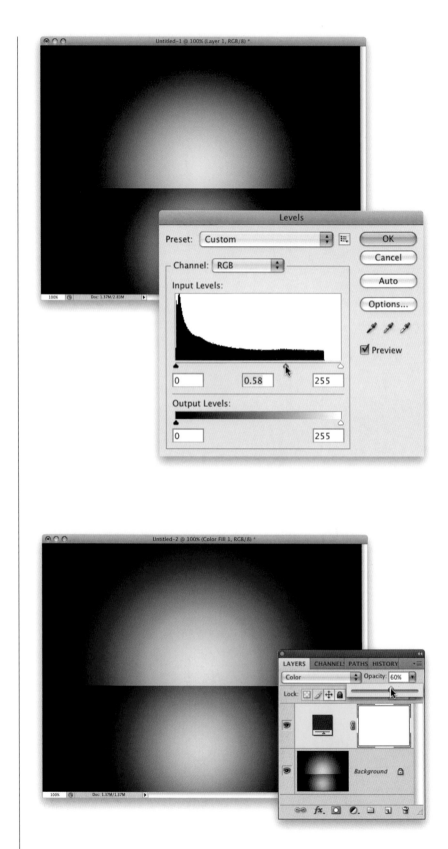

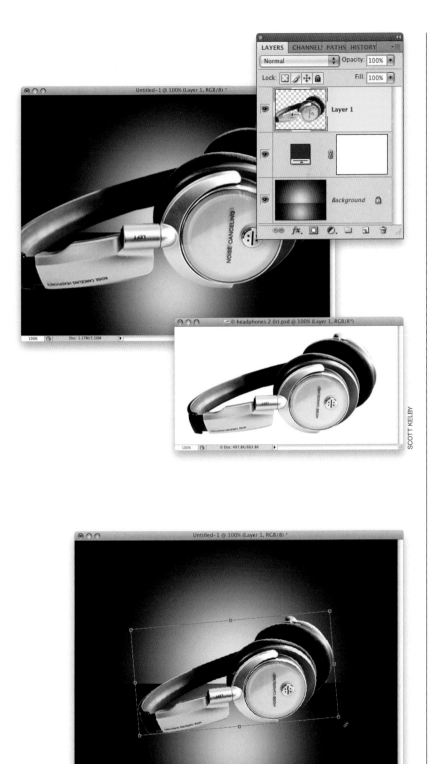

SCOTT KELBY

STEP SEVEN: Open the photo of the product you want on this background. I took a quick photo of some Sony noise-canceling headphones I sometimes travel with, and made it available for you on this book's downloads page. The headphones are on their own layer, so once you open the document, you can just take the Move tool and drag-and-drop those headphones right onto your layout.

STEP EIGHT: If you need to make them smaller, just press **Command-T (PC: Ctrl-T)** to bring up Free Transform, press-and-hold the Shift key, grab a corner handle, and drag inward (if you can't see the corner handles when you enter Free Transform, just press **Command-0 (zero; PC: Ctrl-0)**. Position them so a little bit of the edge of the fake table is visible through the opening in the headphones (as seen here). To angle them, move your cursor outside the bounding box until you see the curved two-headed cursor, then click-and-drag up or down to rotate (as shown here). Press **Return (PC: Enter)** to lock in your changes.

Continued

STEP NINE: Now, let's make the reflection. Duplicate the headphone layer, then bring up Free Transform again. Now, Control-click (PC: Right-click) inside the Free Transform bounding box and a contextual menu will appear. Choose Flip Vertical (as shown here) to flip this duplicate layer upside down.

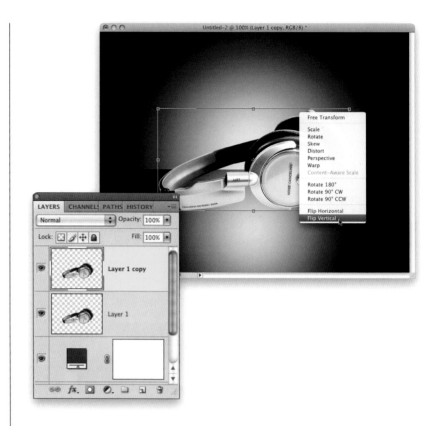

STEP 10: Click inside the bounding box and drag your flipped image straight down until the two sets of headphones are just barely touching, creating the mirror reflection you see here. When it's positioned where you want, lock in your transformation.

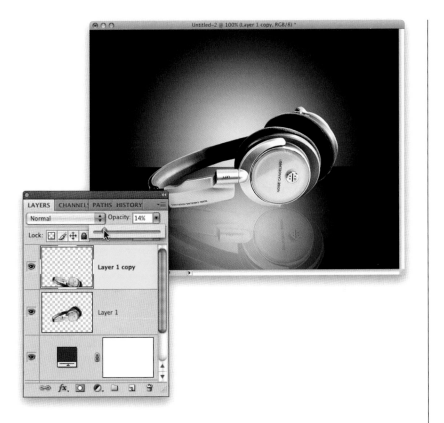

STEP 11: To enhance the reflected effect, lower the Opacity of this layer to around 14% (this will vary from image to image, but anywhere between 10% and 20% will usually work—you have to make the call as to what exactly that percentage will be. I know. The pressure!). The reflection here isn't dead-on with what the real reflection would be if these headphones were really sitting on a reflective surface, but you'd have to tweak the type on them so much (bending and distorting it), that we're getting close enough that folks won't ever even notice. Of course, the whole thing is faked from top to bottom, so that should be the least of our worries, eh?

STEP 12: To make sure the reflection isn't on top of the headphones, click on the reflection layer and drag it below the headphone layer in the Layers panel. Now, we need to apply a "fade away" effect to our reflection, so click on the Add Layer Mask icon at the bottom of the Layers panel (it's shown circled here in red), then get the Gradient tool **(G)**, click on the down-facing arrow to the right of the gradient thumbnail in the Options Bar, and choose the Foreground to Background gradient (the top-left one). Click at the top of your reflected image, and then drag downward to the point where you want your image to fade away (as shown here), and son of a gun, it just fades away.

Continued

STEP 13: Lastly, you actually have control over the brightness and spread of the background, and in the Sony ads, it's usually a little darker and more dramatic, and the glow isn't quite as big, but luckily we can adjust that easily. Click on the Background layer, then in the Adjustments panel, click on the Levels icon (the second icon from the left in the top row), and when the options appear, drag the center midtones slider to the right. As you do, it crunches down the spotlight effect quite a bit (as seen here).

STEP 14: Now you can add some text to finish the project off (as I did here in the final image). The headline (and tiny disclaimer at the bottom) are both done in Helvetica Regular.

3D Video Wall with Live-Updating Reflections

Here, we're going to recreate the very slick 3D wraparound video wall that Apple used for the introduction of AppleTV. This is the longest project in the entire book, but that doesn't mean it's hard. In fact, it's not hard at all—you'll be able to recreate this project, which starts in Bridge CS4, without any problem at all, so don't let the number of steps make you think it's too hard. The thing I like best about this project is the cool way Smart Objects are used to make the whole thing into a template that lets you change the look (once you're done with the initial project) in less than one minute (I have to thank Corey Barker for his suggestion to add Smart Objects to this project, because as you'll see, it takes the technique over the top).

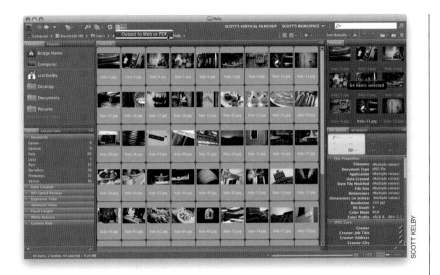

STEP ONE: Put together a folder of 64 low-resolution photos you'd like to have appear in your curved 3D video wall. Your wall will look best if you use all wide photos (rather than a mix of tall and wide photos), and this will work best if you make them all the same width. Open that folder of images in Bridge CS4 (as shown here). Press **Command-A (PC: Ctrl-A)** to select all your photos in Bridge, then click on the Output icon at the top of the Bridge window, and choose Output to Web or PDF from the pop-up menu (as shown here) to bring up the contact sheet feature.

STEP TWO: When the Output workspace appears (shown here), at the top of the Output panel (on the right side), click on the PDF button. Then in the Document section, enter a Width of 16 inches, a Height of 4, and choose a Quality of 300 ppi (as shown here). In the Layout section, choose 16 columns by 4 rows, then set your Horizontal and Vertical spacing to 0.00. One last thing: scroll down to the Overlays section, and make sure the Filename checkbox is turned off. Now, scroll to the bottom of the right-side panels and click on the Save button.

Continued

STEP THREE: Give your PDF a name, and save it on your computer. Now go to Photoshop CS4, under the File menu, and choose Open. Navigate to your PDF and click Open. When you do this, it will bring up the PDF Import dialog you see here. Luckily, you don't have to do anything in this dialog except click OK.

STEP FOUR: When your contact sheet appears, go under the Layer menu, under Smart Objects, and choose Convert to Smart Object (as shown here). When you do this, you'll see a little page icon in the bottom-right corner of your layer's thumbnail, letting you know it is now a Smart Object (as shown in the next step).

STEP FIVE: Create a new blank layer above your contact sheet layer by clicking on the Create a New Layer icon at the bottom of the Layers panel. Click on the Foreground color swatch at the bottom of the Toolbox to bring up the Color Picker, and choose a gray color. Then, get the Rounded Rectangle tool (press **Shift-U** until you have it), and set your Radius (corner roundness) up in the Options Bar to 20. Click on the third icon from the left in the Options Bar, so when you draw rectangles, they're made of pixels, rather than becoming a Shape layer or path. Now, draw a rounded rectangle over the first thumbnail in your contact sheet, and make it a little smaller than your thumbnail (as shown here).

STEP SIX: Load that layer as a selection by Command-clicking (PC: Ctrl-clicking) on the layer's thumbnail. Press **Command-Option-T (PC: Ctrl-Alt-T)** to bring up Free Transform and make a copy of your selection. Press-and-hold the Shift key and click-and-drag this shape copy over until it covers the next thumbnail to the right, then press **Return (PC: Enter)** to lock in your change. Because you used that keyboard shortcut, it actually makes a duplicate of your shape on the same layer.

Continued

STEP SEVEN: Press **Command-Option-Shift-T (PC: Ctrl-Alt-Shift-T)** again and again until you have 16 thumbnails in one long horizontal row. They should perfectly align themselves over each thumbnail on the top row of your contact sheet (well, they will if, when you dragged the second thumbnail over, you carefully positioned it so it covers the second thumbnail). Then, Command-click (PC: Ctrl-click) on the thumbnail for your gray shapes layer to select the entire row. Get the Move tool **(V)**, press-and-hold the Option (PC: Alt) and Shift keys, then click-and-drag one of those gray shapes straight downward, and position this row of gray rectangles so it covers the thumbnails on the second row. Pause a moment, then do this two more times (dragging a copy of your gray shapes), until all your thumbnails are covered. Because of the way you did this, all your rows of shapes will be on one single layer.

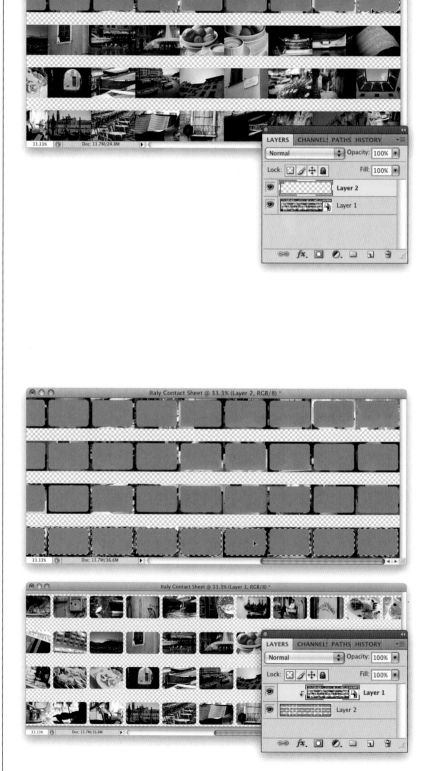

STEP EIGHT: Here's how it should look at this point, with gray shapes covering all your photos, and these shapes all on one layer. Press **Command-D (PC: Ctrl-D)** to Deselect, go to the Layers panel, and drag your gray shapes layer below your photo contact sheet layer. Then, click back on the photo contact sheet layer to make it active. Go up top to the menu bar, under the Layer menu, and choose Create Clipping Mask (or just press **Command-Option-G [PC: Ctrl-Alt-G]**). This puts your photo thumbnails inside the gray rounded rectangles on the layer below it, so now all your thumbnails have rounded corners like a TV (as seen at the bottom here).

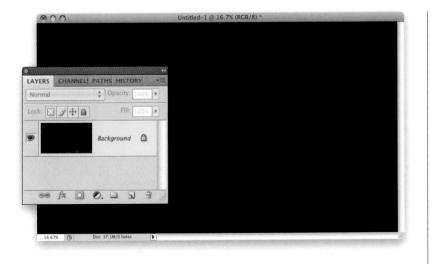

STEP NINE: Press **Command-N (PC: Ctrl-N)** to bring up the New dialog, and create a new document that is 16 inches wide, but rather than using 4 inches again, make the height 9 inches, so we can add a product and some text below the video wall. Set the Resolution to 300 ppi, just like your previous document. Press **D** to set your Foreground color to black, then press **Option-Delete (PC: Alt-Backspace)** to fill this new document's Background layer with black (as shown here).

STEP 10: Go back to your contact sheet document. Go to the Layers panel, Command-click (PC: Ctrl-click) on both layers to select them, then get the Move tool, click-and-drag both of these layers onto your new document, and position them up near the top of the window (as shown here). Go to the Layers panel and drag either of the two selected layers down to the Create a New Layer icon to duplicate both layers.

Continued

STEP 11: Now, press **Command-T (PC: Ctrl-T)** to bring up Free Transform. Then, Control-click (PC: Right-click) inside the Free Transform bounding box, and when the contextual menu appears, choose Flip Vertical (as shown here), to flip these two selected layers upside down.

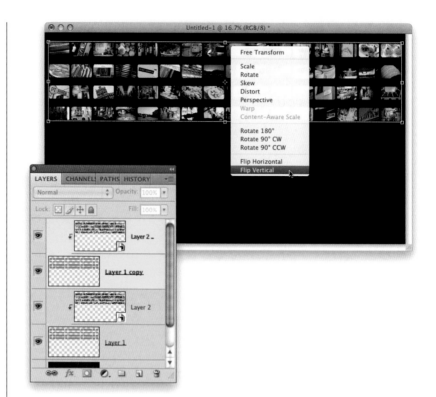

STEP 12: Press-and-hold the Shift key, and click-and-drag these two layers straight downward until the top edge of the flipped layers touches the bottom edge of your original layers (as shown here). This creates a mirror reflection of your contact sheet. When you're happy with the placement, press **Return (PC: Enter)** to lock in your transformation.

STEP 13: In the Layers panel, click on the second layer from the top (the flipped gray rectangles layer), then lower the Opacity of this layer to 20%, so it looks more like a reflection.

STEP 14: Now we need to have this reflection fade away, so click on the Add Layer Mask icon at the bottom of the Layers panel (it's shown circled here in red). Get the Gradient tool **(G)**, click on the down-facing arrow to the right of the gradient thumbnail in the Options Bar to open the Gradient Picker, and click on the top-left gradient (Foreground to Background). Click-and-drag it from the bottom of your upright layer (where the two meet) to the bottom of the flipped layer, so it fades away (as seen here).

Continued

STEP 15: Press-and-hold the Command (PC: Ctrl) key, go to the Layers panel, and click on all the layers (except the Background layer) to select them. Then, Control-click (PC: Right-click) on one of those selected layers, and from the contextual menu that appears, choose Convert to Smart Object (as shown here), to convert all four layers into one Smart Object layer (you'll understand why we did this in just a moment).

STEP 16: Bring up Free Transform again, for this layer you just created. Control-click (PC: Right-click) inside the Free Transform bounding box and, from the contextual menu that appears, choose Warp (as shown here).

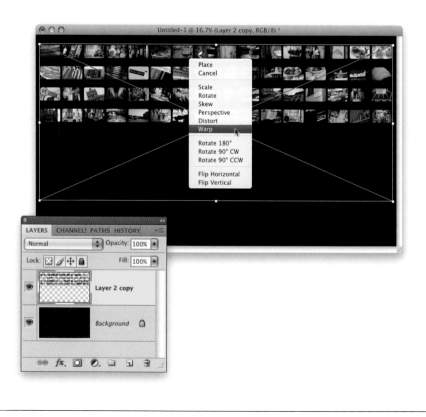

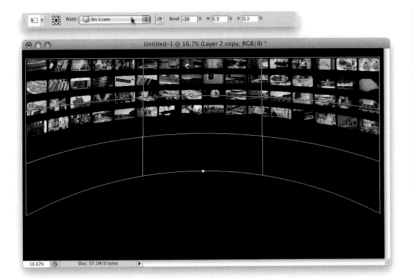

STEP 17: Go up to the Options Bar and, from the Warp pop-up menu, choose Arc Lower (as shown up top here), then set the Bend amount to –30. This bends the thumbnails into a curve.

STEP 18: Adding this warping to your photos tends to make them look a bit stretched, so go back into Free Transform again. Grab the center point on the right side and drag inward (as shown here) to remove some of the stretching. Now do the same thing to the left side, then lock in your side shrinking.

Continued

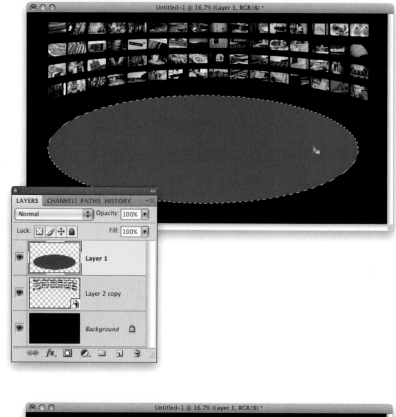

STEP 19: Create a new blank layer. Get the Elliptical Marquee tool (press **Shift-M** until you have it), click-and-drag a huge oval-shaped selection that roughly matches the roundness of your curved video wall, and position it so it overlaps your reflection a little bit (as shown here). Click on your Foreground color swatch and choose a blue color in the Color Picker, then fill your oval-shaped selection with this color by pressing Option-Delete (PC: Alt-Backspace). Deselect by pressing Command-D (PC: Ctrl-D).

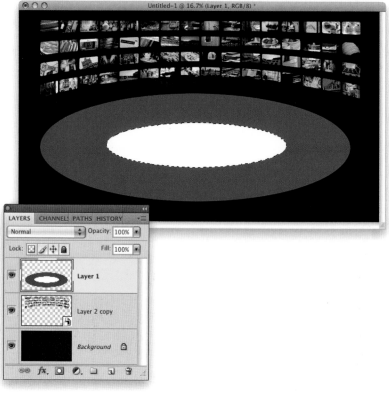

STEP 20: Now, use the Elliptical Marquee tool to draw a smaller oval selection inside your blue oval. Press **D**, then **X** to set your Foreground color to white, and fill that oval with white (as shown here), then deselect.

STEP 21: Go under the Filter menu, under Blur, and choose Gaussian Blur. When the dialog appears, enter 250 pixels to greatly soften the edge of your blue-and-white oval, and make it look like a soft spotlight (as seen here).

STEP 22: Now, open the photo of the product you want to showcase (in our case, it's an Apple MacBook Pro laptop. You can download this photo from the book's downloads page). If you choose to use this one, I put the laptop on its own layer, so all you have to do is get the Move tool, click-and-drag it onto the blurred soft spotlight in your main document, and position it like you see here. Then, get the Magic Wand tool (press **Shift-W** until you have it), and click once inside the blank white screen on the laptop to put a selection around it.

©ISTOCKPHOTO/SERGEY RUSAKOV

Continued

STEP 23: Open the photo you want to appear inside your computer screen (after all, you can't leave that blank white screen there, right?). Press **Command-A (PC: Ctrl-A)** to select the entire photo, then press **Command-C (PC: Ctrl-C)** to Copy this photo into memory. Now, switch to your video wall document, go under the Edit menu, and choose Paste Into to paste the photo in your computer's memory into your selected area inside the computer screen (as seen here). If your image is too large to fit in the screen, bring up Free Transform, then press-and-hold the Shift key, grab a corner point, and drag inward (as shown here) to shrink it down to size (while still staying masked inside the laptop's screen).

STEP 24: Now, let's add a drop shadow directly under the laptop. In the Layers panel, click on the layer with your laptop image on it (it should be the second layer from the top). Choose Drop Shadow from the Add a Layer Style icon's pop-up menu at the bottom of the Layers panel. When the Layer Style dialog comes up, set the Angle to 90°, so the shadow appears directly below the laptop (as seen here). The shadow looks a little too dark, so lower the Opacity to around 55%. Then set the Distance to 28, and to soften it, increase the Size amount to 24. Click OK to apply the drop shadow to the laptop.

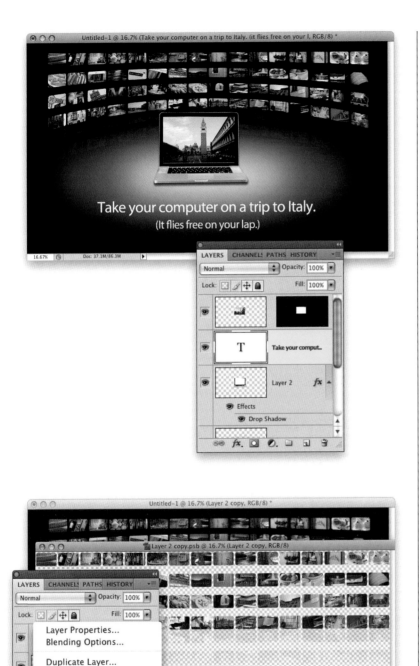

STEP 25: Next, let's add some text below the product (I used the same font that Apple uses, Myriad Pro, which comes installed with Photoshop CS4), so grab the Horizontal Type tool **(T)**, click below the laptop, and type away. Okay, now the look is complete, but we haven't put those Smart Object layers to use yet, and that's where it gets really fun. Here's how: since you used Smart Objects, you can just build another contact sheet (use a different set of 64 photos), and then in just a few clicks, you can not only replace the photos in the video wall (while retaining it's curved video wall look), but it will also automatically create the reflected images, as well. Here's how that's done:

STEP 26: Go to the Layers panel and double-click on the Smart Object layer's thumbnail, click OK in the warning dialog that appears, and a new image window will open with the four separate video wall layers intact (as seen here). Now, Control-click (PC: Right-click) on the top layer, and from the contextual menu that appears, choose Replace Contents (as shown here).

Continued

STEP 27: A standard Open dialog will pop up, and now all you have to do is locate your other photo contact sheet (I created a second contact sheet using photos of daisies), and then click the Place button (as shown here). When your new photos have replaced the old ones, press **Command-S (PC: Ctrl-S)** to save the Smart Objects document, then close it and return to your laptop and video wall document. *Note:* Make sure you don't do a Save As and change the location of the Smart Objects document or your other document won't update.

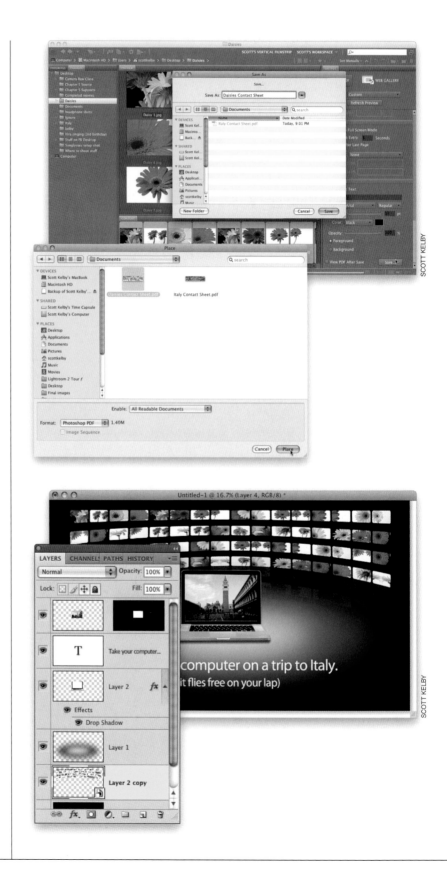

SCOTT KELBY

STEP 28: Now, the photos from the daisy contact sheet have replaced the Italy photos, and the faded off reflection is automatically updated with these new photos (how slick is that!). Of course, we still have a photo of Venice in the laptop, so we'll have to deal with that, too.

SCOTT KELBY

STEP 29: First, let's change the color of the glow (because that blue color just doesn't cut it anymore). In the Layers panel, click on the blue circle layer, then press **Command-U (PC: Ctrl-U)** to bring up the Hue/Saturation dialog. Turn on the Colorize checkbox at the bottom right, then drag the Hue slider to the left, over to the yellow side of the hue gradient, raise the Saturation up to 50, and click OK to change the color of the blue spotlight to more of a yellowish look (as seen here).

STEP 30: Now, let's replace that graphic in the laptop's screen. In the Layers panel, find the layer that has the photo you placed into the screen earlier. Press-and-hold the Command (PC: Ctrl) key and click on that layer's layer mask thumbnail to put a selection around the screen (as shown here).

Continued

STEP 31: Open the photo you want to put inside this laptop (in this case, it's another daisy photo), then select the entire photo, and copy it into memory. Switch back to your video wall document, go under the Edit menu, and choose Paste Into to paste that photo into your selected computer screen (as seen here). If you need to resize the image, use Free Transform to scale it down.

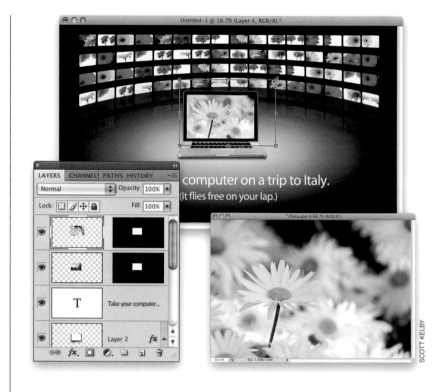

STEP 32: Here's the final image, with the daisies in the video wall and the computer monitor, the spotlight color updated, and new text. Just remember to save a copy of this document with all the layers intact, so any time you want to update it with a new look, it's just a matter of having Bridge make a new contact sheet, then using the Smart Object Replace Contents command to swap out the images for you.

Take your computer out in the garden.
(It could use a break from the office.)

Simple Water Reflection for Photos

Here's a project that takes a little twist on the basic reflection technique we learned at the beginning of this chapter, and adds a little tweak at the end that helps make the effect more realistic.

STEP ONE: Open the photo you want to apply the effect to (you can download this photo from the book's downloads page, listed in the book's introduction). Take the Rectangular Marquee tool **(M)** and make a selection from the horizon line on up to the top of the image (as shown here).

STEP TWO: Press **Command-J (PC: Ctrl-J)** to put this selected area up on its own separate layer. Now, press **Command-T (PC: Ctrl-T)** to bring up Free Transform, then Control-click (PC: Right-click) anywhere inside the bounding box and, from the contextual menu that appears, choose Flip Vertical to flip this layer upside down (as seen here). Press **Return (PC: Enter)** to lock in your transformation.

Continued

STEP THREE: Get the Move tool **(V)**, press-and-hold the Shift key (which keeps things aligned as you drag), and click-and-drag straight downward until the top of your flipped layer touches the horizon of the top layer (to create the mirror reflection you see here). To help the reflection not look so obvious, press **Command-L (PC: Ctrl-L)** to bring up Levels, then drag the Input Levels midtones slider (the gray one in the center) to the right a bit to darken the midtones, and drag the highlights Output Levels slider (on the right) to the left to darken the flipped layer a bit overall.

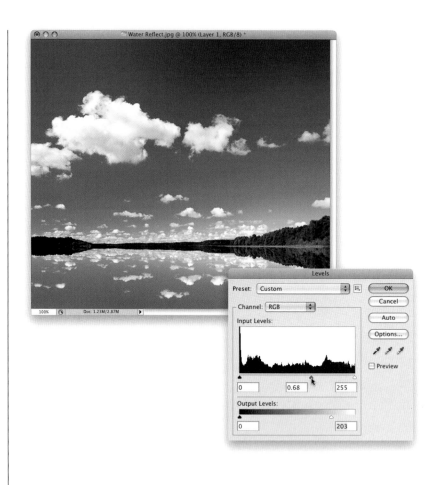

STEP FOUR: Now, click OK to apply your Levels adjustment, which completes the water reflection (as seen here). Press **Command-E (PC: Ctrl-E)** to merge this layer with your Background layer, which flattens the image. Compare this final image with the image in Step One to see what a dramatic difference this 60-second technique can have on the impact of a photo.

Satisfying

CHAPTER 6

Truth in Advertising

advertising effects

This chapter is all about Photoshop effects you see in ads (on the Web, in magazines, etc.), and ads are a great place to find special effects because the ad agency gets to bill the client extra since these aren't just effects—they're "special effects," and anything that's special costs more money, so it's hard to argue the bill when you get it. If you call up the agency and start screaming about a line item on your invoice, they're going to come right back with something like, "Do you have any idea how much high-end special effects cost these days?" and then they'll start using Hollywood movies as an example, and then before you know it, not only have you agreed to pay the invoice, but chances are the agency has now snuck in another line item for a "Special Effects Supervisor" because you can't just let special effects go around unsupervised, right? Besides, clients love special effects. We might look at them and think, "Oh, not that effect again," but clients look at them and say stuff like, "I love that cool thingy you put in the ad" and at that very moment, if you listen carefully, you can hear the sound all advertising executives love to hear. Cha-ching! So, if there's any "Truth in Advertising" (the name of a comedy movie short from 2001), it's the universal truth that no matter how trite, overplayed, or lame we feel an effect may be, clients still love them, and if they love them, my billing department loves them, too!

Multi-Photo High-Tech Look from One Image

I saw this technique used very effectively in downloadable, computer desktop wallpaper for the NFL's Chicago Bears. It works great when you only have one photo, but don't want that "one-photo" look. Plus, in this technique, you'll learn a pretty cool little trick for varying the amount of a filter (in this case, the Halftone Pattern filter) below the lowest setting the filter will allow. You'll also learn a cool way to use the Wind filter (the Wind filter? Yup—there's a Wind filter. It just doesn't work all that great, but don't worry, there's always a way around that, eh?).

STEP ONE: Start by going under the File menu, choosing New, and creating a new document that is 800x600 pixels at a resolution of 72 ppi. Open a photo of the athlete you want to feature on the page (we're using a football shot here, which you can download from the book's downloads webpage, but you could do this same thing with an athlete from almost any sport). Now, you'll need to put a selection around the athlete (if you downloaded the photo shown here, I already selected the running back and put him up on his own separate layer, so he's all ready to go for you. However, if you're one of those "I need a challenge" folks, then choose Flatten Image from the Layers panel's flyout menu to flatten the image file that I provided, and use the Quick Selection tool **[W]**, or any selection tool you like, to put a selection around the player).

STEP TWO: Get the Move tool **(V)** and drag the player over onto your main document, positioning him like you see here. Now, get the Eyedropper tool **(I)**, and click it once on a lighter area of his pants (as shown here) to make that color your Foreground color.

SCOTT KELBY

STEP THREE: In the Layers panel, click on the Background layer, then fill this layer with that blue Foreground color by pressing **Option-Delete (PC: Alt-Backspace)**, so your background is solid blue (as seen here).

STEP FOUR: Click on the Create a New Layer icon at the bottom of the Layers panel to create a new blank layer. In Step Five, we're going to add some horizontal lines using the Halftone Pattern filter, but that filter won't run on an empty layer—you have to have something there for it to run on. So, click on the Foreground color swatch, set a medium gray as your Foreground color, and then fill this new layer with gray using the same shortcut you used to fill the Background layer.

Continued

STEP FIVE: Go under the Filter menu, under Sketch, and choose Halftone Pattern. When the dialog appears, from the Pattern Type pop-up menu on the right, choose Line (as shown here), then leave the Size set to 1 (to get the smallest lines), and set the Contrast to around 23.

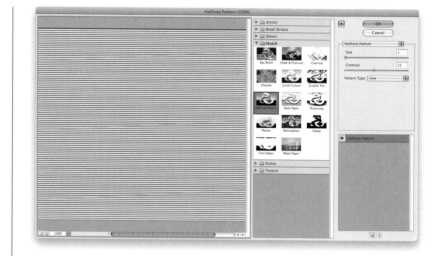

STEP SIX: Click OK and it applies the lines to the layer. To see how your lines will blend in with your blue Background layer, change the layer blend mode of this layer to Soft Light (as shown here).

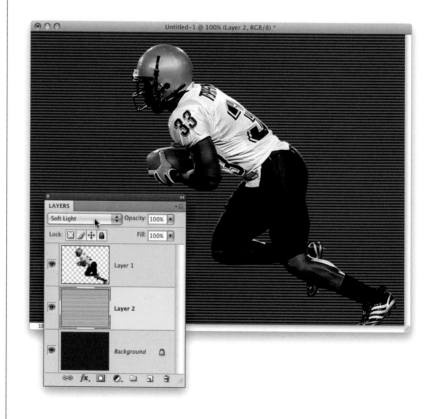

STEP SEVEN: There is one problem, though: with the wallpaper I saw, the lines were much thinner and closer together, but we used the smallest size the filter would allow. So, delete that gray lines layer by clicking-and-dragging it onto the Trash icon at the bottom of the Layers panel, and then use this little workaround trick to get finer lines. Go under the File menu and create a new document that is much larger than your existing document (our existing document is 800x600 pixels, so create a new one that is at least 1152x864 pixels, as seen here, or larger). Then, repeat the process of adding a new blank layer and filling it with gray, then just press **Command-F (PC: Ctrl-F)** to run the Halftone Pattern filter again using the same settings. The lines will pretty much look the same at this point, but it's in the next step that they'll get finer.

STEP EIGHT: Get the Move tool and click-and-drag your gray-lined layer on your larger document over onto your smaller document. It will be way too big to fit fully in your document, so you'll have to use Free Transform to scale it down to fit, which (you guessed it) shrinks the size of the lines, and the width between them, quite a bit. Press **Command-T (PC: Ctrl-T)** to bring up Free Transform, then press **Command-0 (zero; PC: Ctrl-0)** and the window will resize, so you can reach the Free Transform handles (as seen here). Press-and-hold the Shift key, grab a corner point, and drag inward to shrink your lines (as shown here), so that you now have finer, thinner lines (not a bad trick to know, eh?). Press **Return (PC: Enter)** to lock in your transformation.

Continued

STEP NINE: Now, at the top of the Layers panel, change the layer blend mode of this layer to Soft Light (so it blends in with the dark blue background below it), and then lower the layer Opacity to around 30% (as shown here).

STEP 10: Click on your football player layer in the Layers panel, then press **Command-J (PC: Ctrl-J)** to duplicate the layer. Bring up Free Transform again, press-and-hold the Shift key, grab a corner point, and drag out until this copy of the player is really huge (like you see here). To get to this size, you'll probably have to shrink your image size (press **Command-–[minus sign; PC: Ctrl-–]** to zoom out), then grab the bottom-right corner of the image window and drag out, so you see the gray area around the image. Then drag the Free Transform corner point way, way out until the top half of the player fills the image, like you see here. Now, press Return (PC: Enter) to lock in your resizing.

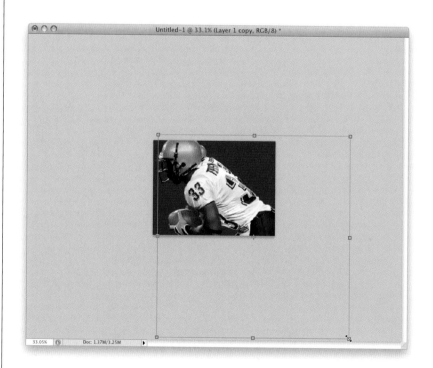

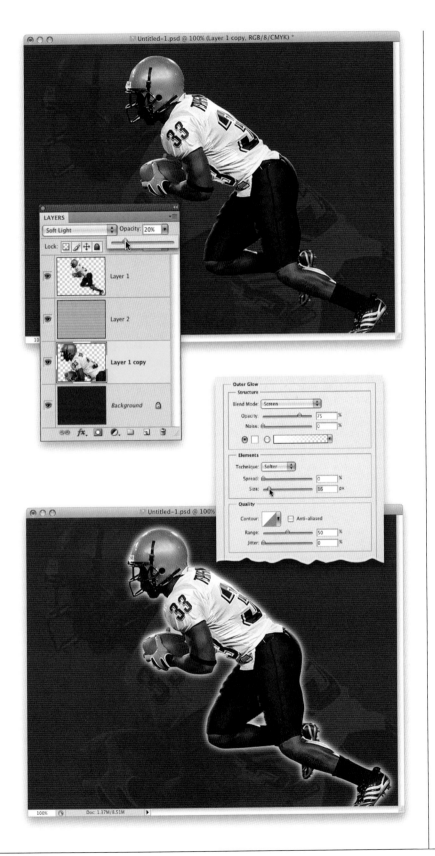

STEP 11: In the Layers panel, drag this giant player layer behind your lines layer, then press **Command-Shift-U (PC: Ctrl-Shift-U)** to Desaturate the layer. Next, change the layer blend mode to Soft Light, and then lower the Opacity of this layer to around 20% (that may be too light, and we won't know for sure until we add some additional things to our layout, but 20% is a good starting place for now).

STEP 12: Now you're going to add a glow around your player, so in the Layers panel, click on the top player layer to make it the active layer, then click on the Add a Layer Style icon at the bottom of the Layers panel, and choose Outer Glow from the pop-up menu. When the dialog appears, click on the color swatch and change your glow color to white, then increase the Size (the amount of glow) to 16 (as shown here), and click OK to apply a white glow around your player (as seen here).

Continued

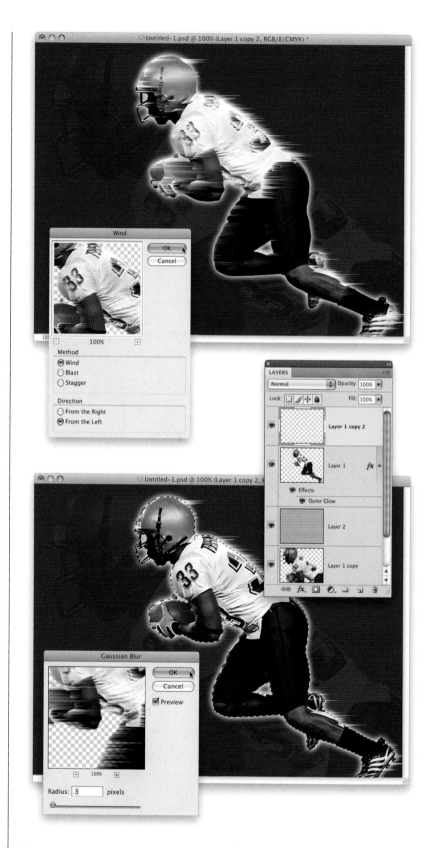

STEP 13: You're now going to add a windblown effect to the edges of your player, but we want to do this on a duplicate layer of our player (you'll see why in the next step), so duplicate your player layer. Now, delete the Outer Glow effect from this duplicate layer by clicking directly on the word "Effects," appearing below your layer's thumbnail, and dragging it down onto the Trash icon at the bottom of the Layers panel, which removes the effect from this layer. Next, go under the Filter menu, under Stylize, and choose Wind. When the dialog appears (shown here), for Method, choose Wind, for Direction, choose From the Left (so the wind appears to blow from left to right), and click OK. Now, to get a more intense effect, reapply that same filter with the same settings, by pressing Command-F (PC: Ctrl-F).

STEP 14: To soften the harsh edges of your Wind effect, go under the Filter menu, under Blur, and choose Gaussian Blur. When the Gaussian Blur dialog appears, set the Radius to 0.3 pixels (so, it's one-third of 1 pixel), then click OK. This little bit of blur does a nice job of softening those rough edges. Now, press-and-hold the Command (PC: Ctrl) key and, in the Layers panel, click directly on the original player's layer thumbnail (as shown here). This loads a selection around the player (but it doesn't select the Wind effect, because that appears outside the player's body). Press Delete (PC: Backspace) and it erases your duplicate player, leaving just the wind in place, which gives you the look you see here. You can now Deselect by pressing **Command-D (PC: Ctrl-D)**.

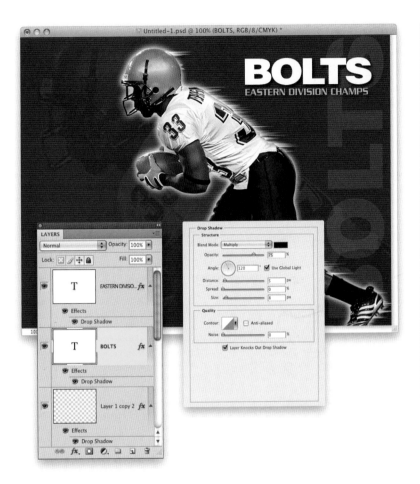

STEP 15: Now, let's add some text. Get the Horizontal Type tool **(T)**, set your Foreground color to white, and type in "BOLTS" in a thick, bold font (I used Helvetica Black) at 165 points. Rotate the text sideways by going under the Edit menu, under Transform, and choosing Rotate 90° CCW, then switch to the Move tool (click on it in the Toolbox), drag this text up against the right side of your image window, and then lower the Opacity to around 10%. So this text appears beneath the player, click-and-drag this Type layer beneath the player layer in the layer stack. Click on the top-most layer in the layer stack, and now add the regular text up top (the word "BOLTS" is in Helvetica Black again, and the line below it is in the font Serpentine). Choose Drop Shadow from the Add a Layer Style icon's pop-up menu at the bottom of the Layers panel to add a drop shadow to your text layer. When the Drop Shadow dialog appears, increase the Size amount to 8 and click OK. Add the same drop shadow to your BOLTS line above it by pressing-and-holding the **Option (PC: Alt) key**, clicking on "Effects," and dragging-and-dropping it onto the "BOLTS" layer.

STEP 16: With everything in place, the background image (the large version of the player) looks too light, so go to the Layers panel, click on that layer, and raise the Opacity up to 40%. Finish things off with a few more lines of text (the player's name, stats, etc.). I did all of this with the font Serpentine at different opacities, which is a very popular choice when you want things to look "high tech," and you see it used in video games, sports graphics, etc., pretty frequently. Here's the final image with the rest of the text added.

Fake Studio Setup with See-Through Glass Trick

Here you're going to use some Photoshop tricks to make it look like you had a complicated lighting setup for a product shot, when all you did was shoot it on a white seamless background. The problem is, though, that our product is glass (a perfume bottle) and if it's glass, it should be see-through, right? Right! So, we'll tackle that along with half a dozen other tricks that give us a realistic setup that's used by commercial photographers and retouchers.

STEP ONE: Go under the File menu, choose New, and create a new document (the one here is 7 inches wide by 8.5 inches high at a resolution of 72 ppi). Click on the Foreground color swatch at the bottom of the Toolbox and, in the Color Picker, set a very light gray as your Foreground color (I chose R: 236, G: 236, B: 236), then fill your Background layer with this light gray by pressing **Option-Delete (PC: Alt-Backspace)**.

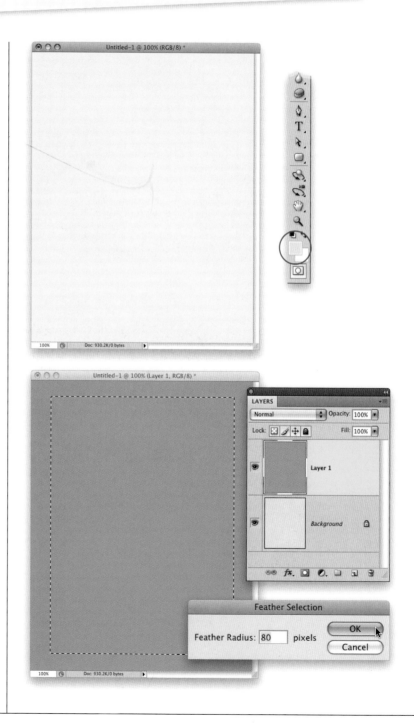

STEP TWO: Add a new blank layer by clicking on the Create a New Layer icon at the bottom of the Layers panel. Click on the Foreground color swatch again, choose a darker shade of gray (I chose R: 181, G: 181, B: 181), and then fill this layer with that darker gray (use the same shortcut you used in Step One). Now, get the Rectangular Marquee tool **(M)**, and draw a large rectangle like the one you see here, leaving only approximately an inch unselected on all sides. To greatly soften the edges of this selection, go under the Select menu, under Modify, and choose Feather. When the dialog appears, enter 80 pixels and click OK.

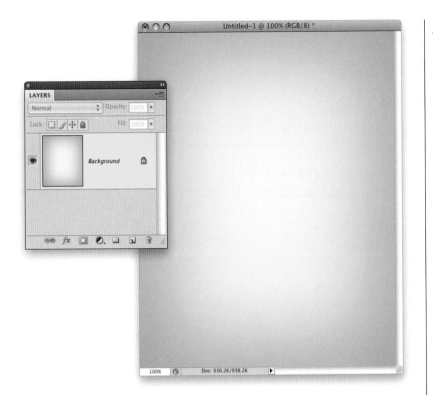

STEP THREE: Now that your edges are softened, just press the Delete (PC: Backspace) key to knock a soft-edged hole out of this darker layer, revealing the lighter layer in the center (as seen here). Press **Command-D (PC: Ctrl-D)** to Deselect and then press **Command-E (PC: Ctrl-E)** to merge these two layers down to just the Background layer.

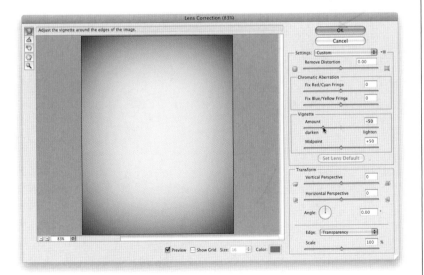

STEP FOUR: It's time to darken just the edges of your Background layer, so go under the Filter menu, under Distort, and choose Lens Correction. When the dialog appears, turn off the Show Grid check-box beneath the preview area. Next, in the Vignette section on the right side of the dialog, drag the Amount slider to the left to darken all four edges of the image (as shown here), then click OK.

Continued

STEP FIVE: Press **Command-J (PC: Ctrl-J)** to duplicate the layer, then press **Command-T (PC: Ctrl-T)** to bring up Free Transform. Grab the bottom-middle point and drag straight upward until you're about one-third of the way up (as seen here), then press **Return (PC: Enter)** to lock in your resizing.

STEP SIX: In the Layers panel, click on Layer 0 (this was the Background layer, but using the Lens Correction filter on the Background layer automatically turns it into a regular layer, and names it Layer 0). Bring up Free Transform again, but this time grab the top-middle point and drag downward until the top of this lower layer touches the bottom of the top layer (as seen here), and then lock in your resizing. Now click on the top layer again, and then merge these two layers into one single Background layer.

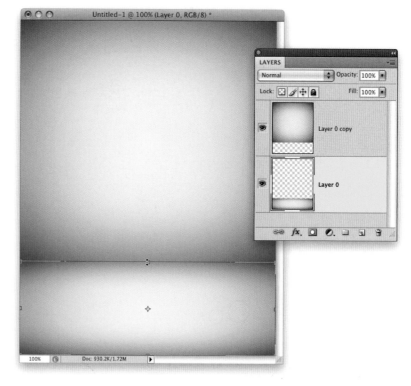

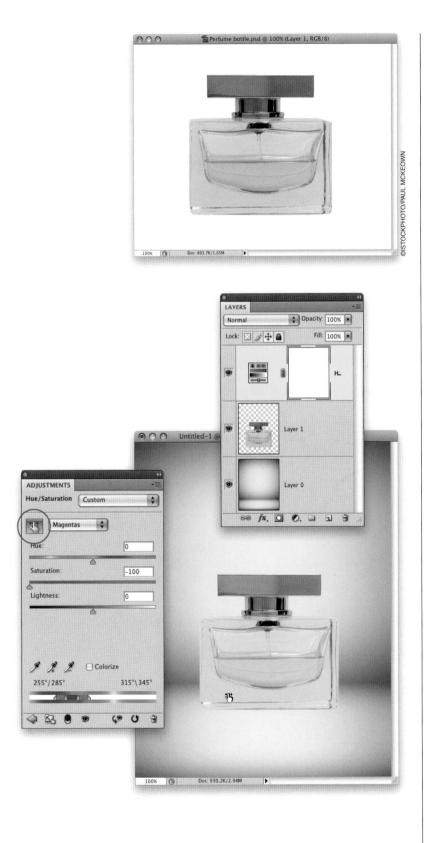

©ISTOCKPHOTO/PAUL MCKEOWN

STEP SEVEN: Open the perfume bottle image (you can download it from the book's downloads webpage). Get the Move tool **(V)** and click-and-drag the image over onto your main document (I've already selected it and placed it on its own layer for you, so you just have to drag-and-drop it). Position it in the document like you see here below. Now, you might notice something that you probably didn't notice when the perfume bottle image was on a white background, and that is the bottle's glass looks a little pinkish (it was that way in the original image). You'll need to get rid of that before we go any further, so go to the Adjustments panel (found under the Window menu) and click on the Hue/Saturation icon (it's the second icon from the left in the second row). In the Adjustments panel, click on the Targeted Adjustment Tool (it's shown circled here in red), then move your cursor over a part of the glass that looks pink, and click-and-drag to the left. This targets the pink color (actually, magenta) in the glass, and as you drag, it removes the color saturation in the magentas, and now your glass looks neutral instead of pink. Shift-click on the Hue/Saturation adjustment layer and the bottle layer and merge them into one layer.

Continued

STEP EIGHT: Your next challenge is that the glass isn't see-through (a dead giveaway), but we're going to use a couple of tricks to make it realistically see-through (just lowering the opacity won't work, because it would make everything see-through, which you don't want). First, we want the center of the bottle, where the perfume is, to stay intact, so click on the bottle's layer, get the Lasso tool **(L)** and draw a selection around that center part of the bottle (as shown here). It doesn't have to be a perfect selection, so don't spend a bunch of time on this—just get kinda close, like I did here.

STEP NINE: Press **Command-Shift-J (PC: Ctrl-Shift-J)** to cut that part of the bottle out and put it up on its own layer (you can see it as the top layer over in the Layers panel, and don't worry, it will still look like it's in one piece—you won't see any seams). Now, in the Layers panel, click on the bottle layer again. Get the Rectangular Marquee tool and select the inside of the glass part of the bottle—stay away from any solid areas, like the heavier glass on the sides or the bottom. You'll also need to press-and-hold the Shift key and put a tall thin selection over on the far-right side (as seen here. Holding the Shift key adds to your selection). One more thing: you don't want that black plastic part at the top center of the glass to be transparent, so press-and-hold the Option (PC: Alt) key and draw a rectangular selection over it, and it will be removed from your selection (holding the Option key does that—it removes whatever you select from your current selection).

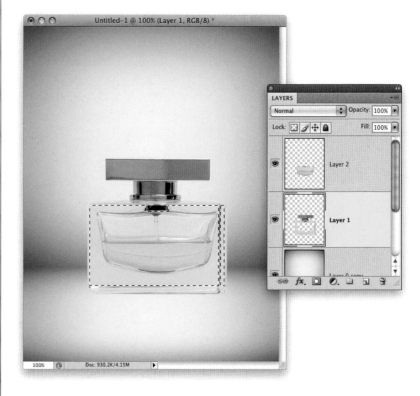

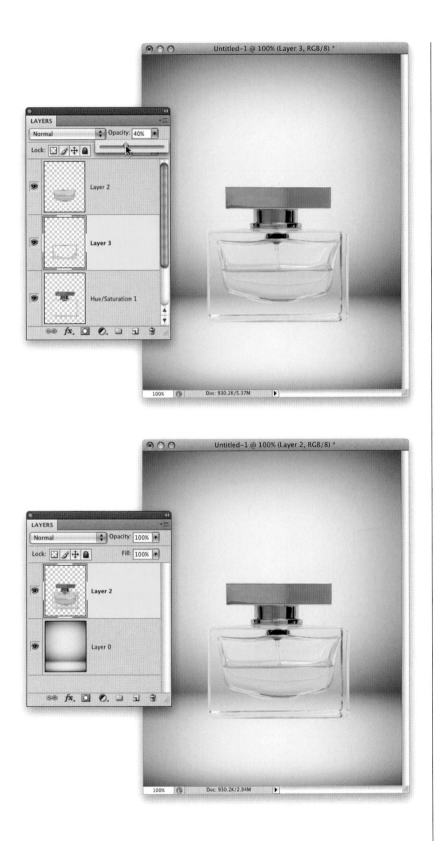

STEP 10: Press Command-Shift-J (PC: Ctrl-Shift-J) again, to cut out those glass parts of the bottle that should be see-through and put them up on their own layer (as seen here in the Layers panel). Now that they're separate, you can lower the Opacity of this layer (I lowered it to 40%, as seen here) and the edges of the bottle stay solid (it's on the layer below, still at 100% opacity), and the perfume is still solid (it's on the layer above, still at 100%). If you look at the bottle now, you can see through it and see the seam in the background, but the rest still looks solid. This is a great trick for situations like this with wine glasses, bottles, eyeglasses, or anything where part of the image should be see-through. Okay, on to the rest of our project.

STEP 11: Although our bottle looks like it's all on the same layer, it's actually on three different layers, so let's pull them all back into one layer. Go to the Layers panel, press-and-hold the Shift key, and click on each of the three layers to select them. Now, merge them all into one single layer (as seen here, where they've all merged into Layer 2).

Continued

STEP 12: You're now going to create a small drop shadow under your bottle. Press-and-hold the Command (PC: Ctrl) key and click on the Create a New Layer icon—holding that key creates your new layer below your current layer, rather than above it, as usual. Get the Rectangular Marquee tool and draw a thin rectangular selection, like the one shown here. Press **D** to set your Foreground color to black, fill your selected area with black (as seen here), and then deselect.

STEP 13: To soften your rectangle (so it looks like a shadow), go under the Filter menu, under Blur, and choose Gaussian Blur. When the dialog appears, enter 2.4 pixels to add a little softening to the edges (as seen here), then click OK.

STEP 14: Get the Move tool, then use the Up Arrow key on your keyboard to nudge that shadow up close to the bottom of your perfume bottle, so just a little bit of the shadow is visible (as seen here).

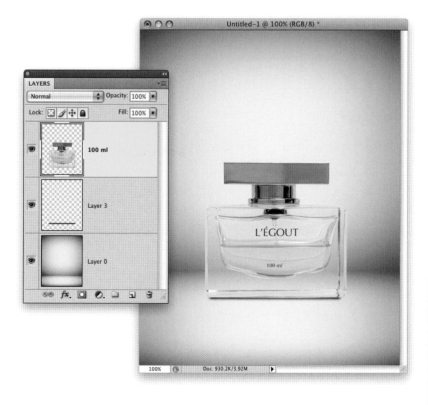

STEP 15: Let's now add our text to the front of the bottle, so get the Horizontal Type tool **(T)**, and then click on the bottle layer in the Layers panel. You can use any sans serif font (in all caps), but I used the font Optima (which is actually a standard business font) for the perfume's made-up name, which is L'Égout (that is actually French, but you'll have to look up what it means—I won't spoil it). (*Note:* To create the É on a Mac, press Option-E, then Shift-E; on a PC, press-and-hold the Alt key, and then type 0201 on your keyboard's number pad.) Then create another Type layer and enter "100 ml" and, with the Move tool, position it near the bottom of the perfume liquid (as shown here). Now, in the Layers panel, select the two Type layers and the bottle layer and merge them into one layer.

Continued

STEP 16: Now, we'll create our reflection (if you read the Reflections chapter [Chapter 5] this part will sound very familiar). Duplicate the layer, then bring up Free Transform. Control-click (PC: Right-click) inside the Free Transform bounding box, and a contextual menu will appear. Choose Flip Vertical (as shown here) to flip this duplicate layer upside down and then lock in your transformation.

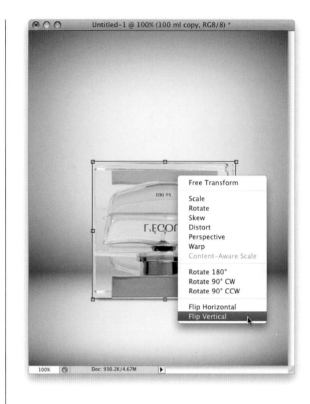

STEP 17: Get the Move tool, press-and-hold the Shift key, and drag the upside down duplicate straight down until the bottoms of the two bottles meet (as shown here). This creates a mirror reflection.

STEP 18: In the Layers panel, click-and-drag your reflected layer down below your bottle layer, and then down below your drop shadow layer (shown here). Now you're going to add a motion blur to the reflected layer, which helps make the effect look more realistic. Go under the Filter menu, under Blur, and choose Motion Blur. When the Motion Blur dialog appears, set the Angle to 90° (so the blur goes straight up/down), increase the Distance amount to 10 pixels, which gives you the effect you see here in the reflection, and then click OK. Now to finish off the reflection, lower the Opacity of this layer to around 40% (as shown here).

STEP 19: Finally, get the Horizontal Type tool and create your text (I used the same font—Optima—at a size of 19 points).

Continued

STEP 20: The main advantage of starting this technique with a background with shades of gray is that you can easily change the color of your shoot at any time by clicking on the Background layer, then going to the Adjustments panel and clicking on the Hue/Saturation icon. In the Hue/Saturation options, turn on the Colorize checkbox near the bottom, then drag the Hue Slider to whatever color you'd like (I chose a Hue setting of 23, which gives you the final image you see here).

3D-Looking Wireframes as Design Elements

I saw this look on the Day Pass ticket for the Los Angeles Metro system, and at first glance, I figured the 3D-looking wireframes were done in a 3D program, but after a closer look, I realized they could be done in Photoshop (and you don't even need Photoshop Extended's 3D features—it's all done with the regular Brush tool).

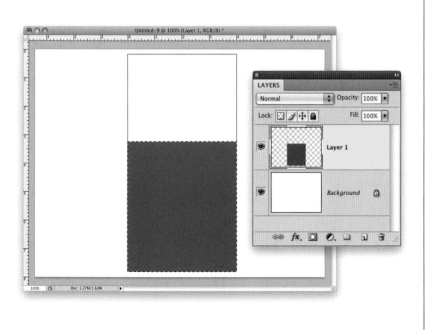

STEP ONE: Go under the File menu, choose New, and create a new document that's 800x600 pixels at a resolution of 72 ppi. Create a new blank layer by clicking on the Create a New Layer icon at the bottom of the Layers panel. Next, take the Rectangular Marquee tool **(M)** and draw a large, tall rectangle that is 4" wide, and nearly as tall as your image (as shown here. Press **Command-R [PC: Ctrl-R]** to turn on the Rulers if you need them). Once it's in place, go under the Edit menu and choose Stroke. When the Stroke dialog appears, set your Width to 2 px, click on the black color swatch and change your stroke color to a medium gray, set your Location to Center (as shown here), and then click OK to add a gray stroke around your selection.

STEP TWO: Press **Command-D (PC: Ctrl-D)** to Deselect. Now, take the Rectangular Marquee tool and put a selection around the bottom section of the rectangle, like the one you see here. Click on the Foreground color swatch and set your Foreground to a blue color (I used R: 57, G: 92, B: 132), fill your selected area with this color by pressing **Option-Delete (PC: Alt-Backspace)**, and then deselect.

Continued

STEP THREE: Create a new blank layer and make a selection around the bottom half of your blue-filled rectangle. Set a teal green as your Foreground color (I used R: 0, G: 123, B: 131), fill your selected area with this color, and then deselect. Create another new layer, and this time create a wide, short rectangular selection up near the top (like the one you see here), and fill it with your teal Foreground color, as well. Go to the Layers panel, lower the Opacity of this thin rectangle layer to 30%, and then deselect.

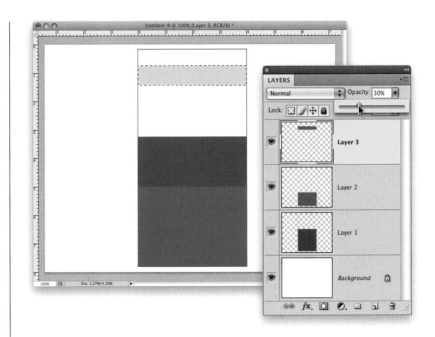

STEP FOUR: Now, let's add some text, and we're going to use the font Myriad Pro Bold for almost all of it (this font is installed when you install Photoshop). Get the Horizontal Type tool **(T)**, type "RTA Fast Pass" (I used a font size of 16 points), and then click on the Move tool in the Toolbox and position it right above the light teal rectangle. Get the Horizontal Type tool again, click somewhere else to create a new layer of type, set your text color to black in the Options Bar, type in "FEB 2010THURSDAY" (as shown here—same point size, but for "THURSDAY," I changed the font to Myriad Pro Regular), and position it inside the light teal rectangle. Then add another line of text and type in "05" in the font Myriad Pro Bold Condensed, make the point size really big (I made mine 160 points), and position it like you see here.

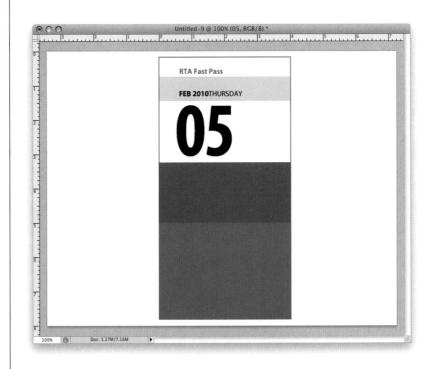

STEP FIVE: You can add the rest of the type (like you see here), which is set with white as the color, using the font Myriad Pro Bold. For the little "R" logo at the bottom, create a new layer, use the Rectangular Marquee tool to draw a square selection (press-and-hold the Shift key to make it perfectly square), fill it with a pink color (I used R: 237, G: 152, B: 185), then type in the letter "R" and put it on a layer above the pink square. Easy enough. Now, press **Command-E (PC: Ctrl-E)** to merge the "R" layer and the pink square layer, then click-and-drag this merged pink square layer down in the layer stack, so that it appears beneath all your Type layers. Then, with the Rectangular Marquee tool, put a selection around everything from the bottom of the blue rectangle on up (as shown here).

STEP SIX: You're going to create a custom brush that we're going to make look like a 3D wireframe. Start by creating a new blank document just like the one you're already working on. Add a new blank layer, then get the Elliptical Marquee tool from the Toolbox (or press **Shift-M** until you have it) and draw a large, wide oval-shaped selection like the one you see here. Go under the Edit menu and choose Stroke. In the dialog, set the Color to black, leave all the other settings as is, and click OK to put a black stroke around your oval. Now you can deselect.

Continued

STEP SEVEN: Go under the Edit menu and choose Define Brush Preset, which brings up the Brush Name dialog you see here. Give your brush a name, and click OK. Even though there's a white background on the layer below your oval, when you make a brush like this, Photoshop ignores the white background, so the background behind your new brush will be transparent (which is a good thing).

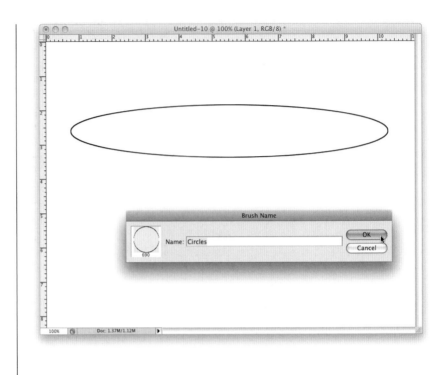

STEP EIGHT: Return to your main ticket document. Get the Eyedropper tool (**I**) and click it once on your pink square rectangle to set that pink color as your Foreground color. Next, get the Brush tool (**B**) from the Toolbox. In the Options Bar, click on the down-facing arrow to the right of "Brush" and, in the resulting Brush Picker, you'll find your newly-created brush is the very last brush. Instead of going there, though, in this case we need the full Brushes panel, so go under the Window menu and choose Brushes. Your new Brush preset will be the last brush in the list (as shown here), so go ahead and click on it to make it your active brush tip. The preview area at the bottom of the Brushes panel shows you what a brush stroke using this brush would look like using the current settings (but, of course, we're going to mess with those settings in the next step).

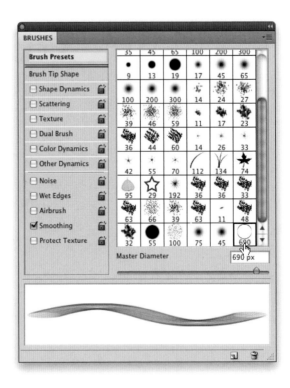

STEP NINE: In the list of Brush options on the left side of the Brushes panel, click on Brush Tip Shape to bring up those options (seen here). The Diameter slider controls the size of your brush, so lower that to around 222 px. The little target-shape (in the white square box, where my cursor is) controls the angle of the brush—you can just click-and-drag it around to rotate your brush, as I did here, where I rotated the Angle to –61° (of course, you could just type in –61° in the Angle field, but where's the fun in that?). The Spacing slider at the bottom controls how much space there will be between each of your oval shapes (the higher the number, the more space will appear between them). For our project, set the Spacing at 20%.

STEP 10: Your selection of the upper two-thirds of your ticket should still be in place. Now, in the Layers panel, scroll down until you reach the pink square layer (all your Type layers should appear above this layer), then create a new blank layer (that way, anything you create on this layer will appear above the rectangles, but below your type). Take the Brush tool, and draw a "C" shape starting just outside the ticket itself. Don't worry—your brush stroke will be contained within your selected area (as seen here). Also, don't worry if your brush stroke doesn't look just like mine—the fun of this technique is coming up with your own look. If you paint and you don't like your brush stroke, just press **Command-Z (PC: Ctrl-Z)** to undo it, then try again until you come up with something you like.

Continued

STEP 11: Now let's paint another stroke, but let's mess with the look a little bit, so it doesn't look exactly the same. Go back to the Brushes panel, and increase the Diameter to 632 px. Next, change the Angle to 20°, then grab one of the little black dots on the side of the brush tip circle and drag inward to flatten the shape of the oval a bit (as shown here). Now, increase the Spacing to 40%. By the way, the changes I did here are pretty arbitrary—I just started moving sliders and stuff, I painted a stroke on the left side of the ticket, and it looked sort of cool. This technique is all about "messing with sliders," so have fun.

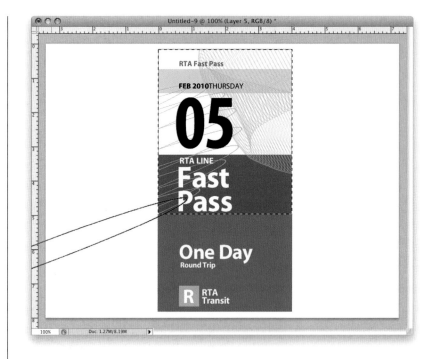

STEP 12: If you want to change your ticket colors, it's easy. Go to the Layers panel, and click on the thin, light teal rectangle layer. Next, go to the Adjustments panel and click on the Hue/Saturation icon (it's the second icon from the left in the second row). Now, just drag the Hue slider to a new color (I dragged over to 100 to get the color scheme you see here—it automatically changes all the rectangles at once, because they are all on layers beneath the adjustment layer). Then, either hide or delete your original brush stroke layer by clicking on the Eye icon to the left of its layer or clicking-and-dragging it onto the Trash icon at the bottom of the Layers panel. You can set your Foreground color to a purple color, create a new blank layer, and start painting with the brush over the top part (as shown here). If the brush strokes look too dark, you can lower the Opacity of this layer in the Layers panel.

Chrome with Photo Reflections

Last year, Walt Disney Pictures redesigned their logo (I have a three-year-old daughter, so as you might imagine, I see that logo fairly often). The logo uses a chiseled-type look, which is easy to recreate, but if you look closely, their logo type has a little something extra—a reflection of the surrounding image (in this case, the background image), which helps give the effect that the type is actually reflective. Here's how it's done:

STEP ONE: Open a background image (you can download the one you see here from the book's downloads page. Of course, it's not entirely necessary to have a background photo at all, but it does look better if there's something kind of dark behind your text [but not solid black], so you could just fill the background with a dark purple or a light purple-to-dark purple gradient).

STEP TWO: Get the Horizontal Type tool **(T)**, click on the Foreground color swatch in the Toolbox and set your Foreground color to a medium gray, choose a script font, and type in "Wade Davey" in a font size of about 23 points. I used one of my favorite fonts for this: it's called Satisfaction, and if you don't have it, you can either: (a) download the file (from the book's downloads page) I made for you with the text already ready to go, or (b) buy the font (it cost me $12 at myfonts.com), and then you can use it for other projects. Use the Move tool **(V)** to move your type into place. Press **Command-T (PC: Ctrl-T)** to bring up Free Transform, grab the right-center point and drag inward a bit to squeeze the font and make it skinnier (the font just looked a little too wide for me, but hey—that's just me), and then press **Return (PC: Enter)** to lock in your transformation.

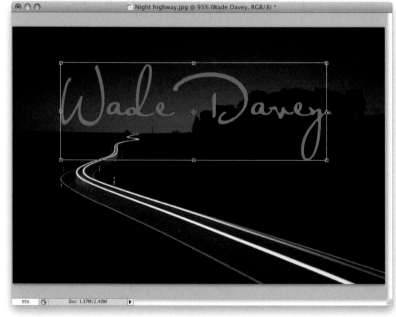

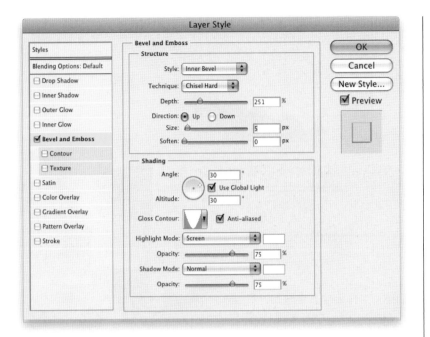

STEP THREE: Click on the Add a Layer Style icon at the bottom of the Layers panel and choose Bevel and Emboss. When the dialog appears, in the Structure section at the top, choose Chisel Hard from the Technique pop-up menu (which puts a hard ridge in the center of your letters), and then increase the Depth to around 250%. In the Shading section, turn on the Anti-Aliased checkbox (so the edges of the metallic effect we're going to apply will appear smoother), then click on the down-facing arrow to its left, and from the Gloss Contour Picker that appears, click on the Cone-Inverted icon (the third icon from the left in the top row—it looks like a valley, as seen here), which adds a bright metallic look to your beveled edges. Change the Shadow Mode from Multiply to Normal, and then click on the color swatch to its right and change the color from black to white. This makes the shadow side of your ridged letters much brighter.

STEP FOUR: Click OK to apply that effect to your type. Now, you're going to add another line of type, so get the Horizontal Type tool, choose the Trajan Pro Bold font (it comes with Photoshop CS4) in 7-point size, and type in "PICTURES." Move your cursor until it turns into an arrow, and then click-and-drag the text into place. Highlight that text, and press **Option-Right Arrow key (PC: Alt-Right Arrow key)** a few times to increase the amount of space between the letters (like you see here). To get that same beveled effect, just press-and-hold the **Option (PC: Alt) key** and, in the Layers panel, drag-and-drop the word "Effects" from the Wade Davey layer onto the "PICTURES" layer (this puts a copy of the effect onto this layer). Now, press-and-hold the Shift key, select both layers, and with the Move tool, drag your text layers up a little higher in the image (like you see here).

Continued

STEP FIVE: In the Layers panel, click on the Background layer, then press **Command-J (PC: Ctrl-J)** to duplicate this layer. Next, click-and-drag the duplicate layer up in the layer stack, so it's directly above your "Wade Davey" Type layer (as seen here). What we're going to do is add a little bit of reflection and depth to our type by having a little bit of this background image appear throughout the type—not enough so you'd know it was there at first glance, but enough so it adds a nice bit of realism to the type, as though it really was chrome and was reflecting its surroundings.

STEP SIX: Now you're going to create a clipping mask, which clips the photo inside your type. To do that, press **Command-Option-G (PC: Ctrl-Alt-G)**, which puts the image inside your type (as seen here). If you look in the Layers panel, you'll see that your duplicate photo's thumbnail has been nudged over to the right, and there's a small arrow pointing down—that's letting you know that the photo is clipped into the layer below it. The type effect actually looks pretty cool at this stage, and you could end it here if you'd like (it's kind of see-through and almost has a liquid quality to it), but if you continue on, we'll get closer to the actual Walt Disney Pictures look.

STEP SEVEN: To have your photo blend in with the type, at the top of the Layers panel, change the layer blend mode from Normal to Overlay (for a more intense effect, as seen here) or Soft Light (for a more subtle look), and now you can see the beveling and chrome coming through the image. Get the Move tool, and click-and-drag right within your image to reposition your photo to where it looks best with your text (in the example shown here, I moved it up and to the left. If you look at the layer thumbnail shown here, you can pretty much see what I did).

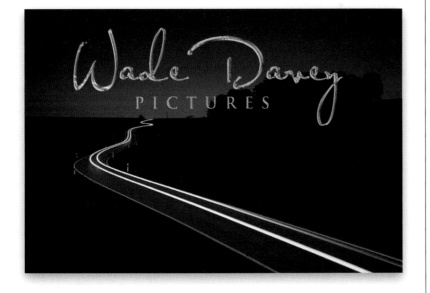

STEP EIGHT: The final step is to lower the Opacity of this layer enough to where you just see a bit of the reflection, without becoming real obvious (as shown here, where I lowered the Opacity at the top of the Layers panel to 60%), to complete the effect.

The Midnight Special

more special effects

The 2010 Sales & Marketing Awards Show

If you recognize *The Midnight Special* as a TV show that aired from 1972 to 1981, then it means you're really like crazy old (not like me, who only has a vague recollection of the show, probably from stories my father told me). *The Midnight Special* (which makes a great name for a chapter on more special effects) was a weekly live concert TV show that featured live performances by everyone from David Bowie to Aerosmith, Elton John to Donna Summer (well, at least I hear those people were on there. Again, I'm very young, so this can obviously only be hearsay). Anyway, if the name rang a bell, it's time for an "I'm really old" pop-quiz. For 100 bonus points (and a chance to play in our lightning round), who was *The Midnight Special* produced by? (Hint: His name was in the title.) No, it's not Don Kirshner (he ran a competing show. At least, that's what they told me at an AARP meeting). Come on, you're so close...(bzzzzzt!) sorry, time's up. It was *Burt Sugarman's The Midnight Special*. Now, you're probably wondering what all this has to do with special effects? Well, besides the obvious tie-in with the name, if you go to www.midnightspecial.com, you'll see a variation of one of the effects that you're going to learn in this chapter (and you'll also see a background effect that you learned in Chapter 3). That is, of course, unless they change the look of their site, and if that happens, well there's goes my perfect tie-in.

The phone you've been waiting for.

the skyone hybrid

Mixing Photos and Vector Art

Mixing photography and vector art is hugely popular right now—you see it everywhere from print ads to commercials to t-shirts. The project we're going to do is based on a fake print ad for the Sony Ericsson W880i cell phone. I originally thought it was a real ad, but later learned (in the ad's small print) that it was a practice project created by Netherlands-based designer Tobias Gommer. What drew me to the ad were the smooth flowing lines in the background, but once I started it, I broke from his layout to add more vector art—in particular, the "garden vines" look that is so popular right now. Here's how to fake the fake ad, with some other fake stuff faked in:

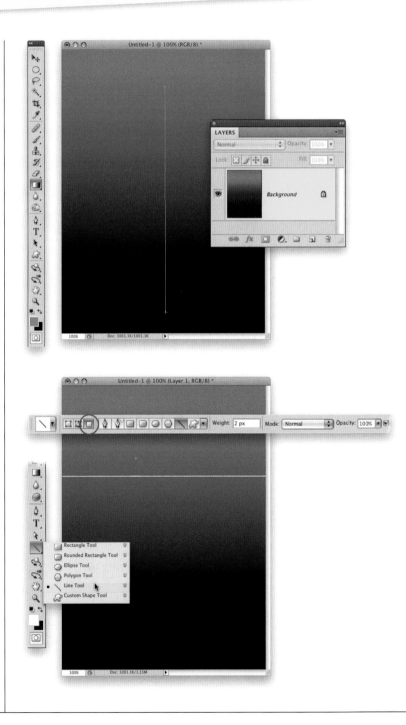

STEP ONE: Start by going under the File menu, choosing New, and creating a new document that is 7 inches wide by 9.5 inches high at a resolution of 72 ppi. Press **D** to set your Foreground color to black, then press **X** to make white your Foreground color. Click on the Foreground color swatch and now change this white Foreground color to a pinkish magenta color (I used R: 224, G: 28, B: 162). Get the Gradient tool **(G)** from the Toolbox, and up in the Options Bar, make sure the Linear Gradient icon is chosen (the first of the five icons), then click on the down-facing arrow next to the gradient thumbnail and choose the top-left gradient (Foreground to Background). Click-and-drag the tool about an inch or so from the top of your image to nearly the bottom (as shown here) to create the pink-to-black gradient.

STEP TWO: Create a new blank layer by clicking on the Create a New Layer icon at the bottom of the Layers panel. Set your Foreground color to white again, then get the Line tool from the Toolbox (or press **Shift-U** until you have it). Go up to the Options Bar and click on the third icon from the left (circled here in red), so the line you create will be made up of pixels (rather than creating a Shape layer or a path), and then set the Weight to 2 pixels. Press-and-hold the Shift key and draw a horizontal line from side to side (as seen here).

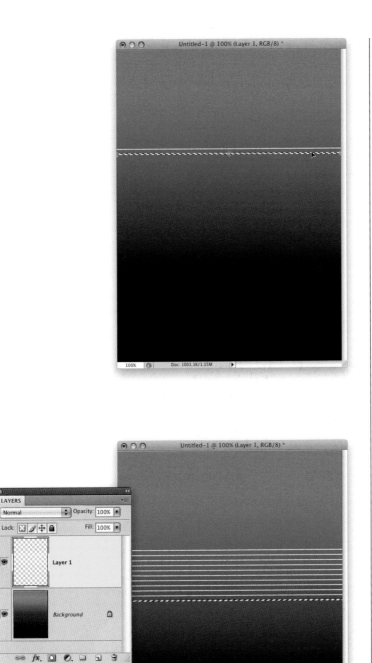

STEP THREE: Press-and-hold the Command (PC: Ctrl) key, then go to the Layers panel and click directly on your line layer's thumbnail to put a selection around your line. Now, press **Command-Option-T (PC: Ctrl-Alt-T)**, which brings up Free Transform in copy mode. Move your cursor over your line until it turns into a tiny black arrow, then click-and-drag straight down just a little bit to add a second line (as shown here). Press **Return (PC: Enter)** to lock in this duplication and move, but don't deselect quite yet.

STEP FOUR: Because you used the keyboard shortcut to copy your line, you can now use a modified version of that shortcut to automatically make a whole row of lines. Press **Command-Option-Shift-T (PC: Ctrl-Alt-Shift-T)** and it makes a perfectly spaced copy just below your two lines. Now, press that shortcut eight more times until you have a row of lines (11 of them) like you see here, and then you can press **Command-D (PC: Ctrl-D)** to Deselect.

Continued

STEP FIVE: Press **Command-T (PC: Ctrl-T)** to bring up Free Transform, Control-click (PC: Right-click) on your image, and from the contextual menu that appears, choose Warp (as shown here).

STEP SIX: From the Warp pop-up menu (up in the Options Bar), choose Flag to apply a wavy look to your lines (as seen here).

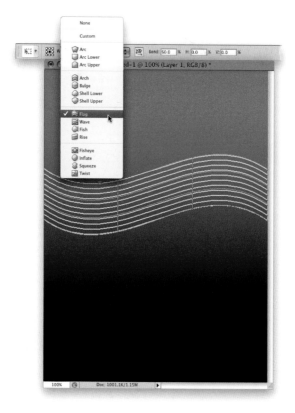

STEP SEVEN: You're going to apply a perspective effect to both ends of your lines. First, start by pressing **Command-T (PC: Ctrl-T)** to switch you from Warp back to Free Transform. Press-and-hold **Command-Option-Shift (PC: Ctrl-Alt-Shift)**, grab the top-left point and drag downward, which pinches that side together, creating a perspective effect (as seen here). Now, do the opposite on the right side of your lines—press-and-hold those keys, grab the top-right point, and this time drag straight up to expand this side out, which enhances the perspective effect (you'll see this side in the next step).

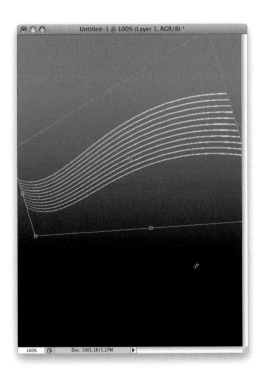

STEP EIGHT: Move your cursor outside the bounding box, and it changes into a two-headed arrow. Click-and-drag in a counterclockwise circular motion to rotate your lines like you see here (it's a pretty small amount of rotation). Of course, this creates a small gap on either side of your lines, so grab the right-center point and drag it to the right just enough to where your lines completely touch the right side of your image window. Now, do the same thing to the left side (dragging the left-center point to the left) until the lines fill the image area from left to right.

Continued

STEP NINE: Now, press **Return (PC: Enter)** to lock in your transformation, so your lines look like the ones here, and then open the cell phone image you see here (you can download it from the book's downloads page—the address is listed in the book's introduction).

STEP 10: Go to the Layers panel and change the layer blend mode from Normal to Overlay to have your white lines pick up the colors from the pink gradient they're sitting over (as seen here). Now, get the Move tool **(V)**, go over to your cell phone document, and drag that phone over onto your main document (I've put it on its own layer for you). Use Free Transform to resize the phone image (while pressing-and-holding the Shift key to keep your re-sizing proportional) and position it like you see here.

STEP 11: Press **Command-J (PC: Ctrl-J)** to duplicate your phone layer, then bring up Free Transform. We're going to create a reflection (for more on reflections, see Chapter 5). Go under the Edit menu, under Transform, and choose Flip Vertical to flip this duplicate layer upside down, then lock in your transformation. With the Move tool, press-and-hold the Shift key (to keep them perfectly aligned while you move things), and then click-and-drag straight downward until the bottoms of the two cell phones touch (as seen here). You can already see we have a problem with the reflection—it doesn't quite line up flush with the phone, so there's a big gap at the right side of the phone image. This is going to happen when your product isn't shot at a straight-on angle, but we can just tweak the reflection to get a better, more realistic look.

STEP 12: Bring up Free Transform again, on this flipped layer. Press-and-hold the **Command (PC: Ctrl) key**, along with the **Shift key** (again, for alignment), and click-and-drag the right-center point upward to skew the right side of your phone reflection upward, so it meets the bottom of the original phone (as shown here). Once you do this, you'll have to move your cursor inside the bounding box and drag downward a bit, because moving this side of the phone reflection up actually covers part of the original phone. Having to do little tweaks like this to reflections is pretty common, and this skew method works wonders for this type of stuff. Now, lock in your changes (you know how by now).

Continued

STEP 13: Go to the Layers panel and drag this reflection layer beneath your original phone layer. Next, lower the Opacity of this layer to 70%, then click on the Add Layer Mask icon at the bottom of the Layers panel (it's shown circled here in red). Get the Gradient tool, make sure your Foreground color is set to white and your Background color is set to black, and click-and-drag from the top of your reflected layer down about an inch and a half or so to have the reflection fade away (as shown here).

STEP 14: Now, open an image with some vector-looking garden elements (you can download this one from the book's downloads page, too). Get the Lasso tool **(L)** and draw a very loose selection around the shape at the top (as shown here). Switch to the Move tool and click-and-drag that area over onto your phone document, and then in the Layers panel, position it beneath your phone reflection layer. We're going to position these garden elements behind the phone, as if they're coming out the sides. This particular shape looks like it should be vertical, and we're going to position it on the left side of the phone, which means we're going to have to: (a) rotate it, so it's tall, (b) flip the image, so the stems are coming out from behind the phone, rather than into the phone, (c) get rid of that white background, and (d) change the color of the elements to white. Luckily, this is a lot easier than it sounds.

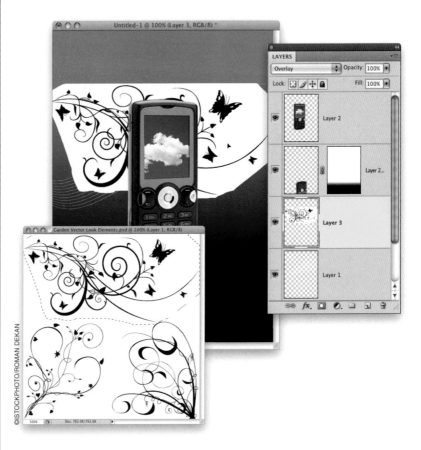

©ISTOCKPHOTO/ROMAN DEKAN

STEP 15: Bring up Free Transform on this garden elements layer, then go under the Edit menu, under Transform, and choose Rotate 90° CCW (counterclockwise) to make your image tall. Go back under that same menu, but this time choose Flip Horizontal, to flip the image so that it now appears as though everything is coming out from behind the phone (as shown here). Now, position your garden elements as seen here, and then lock in your transformation. Two down, two to go.

STEP 16: Press **Command-I (PC: Ctrl-I)** to Invert your image, so now your garden elements are white and your background is black (if you look at the thumbnail of this layer in the Layers panel, you can see that here). To hide that black background (so you just see the white elements), go to the Layers panel and change the layer blend mode to Screen (as shown here), which gives you the look you see here. Now that the elements are solid white, we want them to blend into the background a bit more. We can't change the blend mode to do that, because we're already using Screen mode to ignore the black background, so instead, just lower the Opacity to around 50% (you'll see how this looks in the next step).

Continued

STEP 17: So, that's the process we're going to do for the other two pieces of vector-like art we're going to add. Put a loose selection around each one (my selection around the bottom-left one is shown here), drag each one over to the phone document, see if they need to be rotated or flipped, then invert them (to make them white) or leave them as is (to leave them black, where you'd choose Multiply as your blend mode to ignore the white background). For the art at the bottom right of the phone, I rotated it a bit, inverted it, changed the blend mode to Screen, and lowered the opacity. For the black elements at the top right (selected from the bottom right of the garden elements image), I flipped it horizontally, and scaled it down in size a little (using Free Transform), but didn't invert, because I wanted them to stay black. I just changed the layer blend mode to Multiply.

STEP 18: Now that all the elements are in place, go to the Layers panel, click on your lines layer (Layer 1), and with the Move tool, move them up (or down), so they fit your composition better (I moved them down a bit). If you want to add some more little garden vector shapes, there are some already in Photoshop. Create a new blank layer at the top of your layer stack, then set your Foreground color to a bright green (I used R: 156, G: 199, B: 81). Get the Custom Shape tool (press **Shift-U** until you have it; it's circled here in red), then click on the Shape thumbnail in the Options Bar to get the Shape Picker. In the Picker, click on the little right-facing arrow in the top-right corner. From the flyout menu, choose All to load all the shapes into the Picker, then click OK in the warning dialog. Now, scroll through them and find any shapes you like (I chose Butterfly, Leaf Ornament 3, and Floral Ornament 1), and click-and-drag out these shapes on the new layer (or put each on its own layer if you want more control over where you place them).

STEP 19: It's time to add the text. To make room at the top, you'll have to move everything else down a little. So, go to the Layers panel, and Shift-click on every layer (except the Background layer). Then, get the Move tool and use the Down Arrow key on your keyboard to move all your layers down together. Move everything down enough so you can add two lines of text in the upper-right corner. Get the Horizontal Type tool **(T)**, set your Foreground color to white, your font to Helvetica Neue Light, and in the Character panel, set the Tracking (the space between letters) to –60 to tighten things up. Type, "The phone you've been waiting for." Duplicate that Type layer, and with the Move tool, click-and-drag the text to the bottom of the ad, high-light it, and change it to "the skyone hybrid." You can also add some small text at the bottom, if you like. Finally, the reflection is a little distracting, so lower its Opacity to around 40% to give you the final image, seen here.

STEP 20: Technically, we're done, but I want to show you how easy it is to change your look by using a different gradient style and color for your back-ground. Go to the Layers panel, click on your Background layer, and add a new blank layer above it. Now, Option-click (PC: Alt-click) on the Eye icon to the left of the new layer's thumbnail to hide all the other layers. Set your Foreground color to a dark green (I used R: 99, G: 165, B: 18) and your Background color to a bright green (I used R: 195, G: 218, B: 69), then get the Gradient tool. Click on the second icon from the left (the Radial Gradient) in the Options Bar, then click in the center of the image, and drag all the way to the right—right off the image, about three or four inches outside your window—to get your new background. Just Option-click where the Eye icon used to be to make all your layers visible again, change the color of your Shape layer(s) to magenta, and you've got a new look.

Fashion Warped Grid Technique

I saw this cool, swooshing, warped grid effect in a print ad for Lancôme's Rénergie Microlift Eye cream, but besides just the cool grid, there are a lot of other elements here (like see-through panels that hold text) that are found in lots of graphics and layouts (but it was that warped grid that drew me to the ad in the first place, which is really kind of sad because most people would be drawn to the ad by the photo of a beautiful woman. This is what happens if you use Photoshop too much).

STEP ONE: Go under the File menu, choose New, and create a new document that is 7x8.5" at a resolution of 72 ppi. Press **D** to set your Foreground and Background colors to their defaults of black and white, then click on the Foreground color swatch and change your Foreground color to a light pink color (I used R: 197, G: 160, B: 167). Get the Gradient tool **(G)**, click on the Linear Gradient icon in the Options Bar (the first icon on the left, circled here in red), then click on the down-facing arrow next to the gradient thumbnail and choose the top-left gradient in the Gradient Picker (Foreground to Background). Now, click the Gradient tool about an inch or so from the top of the image window, and drag straight downward (as shown here) to create a pink-to-white gradient for your background. Next, open the headshot that we'll be adding (as seen in the next step).

STEP TWO: We only want the subject in the image, not the white background behind her, so take the Magic Wand tool (press **Shift-W** until you have it) and click it once on the white background area to select it (if part of her face becomes selected, just press-and-hold the Option [PC: Alt] key and click there to remove it from the selection). Now, we have the opposite of what we want (we have the background selected, rather than the woman). To switch the two, go under the Select menu and choose Inverse (or press **Command-Shift-I [PC: Ctrl-Shift-I]**), which inverses your selection, so now only the woman is selected (as seen here).

©ISTOCKPHOTO/EKATERINA SOLOVIEVA

STEP THREE: Get the Move tool **(V)**, and click-and-drag her over onto the pink-to-white background image, positioning her on the left. You'll probably notice a little white fringe around the edges of her hair (this usually happens when you use the Magic Wand tool for things like this), and there are a couple of different ways to get rid of that edge fringe. One way is to go under the Layer menu, then go all the way to the bottom under Matting, and choose Defringe. When the dialog appears, just click OK and that'll usually do the trick. Of course, you can try what I did here, which is my favorite way to remove edge fringe: Press-and-hold the Command (PC: Ctrl) key and, in the Layers panel, click directly on the layer thumbnail for your subject. This puts a selection around her. Go under the Select menu, under Modify, and choose Contract. When the dialog appears, choose to contract (shrink) your selection by 1 pixel, then click OK. Now, your selection around her has contracted one pixel into her skin and hair. Press Command-Shift-I (PC: Ctrl-Shift-I) to Inverse the selection (so just that one edge pixel is selected), then press Delete (PC: Backspace), and the fringe is gone!

STEP FOUR: Deselect by pressing **Command-D (PC: Ctrl-D)**, and you can see the nice smooth edges no longer have any visible edge fringe. Now, on to creating our grid: Create a new document that is 100 pixels wide by 100 pixels high, at a resolution of 200 ppi. I'm using a higher resolution, so my final grid is smaller in size (you'll see this new document in the next step).

Continued

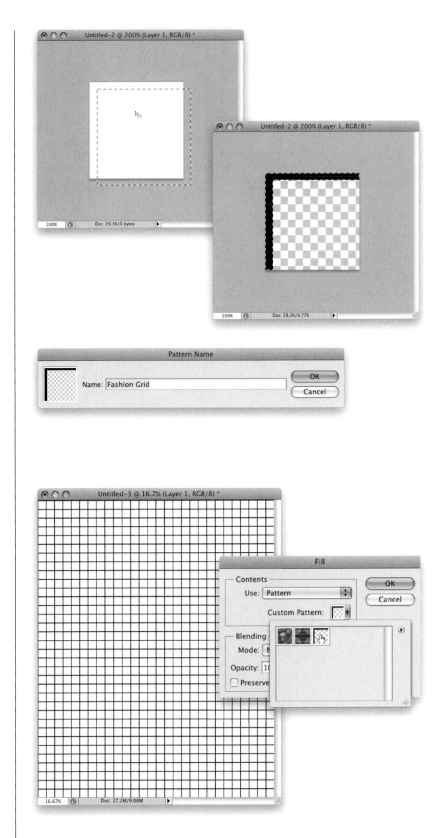

STEP FIVE: Create a new blank layer by clicking on the Create a New Layer icon at the bottom of the Layers panel. Press **Z** and click in your document to zoom in a bit, then grab the bottom-right corner of your image window and drag it out to expand the window, revealing the gray area surrounding your image area. Press **Command-A (PC: Ctrl-A)** to select your entire image area. Now, get the Rectangular Marquee tool (**M**; actually, you can use any selection tool), move your cursor inside your image area, and click-and-drag down and to the right a few pixels, so your selection extends off the canvas (as shown here, on the left). When you move this selection, you're choosing how thick your grid lines will be. Inverse your selection, so now only a thin area of the top and left sides are selected. Set your Foreground color to black, then press **Option-Delete (PC: Alt-Backspace)** to fill your selected area with black (as shown here, on the right). Now, to make the background behind your grid transparent, in the Layers panel, drag the Background layer onto the Trash icon at the bottom of the panel to delete it. Deselect, and then go under the Edit menu, choose Create Pattern, give your pattern a name in the Pattern Name dialog, and click OK.

STEP SIX: To get our grid really small, we're going to cheat: create a new document that is 14x17" (double the size of your main document), but at a higher resolution (200 ppi). Now, create a new blank layer, then go under the Edit menu and choose Fill. In the Fill dialog, choose Pattern from the Use pop-up menu in the Contents section at the top, and then click on the Custom Pattern thumbnail to bring up the Pattern Picker (shown here). Click on the last pattern in the Picker (that's the one you just created—the latest one created always appears in the last position). Click OK and it fills your layer with that black grid pattern (you can see the grid it creates here).

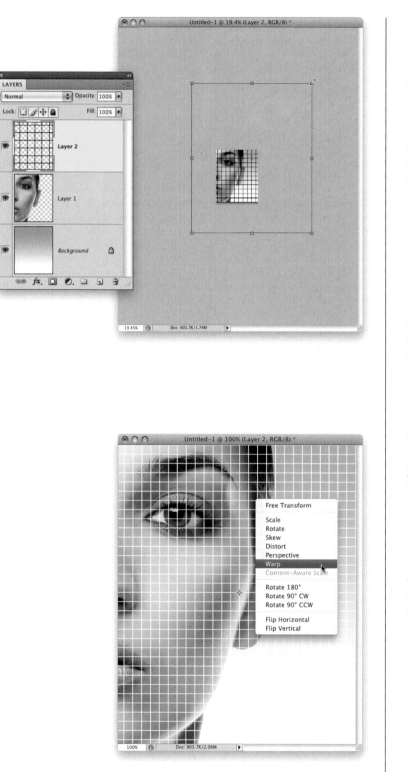

STEP SEVEN: Get the Move tool and drag this grid layer over onto your main document. It won't look like the grid is very small when it first appears, but that's just because you're only seeing a small part of the grid layer (it extends way beyond the boundaries of your image). Press **Command-T (PC: Ctrl-T)** to bring up Free Transform, then press **Command-0 (zero; PC: Ctrl-0)** to have Photoshop automatically resize the window, so you can see the Free Transform handles (and you can see how big the layer really is). Grab any one of the corner handles, press-and-hold the Shift key (to keep your grid proportional as you scale it), and drag inward (as shown here). Keep dragging inward until your grid is just a tiny bit larger than your image area, then press **Return (PC: Enter)** to lock in your transformation. Now, press **Command-0** again, to return your window size to a normal view.

STEP EIGHT: We actually want white grid lines (rather than black—the white just fits so much better with the overall look of the ad), so press **Command-I (PC: Ctrl-I)**, which inverts your black grid to white (as seen here). Now, bring up Free Transform again, then Control-click (PC: Right-click) inside your image area, and from the contextual menu that appears, choose Warp (as shown here). In the next step, you're going to bend your grid to give it a flowing look.

Continued

STEP NINE: Click on the far-right side of your grid, up in the top third, and just drag to the right. The grid will move just like liquid. You don't have to move the control handles or any of that stuff—just click on the right side of the grid, drag right, and you'll see the grid bend and move as you drag it. Now, click on the top-left side of the grid and drag to the right, and then click a little lower (my cursor is shown circled here in red) to move the bottom part over to create more of a curve. If you mess things up, don't sweat it, just hit the **Esc key** on your keyboard to cancel your transformation, then bring up Free Transform again, choose Warp from the contextual menu, and try again. Remember, it moves like liquid (well, more like molasses, actually), so just mold it like you want it by dragging. When you're done, lock in your changes.

STEP 10: To make the bottom of your grid lines fade away, click on the Add Layer Mask icon at the bottom of the Layers panel (it's shown circled here in red), then get the Gradient tool, make sure your Foreground is white, and click-and-drag a gradient from the middle of the grid to just below her ear (as shown here) to have the bottom of the grid fade out.

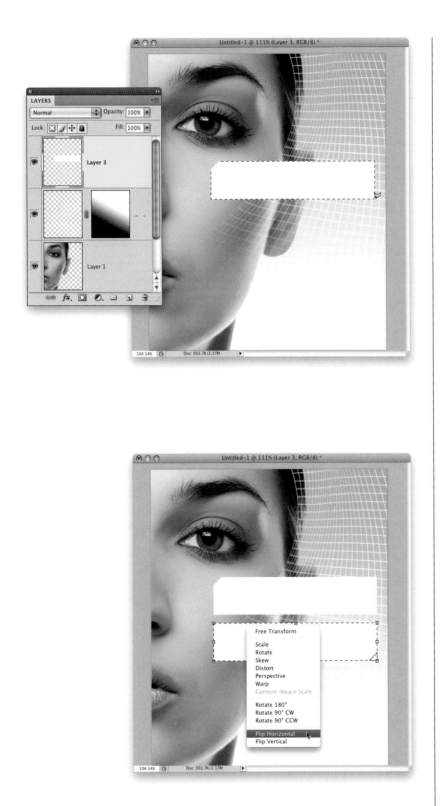

STEP 11: Now, you're going to add some boxes for text (advertising copy), so create a new blank layer, then get the Polygonal Lasso tool from the Toolbox (or press **Shift-L** until you have it; it draws straight-line selections). Press-and-hold the Shift key, and draw the shape you see here (it's basically just a rectangle, but before you get to the top-left corner of the rectangle, you angle to the right. Holding the Shift key makes that an exact 45° angle). When you get back to where you started your shape, a little circle appears at the bottom of the tool to let you know you've come "full circle." Just click once and it completes your selection. Press **D**, then **X** to set your Foreground color to white, then fill this selection with the white Foreground color (as seen here). Don't deselect quite yet.

STEP 12: Here, you're going to duplicate your white rectangle, and flip it both horizontally and vertically. Get the Move tool, press-and-hold Option-Shift (PC: Alt-Shift), then click inside the white selected rectangle, and drag down a copy (holding the Option key while you drag makes a copy; the Shift key keeps it perfectly aligned with the first one). Drag it down, and leave a little gap between the two shapes. Don't deselect, but instead, bring up Free Transform again, Control-click (PC: Right-click) inside the bottom rectangle, and from the contextual menu that appears, choose Flip Vertical. Control-click (PC: Right-click) again, but this time, choose Flip Horizontal, which gives you the flipped rectangle you see here (which is what they had in the ad). Now, lock in your transformation and deselect.

Continued

STEP 13: To make your two rectangular boxes a bit see-through, go to the Layers panel and lower the Opacity of that layer to around 80%. Now, open the eye cream image (available on the book's downloads page), get the Move tool, and drag it over onto your main document, positioning it in the bottom-right corner (as shown here), so the right side of the jar is extending off the side and is cut off from view. In the next step, you're going to add all the text, so set your Foreground color to white, then get the Horizontal Type tool **(T)**.

STEP 14: Starting from the top right of the ad, the font is Trajan Pro (which comes installed with Photoshop CS4) and then Copperplate, and the rest of the text is Arial Narrow (which is preinstalled on about every computer on earth, but if you don't have it, try Helvetica Condensed). The final thing to finish this off is to move the two white rectangles (and the text inside them) down a bit, so they're closer to the product shot at the bottom. Go to the Layers panel, press-and-hold the Shift key, click on all the Type layers (well, the ones that appear in those two white rectangles anyway), along with the white boxes layer, too. Now, using the Move tool and with the Shift key still held down, drag everything straight down until they're in the position you see here, which completes the project.

Color Spiral Collage Technique

This is based on a collage created to support a piece in a magazine (the original was created by designer Hue Man. I'm not making that up). It was the subtle spiral over each person that caught my eye, along with the white border around them, which is very trendy right now. One thing I noticed was that none of the people were facing the camera. Now, in the original collage in the magazine (which was about the best unlikely movie scientists), the photos were all taken from movies, so they weren't posed with the subject looking at the camera. The hardest part of this (for me, anyway) was finding stock photos of people not looking straight at the camera.

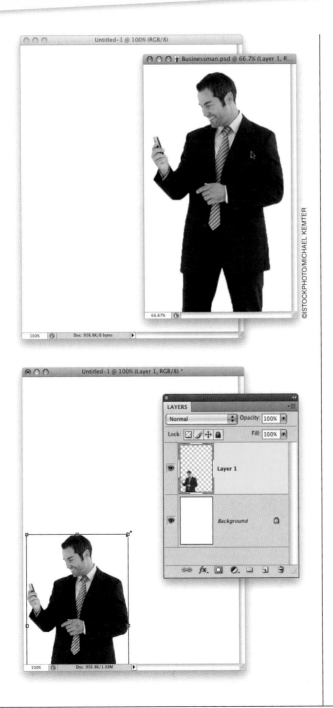

STEP ONE: Go under the File menu, choose New, and create a new document (the one here is 7 inches wide by 10 inches high at a resolution of 72 ppi). Open the first photo you want to use in your collage (I have all six photos used in this project posted on the book's downloads page, and I already put each photo up on its own separate layer for you. See, I care).

STEP TWO: Get the Move tool **(V)** and drag the first image (the businessman) onto your main document, then press **Command-T (PC: Ctrl-T)** to bring up Free Transform. Press-and-hold the Shift key, grab the top-right corner point, and drag inward to scale the image down in size (as shown here). Position him in the bottom-left corner, as seen here, then press **Return (PC: Enter)** to lock in your transformation.

Continued

STEP THREE: Now, open the next photo, and with the Move tool, drag her over onto your main document. Use Free Transform to scale her down in size (as shown here), but don't make her as small as the businessman (*Note*: Her file's name is "Woman in Front.") Position her like you see here, then lock in your transformation.

STEP FOUR: You're going to continue this process of opening a photo, dragging it over to your document, and scaling it down to size until all six photos are in the document. In the Layers panel, arrange their layers, so they appear (from the top of the layer stack to the bottom) with the "Woman in Front" on the top of the stack (so she appears to be in front), then the businessman and business-woman should be on the layers directly below her. The confused-looking woman and the rock star should be on the layers below that, and the man with the megaphone (the file is called "Megaphone man") will be at the bottom of the layer stack (right above the Background layer). Use the Move tool to arrange your people in your main document, so they pretty much look like what you see here.

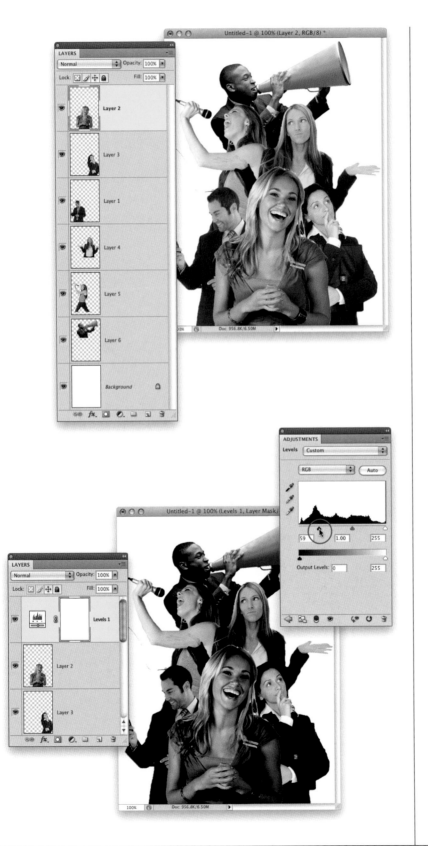

STEP FIVE: Now you're going to remove the color from each layer, so click on the top layer in the Layers panel (the woman in front), and press **Command-Shift-U (PC: Ctrl-Shift-U)** to Desaturate the image (which removes all the color). Do this for all the layers, so they're all in black and white (as shown here).

STEP SIX: You're now going to "crush the black," which is what we call pumping up the shadow areas big time. You can do this once, and have it affect all your layers, by going to the Layers panel and clicking on the top layer. Now, go to the Adjustments panel and click on the Levels icon (it's second from the left in the top row). Grab the far-left (shadows) slider (beneath the histogram and shown circled here in red) and drag it quite a bit over to the right to make the shadows really dark and rich (like you see here).

Continued

STEP SEVEN: You're going to start tinting each layer individually, and since each layer has to be a different color, we can't just add a Hue/Saturation adjustment layer at the top of the layer stack, or all the layers would be the same color. Instead, we have to apply the Hue/Saturation adjustment directly to each layer. So, click on the top layer (the woman in front), then press **Command-U (PC: Ctrl-U)** to bring up the Hue/Saturation dialog (shown here). Turn on the Colorize checkbox, then drag the Hue slider to a yellowish hue. The look we're going after uses very saturated colors, so for each person you're going to increase the Saturation amount to somewhere between 30 and 50 (in this case, all the way to 50, but it just depends on the photo, and the color choice). Once your Hue and Saturation amounts are set, click the OK button.

STEP EIGHT: Do the same thing for the other five layers, choosing a different Hue setting for each person, and then deciding how much saturation to give the color (the higher the Saturation amount, the more vivid the colors will be).

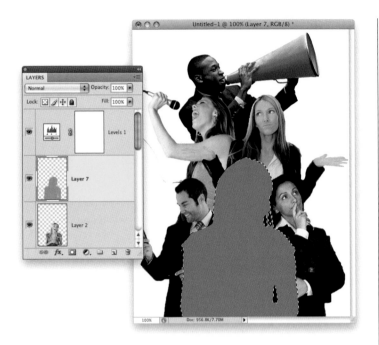

STEP NINE: Once all your layers have been tinted, you're going to go to each layer and apply a spiral effect over the image. You're going to run a filter that creates the spiral effect, but you can't run it directly on the person, because applying the filter will remove the color, so here's what we do: In the Layers panel, click on the first person's layer, then Command-click (PC: Ctrl-click) directly on the layer's thumbnail to put a selection around the person. Now, click on the Create a New Layer icon at the bottom of the Layers panel to create a new blank layer, click on the Foreground color swatch and set your Foreground color to a medium gray, then fill this selection with that color by pressing **Option-Delete (PC: Alt-Backspace)**, as seen here.

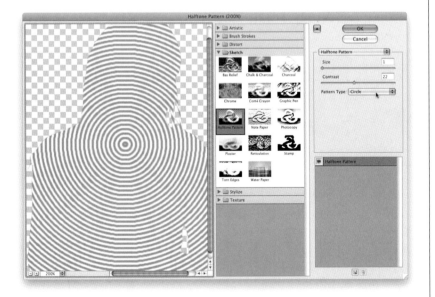

STEP 10: To apply the spiral effect, go under the Filter menu, under Sketch, and choose Halftone Pattern. When the dialog appears, from the Pattern Type pop-up menu on the right, choose Circle (as shown here), and lower the Size to 1. (*Note:* We're applying this spiral to a low-resolution image here, so the lines are fairly big, even at a Size setting of 1, but when you apply this to a regular high-resolution image of 200 or 300 ppi, the lines are much finer, and the effect looks better.) Set your Contrast amount to around 22, click OK to apply this spiral effect to your gray layer, and then press **Command-D (PC: Ctrl-D)** to Deselect.

Continued

STEP 11: To blend the spiral effect in with your color image, go to the Layers panel and change the layer blend mode of your gray layer to Soft Light, and then lower the Opacity to 30% (as seen here). Now, press **Command-E (PC: Ctrl-E)** to merge this gray layer permanently with your person layer below it.

STEP 12: You're going to continue that same process for each person layer—put a selection around the person, make a new layer, and fill it with gray, but once you're ready to add the filter, you can just press **Command-F (PC: Ctrl-F)** to reapply the Halftone Pattern filter using the exact same settings. Then, do the whole change-to-Soft Light-and-lower-the-Opacity thing and then merge the layers. So, go ahead and add the filter for each person layer (it take less time than you'd think).

STEP 13: Here, you're going to add a white stroke around each person layer. In the Layers panel, click on the top person layer, then click on the Add a Layer Style icon at the bottom of the Layers panel, and choose Stroke from the pop-up menu. When the Layer Style dialog appears, set the Position of the stroke to Inside (so the stroke appears inside your people, instead of outside them), choose white as your Color, click OK, and it adds the white stroke you see here.

STEP 14: To finish things off, you're going to go to the Layers panel, press-and-hold the **Option (PC: Alt) key**, click directly on the word "Effects," which appears below your woman in front layer, and drag-and-drop that effect (the white stroke) right onto your other layers (holding the Option key duplicates the effect you're dragging). Lastly, add some text (I used the font Rockwell here) and you're done.

Fading People in the Background

I saw this in a Web ad for a running shoe company. In their version, it had runners on a track, and the runner in front looked regular, but the runners behind him were transparent. At first I thought, "Man, that had to take a lot of masking," but then I realized that as long as you took three different shots, you could pull off that same look surprisingly easy, with barely any masking at all. In fact, it could be a 30-second job in Photoshop if you do the shoot right, and even that part is easy. So, you know what that tells me? The art director for that ad is really clever! (By the way, in their ad, they totally used the desaturated-look technique in Chapter 1.)

STEP ONE: You have to take three photos for this technique, and ideally you'd shoot all three on a tripod. If you don't have a tripod (or are at a location where you can't use a tripod), you can hand-hold the three shots and use Photoshop CS4's Auto-Align Layers feature, which works brilliantly in most cases like this, but if you use a tripod, it's guaranteed to work. Start by taking an empty photo of your background (so, for example, if you're shooting at a table in a restaurant, the first shot would be of the empty table, with no one sitting at it). In this case, we shot an empty soccer field (you can download all three of these from the book's downloads page).

STEP TWO: The second shot will be of the people you want to have fade out (by the way, this works equally well with objects you want to fade out—you don't have to use people). One thing that will make your job easier is to position these people so they won't overlap the person that is the focus of the shot. For example, we knew that we wanted our main soccer player in the middle, so we had the other players leave a gap in the middle. You don't have to leave a gap, but if the faded people in the background and your main subject don't overlap each other, then it makes your job really, really easy.

STEP THREE: Here's the third shot—the person who will be the main focus of our shoot. The idea is she is running down the field, and the other players behind her are just fading away. If you have clouds in the background (like we do here) which are moving, albeit pretty slowly, you don't want to take long between your three shots (of course, if you're shooting indoors, you can take as long as you like). One more thing: the key to this is to make sure that nothing on "the set" gets moved in the background or foreground during these three shots except your subjects. For example, if you're shooting in a restaurant, and you shoot an empty table, then you have two people sit down, they can't move the silverware, or drink glasses, or anything else. Same thing when the third person enters the scene.

STEP FOUR: Now, you're going to put all this together in Photoshop. Open the first photo (the empty soccer field), then open the second photo (the people who are going to fade out). Get the Move tool **(V)**, press-and-hold the Shift key (that's important), and drag your second photo over onto your empty field image (as shown here). Holding the Shift key is important because that's what ensures that your top layer is exactly aligned with the layer below it (this works, providing you shot all three shots on a tripod). If you hand-held your shots, I'll show you something in Step Six to get them all aligned automatically.

Continued

STEP FIVE: At the top of the Layers panel, lower the Opacity of this layer to 35% (as shown here) to make the players appear to fade out. Everything else stays 100% solid, because the backgrounds in the two shots didn't move (well, the clouds shifted a tiny bit in this case, but you really can't tell).

STEP SIX: Open the third photo (the photo of your main subject), press-and-hold the Shift key, and drag-and-drop this image onto your main document, on top of your other two images (as seen here). If you hand-held the shots when you took them, you'll have to have Photoshop align them for you, so go to the Layers panel, press-and-hold the Shift key, and click on all three layers to select them. Now, go under the Edit menu and choose Auto-Align Layers. When the dialog appears, leave it set to Auto and just click the OK button (the dialog is shown here, but again, you'll only use this feature if you didn't shoot on a tripod). Now, just for fun, if you want to test this feature, use the three shots taken here, but when you drag them over into the same document, don't hold the Shift key, so they're alignment is off by quite a bit. Then run Auto-Align Layers and watch it do its thing. It's pretty darn amazing.

You're going to hide the top layer behind a black mask, then paint back in just your player. Press-and-hold the Option (PC: Alt) key and click on the Add Layer Mask icon at the bottom of the Layers panel (shown circled here in red) to put a black mask over your top layer (which hides the layer from view). Get the Brush tool **(B)**, choose a medium-sized soft-edged brush from the Brush Picker in the Options Bar, and with your Foreground color set to white, just paint over where the main player used to be (don't forget to paint back in the soccer ball, too). If your player doesn't overlap the other players, this couldn't be easier, because you don't have to worry about "staying inside the lines"—just start painting. In our case, the player's hand on the right side of the image overlaps the player behind her, but outside of that, it's a 10-second job. When you get to the fingers on her hand on the right side, you'll just need to shrink your brush size down a little and paint over her fingers, but this is about as easy a masking job as you'll ever get to do.

STEP EIGHT: Here's the final image. If you want the players in the back to be more (or less) transparent, just click on the middle layer and adjust them using the Opacity slider.

Instant Glassy Talk Bubbles

This is just a two-page quickie, and I'm adding it because I saw it last week on a website, and I had to smile at how simple, yet effective, the look was that the designer created as headers for different sections of the web-page. The whole thing is created using built-in talk bubble shapes that are already installed on your computer, that you just have to load into Photoshop's Shape Picker. The rest is creating a "Down & Dirty" reflection.

STEP ONE: Go under the File menu, choose New, and create a new document that's 800x600 pixels at a resolution of 72 ppi, then create a new blank layer by clicking on the Create a New Layer icon at the bottom of the Layers panel. Press **D** to set your Foreground and Background colors to their defaults of black and white, and then click on the Foreground color swatch in the Toolbox and set your Foreground color to a medium gray (I used R: 96, G: 107, B: 110). Get the Custom Shape tool from the Toolbox (or just press **Shift-U** until you have it), go up to the Options Bar, click on the third icon from the left so your shape will be made up of pixels, then click on the Shape thumbnail to bring up the Shape Picker. Click on the little right-facing arrow at the top-right corner of the Picker to bring up the flyout menu you see here. Choose Talk Bubbles to add the talk bubble shapes to your Picker. You'll get a warning dialog asking you if you want to replace the current shapes; just click Append.

STEP TWO: In the Shape Picker, scroll down until you come to the talk bubbles you just loaded. Choose the wide rectangular shape (I chose Talk 10, as shown here), and then click-and-drag out a long, thin talk bubble like you see here. Now, press the letter **X** to swap your Foreground and Background colors (so white is now your Foreground color, and gray your Background color).

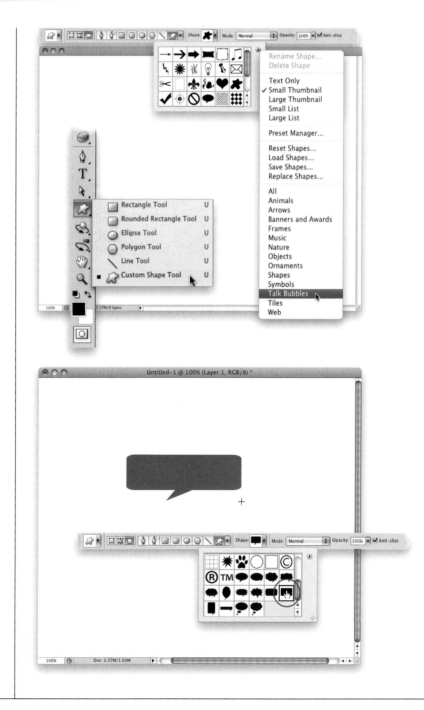

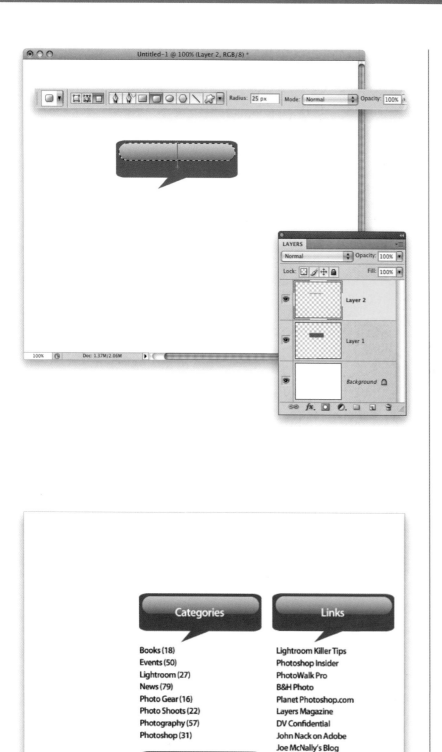

STEP THREE: Create a new blank layer, then switch to the Rounded Rectangle tool (it's one of the shape tools; press **Shift-U** until you have it), then go up to the Options Bar and set the Radius (the roundness) to 25 pixels. Now, click-and-drag out a horizontal rounded rectangle that extends nearly halfway down your talk bubble (like you see here). It will be filled with white, but you need to delete that white, so go to the Layers panel, and Command-click (PC: Ctrl-click) directly on that layer's thumbnail. This puts a selection around your white pill shape. Press Delete (PC: Backspace) to delete your white fill, but leave your selection in place. Get the Gradient tool **(G)**, click on the down-facing arrow next to the gradient thumbnail, and choose the top-left gradient (Foreground to Background) from the Gradient Picker. Click-and-drag a gradient through your selection from the top to just about ⅛" or so past the bottom of the pill shape (as shown here). This gives you a white-to-light-gray gradient in the pill shape.

STEP FOUR: Deselect by pressing **Command-D (PC: Ctrl-D)**. Next, go to the Layers panel and lower the Opacity of this pill-shaped gradient to 70% to help it blend with the gray shape below it. Now you just need to add some text (here, I switched to the Horizontal Type tool **[T]** and typed the word "Categories" in the font Myriad Pro Semibold, which comes with Photoshop CS4, in white at 24 points). I added a couple of other copies of the talk bubble (by clicking on the bubble layer and pressing **Command-J [PC: Ctrl-J]**, and then doing the same thing for the gradient layer), so you can see it in use on a webpage layout similar to when I first saw this quick and simple little glassy effect in use.

Photo Finish

photo effects, part 2

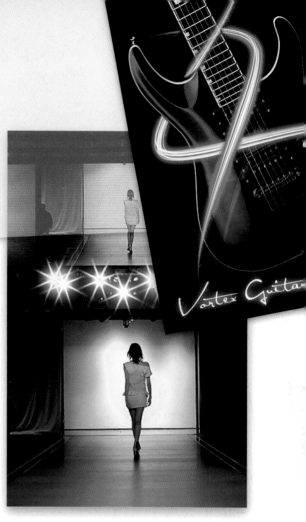

I had a lot of choices for the name of this chapter, because not only is there a movie named *Photo Finish* (2003, from writer and director Douglas McFerran), but there was a song named "Photo Finish" by Chris LeDoux (whose French-sounding name doesn't sound at all like a guy who sings rodeo songs), and an album "Photo-Finish" by rocker Rory Gallagher. But the one I actually chose for this chapter was the song "Photo Finish" from French pop musician Maxime Le Forestier. Now, Monsieur Le Forestier has 17 different albums available on Apple's iTunes Store, and I listened to a number of tracks from several of his albums, and I have to be honest with you—I couldn't understand what in the heck he was saying. I was lucky to understand every 50th word or so, but some of his words were unmistakable, like croissant, Gerard Depardieu, fries, the Louvre, and a vague reference to Jerry Lewis. Anyway, my editor wanted me to choose this French version, because she thought it would make me seem more international, especially if I could work some legitimate Photoshop-related French phrases into the book, like "La chaise est vide" or "Là où est la pharmacie locale," so I assured her they would find their way in somehow. Hey, it's like they say in France, "Le chat est sur le lit." Oui!

Creating Sports Wallpaper

I got the idea for this layout from a series of free wallpaper downloads from Nike Football (www.nike.com/usnikefootball/), and the look has a darkened football field (like outdoors at night, or indoors with the stadium lights off) with a small part of the field lit by your flash (or on-location studio strobes). I thought of figuring out a way to get permission to shoot the setup shot at a local stadium, but then I figured you might be able to just take a daylight shot and make it into a nighttime shot. Luckily, it was easier than I thought, but besides the night look, the cooler trick might be how to drop out the black background behind our football player. Here's how both are done:

STEP ONE: Start by opening the football field shot you see here. The shot is obviously taken in daylight (or in a domed stadium with all the lights on), but we're going to fix that soon enough.

STEP TWO: Go to the Layers panel and double-click on the Background layer. When the New Layer dialog appears, just click OK, and it will convert your Background layer into a regular layer. Now get the Move tool **(V)**, press-and-hold the Shift key (to keep it aligned), and click-and-drag the image straight downward a few inches, so it's positioned like you see here. The reason we're pulling it down is that we want to see the 20-yard line in the final image, and if it's up high (like it was when it was just the Background layer), it will get covered up by the "night" effect.

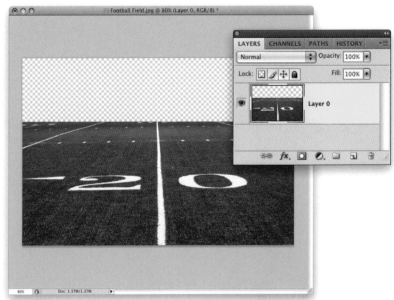

STEP THREE: Create a new blank layer by clicking on the Create a New Layer icon at the bottom of the Layers panel. Press **D** to set your Foreground color to black, then fill this layer with black by pressing **Option-Delete (PC: Alt-Backspace)**. Now, lower the Opacity of this layer to 80%, so you can see the field on the layer below it. Next, you're going to need to have this solid black layer fade about three-quarters of the way down the image, and we'll use a layer mask to do that. So, click on the Add Layer Mask icon at the bottom of the Layers panel (it's shown circled here in red) to add a layer mask to your black layer.

STEP FOUR: Get the Gradient tool **(G)**, click on the down-facing arrow next to the gradient thumbnail up in the Options Bar, and choose the top-left gradient (Foreground to Background) in the Gradient Picker. Then, take the tool, click it about three-quarters of the way from the bottom of the image, and drag upward until you're just above the number 2 on the field (this is why you needed to lower the opacity of this black layer—so you could see where the numbers are). Dragging the Gradient tool like this reveals the lower part of your image, then graduates up to solid black (of course, you can't see that clearly because your layer opacity is still at 80%).

Continued

STEP FIVE: Go to the Layers panel and raise your Layer Opacity to 100%, and now you can see how the top two-thirds of your image is black (as seen here). Next, we need to add a much smaller black gradient to the bottom of our image, so add another new blank layer, then fill this new layer with black. Add a layer mask to this layer, and this time you're going to drag your gradient from the same spot, but in the opposite direction (so you're dragging down to the bottom, as shown here). You've now got just that spot open in the center that looks like it's lit by a flash at night in a darkened stadium. (*Note:* If you think your field looks too dark, click on Layer 0, then press **Command-L [PC: Ctrl-L]** to bring up Levels, drag the top-center slider to the left until it reads 1.40, and drag the far-left slider to the right until it reads 27. Again, this is totally your call.) Now, open the photo of the player you're going to add to your field document (as shown here).

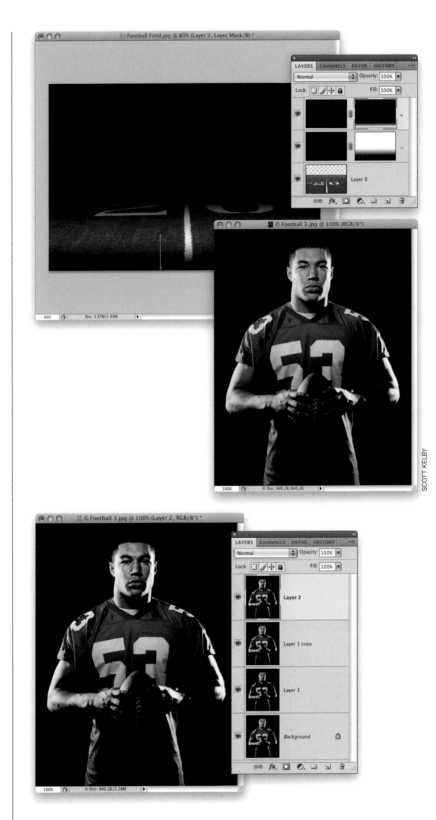

SCOTT KELBY

STEP SIX: The original Nike wallpapers used a desaturated look for their athletes, so we're going to apply the desaturated look from Chapter 1 here in the book, which, in short, is this: Press **Command-J (PC: Ctrl-J)** twice to duplicate the Background layer two times. Click on the middle layer, then press **Command-Shift-U (PC: Ctrl-Shift-U)** to remove the color. Lower the Opacity of this layer to 80%. Then, on the top layer, change the layer blend mode to Soft Light. Now, press **Command-Option-Shift-E (PC: Ctrl-Alt-Shift-E)** to create a new layer on top that looks like a flattened version of your file (as shown here). Get the History Brush tool **(Y)** and paint over his jersey and the ball to bring back their original colors. That way, the jersey looks right, but the new desaturated skin color stays there, as seen here.

STEP SEVEN: Get the Move tool and click-and-drag your top layer over on top of the field document, and make sure it's the top layer in the panel. Now, duplicate this layer, then go to the Layers panel and hide the top layer from view by clicking on the Eye icon that appears to the left of the layer's thumbnail, then click back on the next layer down (the first layer of the player).

STEP EIGHT: This next step is a really slick move you can use to get rid of the background behind your subject when that background is either solid black, solid white, or solid gray. You're going to toggle through the layer blend modes, until you find the one that makes your background transparent. There's a keyboard shortcut for this: it's **Shift-+ (plus sign)**. Each time you press this, it toggles to the next blend mode in the list of layer blend modes, so go ahead and do that now, and you'll see that at least one of them will drop out the background. In this case, both Lighten and Screen mode did it, but Screen kept more of his body intact, so we'll go with that one. You can see in the image shown here that part of his body is now see-through, but that's why you created that duplicate layer back in Step Seven—so we can use that to bring back any missing parts.

Continued

STEP NINE: Make your top layer visible again by clicking where the Eye icon used to be (this layer will still be in Normal mode, so when you make it visible, you'll see the black background behind him again), and then click on the layer to make it active. Press-and-hold the Option (PC: Alt) key and click on the Add Layer Mask icon. This adds a black layer mask to this layer and hides your normal layer behind it. Now, get the Brush tool **(B)**, choose a hard-edged brush (since the areas we're painting have well-defined edges, like his arms and his uniform) from the Brush Picker in the Options Bar, make sure your Foreground color is white, then paint directly over any areas of his body that are missing, and they start to paint right back in, as seen here, where I'm painting just below and to the left of the ball. What you're doing is revealing parts of him from the top layer. Just keep painting until he's fully solid (you may have to shrink the size of your brush when you get to his arms). If you paint too far, press **X** to switch your Foreground color to black, and paint over your mistake.

STEP 10: Here's how he looks after I've painted in those areas (mostly in his stomach and arms) that were missing. Now, is it possible you missed a few areas? Absolutely, but in the next step, you'll learn a great trick to see if you missed any spots where you should have painted.

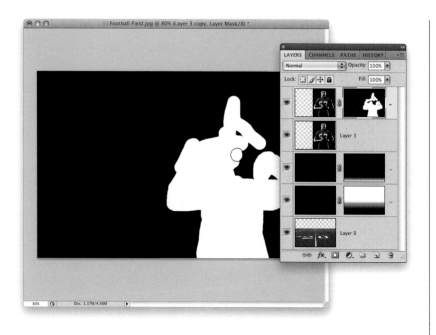

STEP 11: Press-and-hold the Option (PC: Alt) key and click once directly on the layer mask thumbnail that appears to the right of your top layer's regular layer thumbnail. This shows you just the layer mask itself, and you can quickly see which parts you missed when painting (any parts that appear inside your white area that are black are spots you missed). So, just paint over them in white (as shown here), and it paints in those missed spots. I use this trick nearly every time I make a mask, because it's usually too hard to see if you missed a spot because the photo is in color. Option-click on the mask again to go back to seeing your full image.

STEP 12: The last step is to add your player's name and position. Get the Horizontal Type tool **(T)**, make sure you Foreground color is still white, and type in your player's name in all caps (I used the font Helvetica Bold Condensed Oblique at a point size of 42. By the way, Oblique means italic in "font talk"). Then, create the line of text with his position and school (or team), and make this text a medium gray. For this I used the same font, but without the italic (I mean, without the Oblique), to give you the layout you see here.

Adding Window Light to Flat-Looking Photos

Here's a pretty darn easy way to add the look of window light hitting a wall behind your subjects. In this project, you're going to get to decide whether the window light falls across your subjects (and if you do choose this route, you'll learn how to bend the window panes around your subjects for a more realistic look), or if the window light appears behind them (so it's coming from a side angle), plus a few other little tricks thrown in just for good measure (like how to blur just one side of an object, so it looks like it's moving away from you).

STEP ONE: Open the photo you want to add a window light to (you can download the one you see here from the book's downloads page, mentioned in the book's introduction). Press **D**, then **X** to set your Foreground color to white, then create a new layer by clicking on the Create a New Layer icon at the bottom of the Layers panel. Now, get the Custom Shape tool from the Toolbox (it's two tools down from the Horizontal Type tool—click-and-hold on the Shape tools, and choose Custom Shape tool from the menu that pops out, or press **Shift-U** until you have it).

STEP TWO: Go up to the Options Bar, and click on the third icon from the left (shown circled here in red), which sets things up so your shape will be made up of regular pixels (rather than a Shape layer or a path). Now, click on the Shape thumbnail to bring up the Shape Picker (seen here). Choose the shape that has a grid made up of three rows of three (as shown here).

©ISTOCKPHOTO/NICHOLAS MONU

STEP THREE: Press-and-hold the Shift key (so the shape stays proportional), then click-and-drag out the grid square shape made up of white lines, like you see here. Once it's in place, switch to the Magic Wand tool (press **Shift-W** until you have it) and click once inside the top-left square (as seen here) to select just that one square. Now, press-and-hold the Shift key (to add to your existing selection) and click in each of the other eight squares, until all nine are selected (as shown here).

STEP FOUR: Now that your selection is in place, you don't need that shape any longer, so delete that layer by going to the Layers panel and dragging it onto the Trash icon at the bottom of the panel. Create a new blank layer, then press **Option-Delete (PC: Alt-Back-space)** to fill your selected squares with your Foreground color (which should still be white, as shown here) and create the shape of our window. Now you can Deselect by pressing **Command-D (PC: Ctrl-D)**.

Continued

STEP FIVE: To make the window shape look more realistic, you're going to want to apply a blur to the right side, so the window looks more blurry as it moves farther away from where the window light starts. The easiest way to do that is to press the letter **Q** to enter Quick Mask mode (this mode lets us apply things like blurs or filters to a selection). Now that you're in Quick Mask mode (you'll see it say "Quick Mask/8" up in the title bar of your image window), get the Gradient tool **(G)**, make sure the Foreground to Background gradient is chosen in the Gradient Picker, then click it on the left edge of your window and drag it over to the right edge (as shown here). You'll see the left side of your image turn red, which just indicates which part of the photo won't be affected when we add our blur. You'll see it slowly graduates over to clear (the clear areas will get the full blur).

STEP SIX: Press the letter **Q** again, and you'll see your selection is now in place (and the part of the window that you want to blur is the selected part. What you can't see is the smooth transition between the area you're going to blur and the rest of the window, but thanks to Quick Mask mode, and using that Gradient tool, it's there). To blur that side of the window shape, go under the Filter menu, under Blur, and choose Gaussian Blur. When the dialog appears, set the Radius (blur amount) to 3 pixels (as shown here) and click OK to blur the right side of the window. Now you can deselect.

STEP SEVEN: Press **Command-T (PC: Ctrl-T)** to bring up Free Transform around your window shape. Drag the right-center point quite a ways over to the right to stretch the window across the wall (as seen here). Don't lock in your transformation yet—we've still got a couple of tweaks to do.

STEP EIGHT: To create a perspective effect, press-and-hold **Command-Option-Shift (PC: Ctrl-Alt-Shift)**, then grab the bottom-left corner point and drag upward (as shown here) to add perspective and squeeze that side closer together. Now, press **Return (PC: Enter)** to lock in your transformation.

Continued

STEP NINE: To blend the window in with your photo, go to the Layers panel and do two things: (1) change the layer blend mode to Overlay, and (2) lower the Opacity of this layer to 30%. To me, the left side of the window looks too sharp and well-defined, but there's an easy way around that: just go under the Filter menu, under Blur and choose Gaussian Blur. When the dialog appears, add a 1-pixel Gaussian blur (as shown here) to the entire window shape layer. Now you have a decision to make. At this point, the window shadow goes right over your subjects, but if it was really going over their faces, the lines wouldn't be perfectly straight like they are, right? So, in the next step, we'll use a trick to move 'em around just enough so they don't look so straight. However, if you'd prefer the window reflection was only on the wall behind them, then jump over to Step 12 now.

STEP 10: To move the lines a little, click on the window layer, then go under the Filter menu and choose Liquify. When the Liquify dialog appears, make sure the Show Backdrop checkbox is turned on, so you can see the people on the Background layer (it's circled here in red). Now get the Forward Warp tool (it's the top tool in the Toolbox on the left), choose a small-sized brush (use the Brush Size slider in the Tool Options section on the right side of the dialog), and wherever a line goes over your subjects, simply click and move the line a little bit over to the left or right (or up or down, if they're horizontal lines). They move like they're liquid, so just move 'em around a little bit. Don't make big movements—just a few small "bend the line to the left or right" nudges should do it. Don't worry about trying to follow the contours of the face—it's not necessary—just push 'em around a little to help sell the idea that the lines are being affected when they fall on your subjects.

STEP 11: Now click OK to apply the Liquify filter to the parts of the window that extend over your subjects, and as you can see here, while it's fairly subtle, the lines are definitely not straight and that helps sell the illusion that the window light is falling upon them. Now, if you go on to the next step, it shows you how to mask the window so it only appears behind them, in which case there's no sense in doing Step 10 or this step (Step 11)—you should just jump from Step Nine to Step 12. But, hey, if you want to continue on, I won't tell anybody.

STEP 12: To put the window behind your subjects, click on the Add Layer Mask icon at the bottom of the Layers panel (it's shown circled here in red). Then get the Brush tool **(B)**, choose a small, soft-edged brush, make sure your Foreground color is set to black, and paint over your subjects (as shown here). The areas you paint over are now hidden from view, leaving only the window on the wall behind them still visible for the final image you see here.

Creating Realistic Photo Starbrights

You've seen this effect of a light in the background of a photo bursting into a bright star shape because the in-camera effect has been around for years, and it's very popular in Hollywood photos because it adds a sense of excitement. This effect is usually created by attaching a screw-on star filter to your camera's lens. This filter has a thin grid of wires that refract the light and create anywhere from four to eight stars per light source. I've seen folks over the years try to replicate this look in Photoshop, and it always looks fake. I tried myself with no luck, but Corey Barker (my contributing author, who wrote the 3D chapter in this book) came up with an amazingly realistic (and very clever) technique that beats them all. Here's how he does it:

STEP ONE: Go under the File menu and choose New to create a new document that is 8x8" at a resolution of 100 ppi. Press **D** to set your Foreground color to black, then fill the Background layer with black by pressing **Option-Delete (PC: Alt-Backspace)**. Now create a new blank layer by clicking on the Create a New Layer icon at the bottom of the Layers panel. Get the Elliptical Marquee tool (press **Shift-M** until you have it), press-and-hold the Shift key (to make a perfect circle), and draw a small circular selection in the center of your image area (as shown here). Press **X** to make white your Foreground color, then fill your selection with white the same way you filled your Background layer with black, and Deselect by pressing **Command-D (PC: Ctrl-D)**. Now you'll need to soften the circle by going under the Filter menu, under Blur, and choosing Gaussian Blur. When the dialog appears, set the Radius to 5 pixels and click OK.

STEP TWO: You're going to create the points of your starbrights by using the Smudge tool, so choose it from the Toolbox (as shown here). Before you use the tool, you need to do a little setup in the Brushes panel, so click on the Brushes panel icon toward the right side of the Options Bar (it's shown circled here in red). When the Brushes panel appears, in the list of options on the left side of the panel, make sure all the checkboxes beside the options are turned off (as shown here). Now you're ready to start smudging.

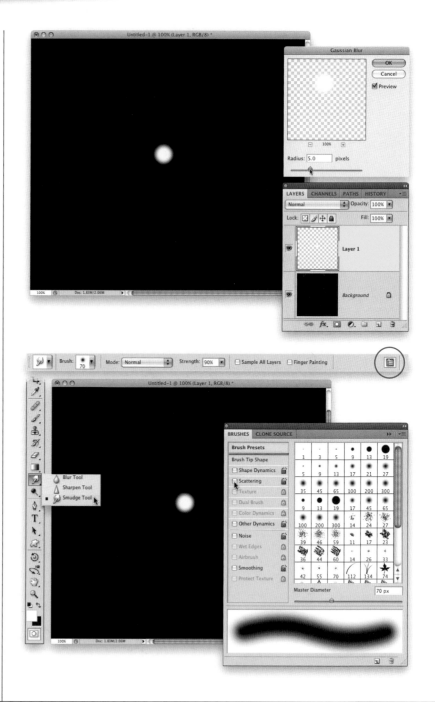

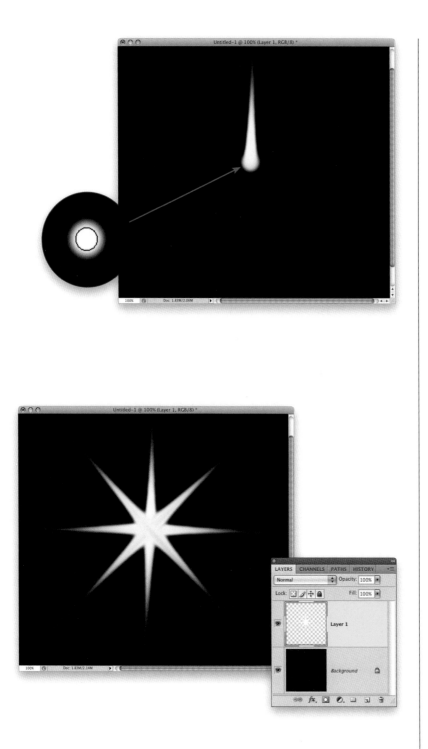

STEP THREE: Choose a brush size that's a bit smaller than the round circle in the middle of your image (take a look at the size of the brush you see here in the overlay. That's how big it should be when you put your brush in the center of the white circle in the center of your screen). By the way, you can change the size of your brush by using the **Left and Right Bracket keys** on your keyboard (they're just to the right of the letter P on your keyboard). Once your brush size looks like the one shown in the overlay, click once in the center of the white circle, then move your cursor up near the top of your image window, just Shift-click once, and it draws a straight smudge between the white circle (where you clicked first) and where you just clicked, which gives you the shape you see here.

STEP FOUR: You're going to repeat that same "two-click tango" all the way around your image (as shown here). You do the same thing every time—start by clicking once in the center of the white circle, then move your cursor out near the edge of your image and just Shift-click once again. That's it. So, go ahead and add seven more "sprites" around the center (as seen here).

Continued

STEP FIVE: Now that your eight sprites are in place, we're going to add a little blur effect to the center of the image. Get the Gradient tool **(G)**, then go up to the Options Bar and click on the second gradient from the left (it's shown circled here in red), which gives you a Radial gradient (a circular gradient). Next, click on the down-facing arrow next to the gradient thumbnail to get the Gradient Picker, and choose the second gradient in the picker (the Foreground to Transparent gradient, as shown here). Take the tool, click it in the center of the image, and drag straight down about an inch. When you release the mouse button, it creates a white gradient in the center that radiates out to transparent, so it looks like a small blur (as seen here).

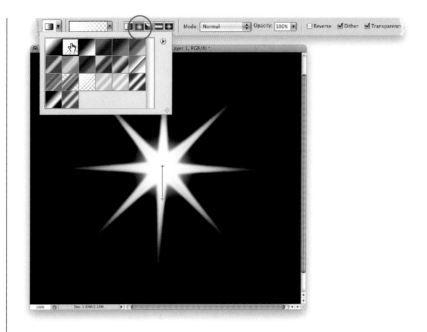

STEP SIX: If you look at real starbrights, created using a traditional star filter, they have a prism of colors at the end of each of the eight sprites. This is a key part of the look, and we can get that look here by adding a new layer, then going up to the Gradient Picker and clicking on the Transparent Rainbow gradient (as shown here). Now take the Gradient tool, go up to the Options Bar and click back on the first gradient icon (the regular Linear gradient), then go down to the bottom half of your image window, and click-and-drag downward to create the rainbow bar you see here.

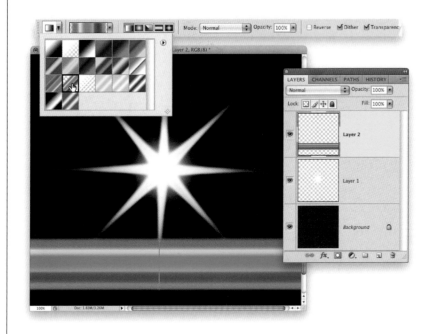

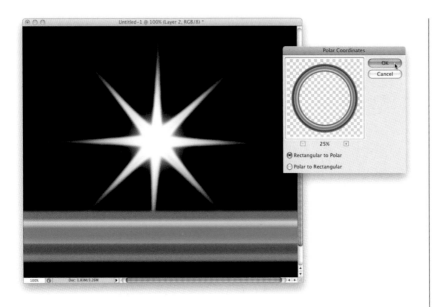

STEP SEVEN: We need that bar to be circular, so go under the Filter menu, under Distort, and choose Polar Coordinates. When the dialog appears, make sure Rectangular to Polar is selected. If you click the minus sign a couple of times under the left side of the filter preview, you'll see a preview of what this filter is going to do—it turns your rainbow bar gradient into a perfect circle gradient. So, click OK (as shown here) to make that circular rainbow gradient.

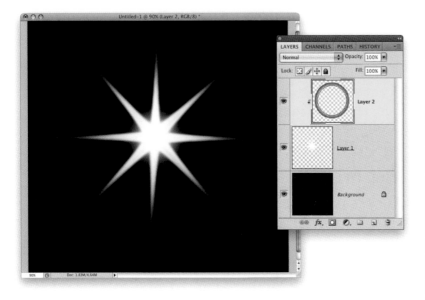

STEP EIGHT: When the rainbow circle appears, get the Move tool **(V)** and position it so the circle is over the ends of your starbright. You may need to use Free Transform (press **Command-T [PC: Ctrl-T]**) to make your circle a little larger (or smaller) so it covers the ends of your starbright. When it covers them, press **Command-Option-G (PC: Ctrl-Alt-G)**, which puts that rainbow circle inside your starbright (as seen here). Since the center of your circle was empty, only the tips of your sprites get the rainbow color (just like the real thing!).

Continued

STEP NINE: This simple step adds another big level of authenticity to the look of your starbright. In the Layers panel, click on the starbright layer, then go under the Filter menu, under Blur, and choose Radial Blur. When the filter dialog appears, set the Amount to 5, and make sure the Blur Method is set to Spin, then click OK to blur the edges in a circular fashion (as seen here).

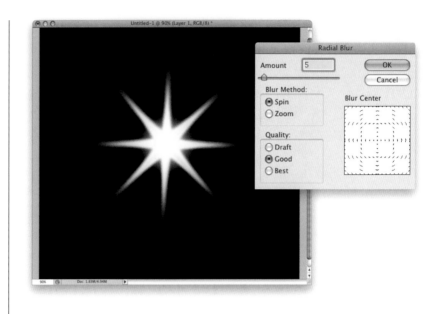

STEP 10: Now we're going to add a glow behind your starbright to help enhance the effect. Click on the Add a Layer Style icon at the bottom of the Layers panel, and choose Outer Glow from the pop-up menu. When the Layer Style dialog appears, lower the Opacity to 50%, leave the glow color as is, but increase the Size setting to 200 pixels, and click OK to give you the glow effect you see here.

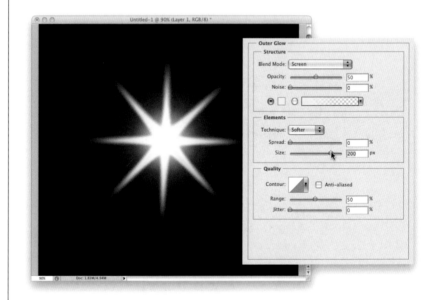

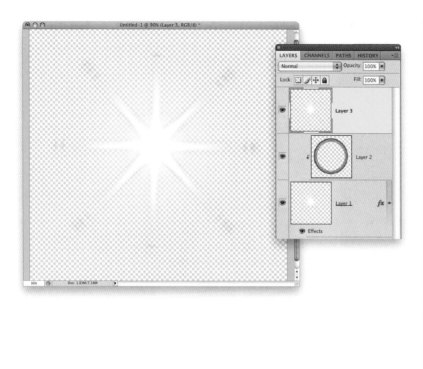

STEP 11: The black background we started with was just there so you could see the starbright as it was being created (after all, it's hard to see a white starbright on a white background, eh?). At this point, you'll need to get rid of the black background, so go to the Layers panel and drag the Background layer onto the Trash icon at the bottom of the panel to delete it. Now only your starbright layer, and the layer with the circular rainbow that is clipped inside it, are visible. Click on the top layer, and press **Command-Option-Shift-E (PC: Ctrl-Alt-Shift-E)** to create a new layer that is a combination of your other visible layers. Now your starbright is done, and it's time to put it to work. (*Note:* At this point, I would save this file as a PSD with all its layers intact, and use this as a template. Anytime you have a photo that you want to add starbrights to, you just open this document and start dragging them in.)

STEP 12: Open the photo you want to apply the starbright effect to (in this case, it's a shot from a fashion show, but this effect is often applied to nighttime shots taken in a downtown area, or theater shots, concert shots, or in a photo where you see lights aiming directly at the camera). Go to your starbright document, get the Move tool, and drag your top layer over onto your fashion show document. Bring up Free Transform, then press-and-hold the Shift key, grab a corner point, and drag inward to scale the starbright down to the size of your lights (as seen here). If you can't see the corner handles, press **Command-0 (zero; PC: Ctrl-0)**. Then move your cursor outside the Free Transform bounding box, and it turns into a two-headed arrow. Click-and-drag in a circular motion to rotate the starbright like you see here. Okay, now you can press **Return (PC: Enter)** to lock in your transformation.

Continued

STEP 13: There is normally more than just one starbright in a photo, so press-and-hold the Option (PC: Alt) key, click on a starbright, and drag yourself a copy, and keep dragging out as many copies as you'd like. Don't be afraid to have two or more of them really close to each other, as this look is fairly common (as seen here).

STEP 14: If you want your starbrights to appear even brighter, with a larger glow, all you have to do is duplicate each starbright layer (press **Command-J [PC: Ctrl-J]**), and that's it—you don't have to change blend modes or make any other changes. If you have several starbrights and you want them all to be brighter, simply Shift-click on each start-bright layer, then press **Command-E (PC: Ctrl-E)** to merge them together, and duplicate the merged layer. Just duplicating the layer builds up the brightness behind the layer, which gives you the final (yet totally optional) look you see here.

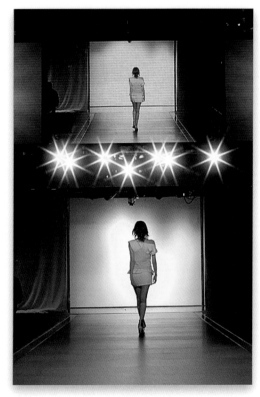

Composing Made Easy Using a Green Screen

To put people or products onto a different background, shooting them on a green screen is the way to go. The problem has been that shooting on a green screen took a lot of effort, really exact lighting, and an expensive plug-in to remove your subject from the background. Two things have changed that made me add this technique to the book: (1) The F.J. Westcott Company came up with an inexpensive, easy-to-use green screen kit; and (2) my colleague Dave Cross came up with a way to remove someone from a green screen in Photoshop, without a plug-in and without breaking a sweat.

BRAD MOORE

SCOTT KELBY

STEP ONE: Here we're going to use the green screen to create a skateboarding event poster. I'm going to start with the shoot we did using the Westcott kit on a green-screen backdrop (held up by two light stands). The scoop on Westcott's kit is it's just $300 and comes with the green screen background, two continuous lights, stands, and everything you need to get a good green-screen shot, except the camera itself, of course. You simply hang the green-screen cloth behind your subject, then position the two lights in front of your subject on either side of the camera (as shown here), then take your shot. I know, it seems like it should be harder than that, but it's just not. (More info on the kit is at www.photobasics.net/details.cfm?id=r&itemnum=401.)

STEP TWO: Now, open your green-screen photo in Photoshop CS4 (you can download the photo you see here, shot on that green screen setup, from the book's downloads page). There are a number of different ways to get your subject off the green-screen background, the most popular being the use of an expensive plug-in, but my buddy (and my *Photoshop User TV* co-host) Dave Cross invented a green-screen technique that is just astounding, and he agreed to let me share it here. You start by converting your image to Lab Color mode (which is a non-destructive move), so go under the Image menu, under Mode, and choose Lab Color (as shown here).

Continued

STEP THREE: Go under the Window menu and choose Channels to bring up the Channels panel. You'll see four channels here: the Lab channel, the Lightness channel, the "a" channel, and the "b" channel. Click on the "a" channel to make it the active channel, then duplicate this channel by dragging it onto the Create New Channel icon at the bottom of the Channels panel (it's shown circled here in red). Next, go under the Edit menu and choose Fill. When the Fill dialog appears, for Contents, choose White from the Use pop-up menu. In the Blending section, change the Mode from Normal to Overlay (as seen here). Now click OK to fill the white areas of this channel with white. (*Note:* When you build a mask of an object, or in this case a person, you want your subject to be solid white, and the background around them to be solid black. When you have that, you have a perfect mask, and that's what you're building here.)

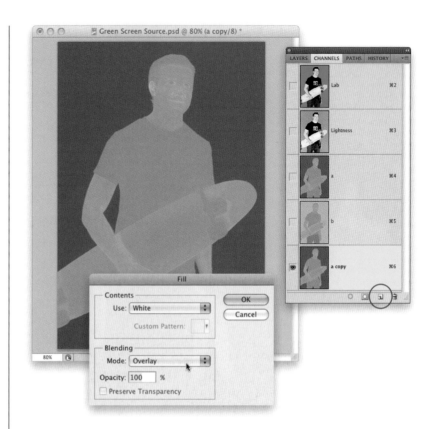

STEP FOUR: You can see that your subject, who was different shades of gray in the previous step, is now white. If it's not perfectly white, we'll fix that in a minute. Now you're going to change the dark gray around him to solid black. Go under the Edit menu again and choose Fill. This time, for Contents, choose Black from the Use pop-up menu, then click OK. This fills the background with black, but the first time you do this, it probably won't be solid black. You'll have to do this at least one more time—maybe even twice—to get the nice solid black fill you see here. If your subject isn't solid white, run Fill again with White chosen in the Use pop-up menu.

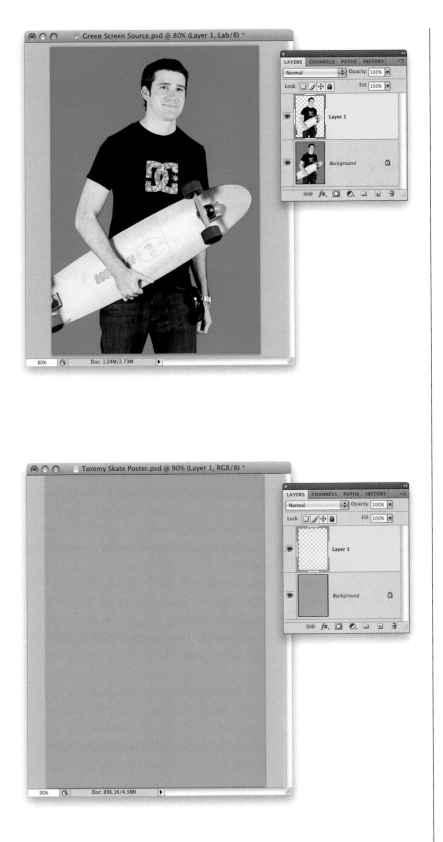

STEP FIVE: Now your mask is complete, and you'll use it to get your subject off that green background. Press-and-hold the Command (PC: Ctrl) key and, in the Channels panel, click directly on the thumbnail for the "a copy" channel (the channel you've just been editing). This loads the channel as a selection. Scroll up to the top of the Channels panel, and click on the Lab channel to return to the full-color view of your image (your selection will still be in place). Now, go under the Image menu, under Mode, and choose RGB Color. Return to the Layers panel (your selection is still in place), and press **Command-J (PC: Ctrl-J)** to put this selected area (your subject) up onto its own separate layer (as seen here). That's it—your subject has been removed from the green-screen background and is up on his own layer. (*Note:* Click on the Eye icon next to your Background layer to make sure there is no green on your subject's edges. If there is, press **Command-Z [PC: Ctrl-Z]** to undo your duplication, then go under the Select menu, under Modify, and choose Contract. In the Contract Selection dialog, enter 1 pixel and click OK. Then, duplicate your selection.) By the way, if you're familiar with actions, this is a great technique to save as an action, and then apply with just one click in the future.

STEP SIX: Now, let's put our subject to use in our poster. Go under the File menu and choose New to create a new document that is 6.5" wide by 9" tall at a resolution of 72 ppi. Click on your Foreground color swatch and set orange as your Foreground color (I used R: 236, G: 146, B: 47), then fill your background with that orange by pressing **Option-Delete (PC: Alt-Backspace)**. Next, create a new blank layer by clicking on the Create a New Layer icon at the bottom of the Layers panel.

Continued

STEP SEVEN: Press **D**, then **X** to set your Foreground color to white, then get the Gradient tool **(G)** from the Toolbox. Up in the Options Bar, make sure the Liner Gradient icon is selected, then click on the down-facing arrow next to the gradient thumbnail to bring up the Gradient Picker. Click on the second gradient in the top row—the Foreground to Transparent gradient (as shown here). Next, take the Gradient tool, click it about 25% of the way up from the bottom of your image, and drag upward to nearly halfway up your image to create a white-to-transparent gradient on this layer (the transparent part reveals the orange on the layer below). Now, to get the little specks throughout the bottom of your gradient (like the ones you see here), just go to the Layers panel and change the blend mode of this layer from Normal to Dissolve (as shown circled here).

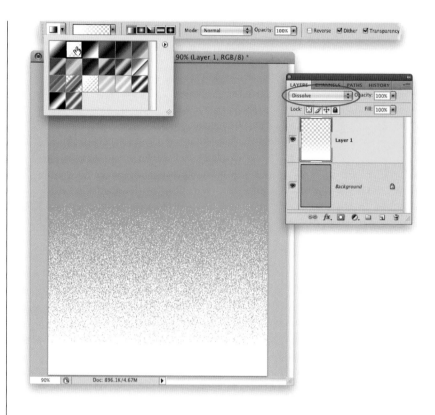

STEP EIGHT: Get the Move tool **(V)**, go to your green-screen image, click-and-drag your subject over onto your orange gradient document (as shown here), and position him way over to the left, like he's positioned here. You'll notice that he's completely separate from the green-screen background (thanks to what you did earlier). If you need to resize him, simply press **Command-T (PC: Ctrl-T)** to bring up Free Transform. Now, to add a posterized effect, go under the Image menu, under Adjustments, and choose Posterize. When the dialog appears, set the Levels to 7, and click OK to create the look seen here.

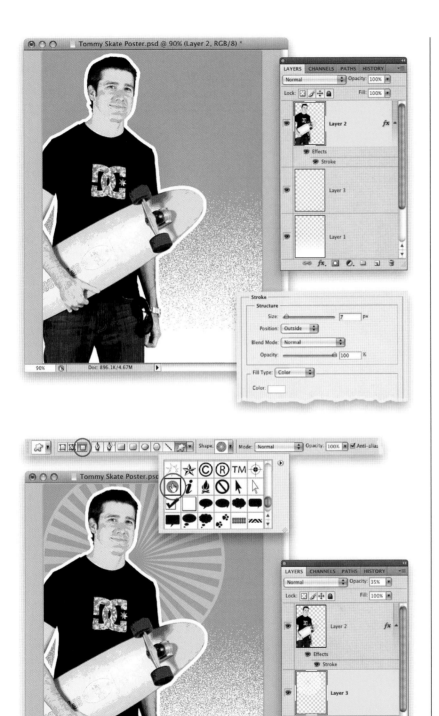

STEP NINE: You're now going to add a white stroke around your subject. Choose Stroke from the Add a Layer Style icon's pop-up menu at the bottom of the Layers panel. When the Layer Style dialog appears, increase the Size to 7, and change the Color to white (click on the color swatch and choose white in the Color Picker) to give you the effect you see here. Now click OK. Next, you're going to add some vector background elements behind your subject. In the Layers panel, click on your white gradient layer, then create a new blank layer above it.

STEP 10: Now get the Custom Shape tool from the Toolbox (it's two below the Horizontal Type tool, or press **Shift-U** until you have it). Go up to the Options Bar and click on the third icon from the left (so you create pixel-based shapes, and not a path or Shape layer), then click on the Shape thumbnail to bring up the Shape Picker (shown here). Click on the right-facing arrow in the top-right corner of the Picker, and from the flyout menu that appears, choose All to load all the shapes that come with Photoshop. Click Append in the warning dialog. Next, scroll through the shapes and choose the Registration Target 2 shape you see here (it's right before the italic "i" shape). Make sure your Foreground is still white, click-and-drag out this shape at a large size, and position it behind his head, like you see here. Now lower the Opacity of this layer to 35% to help it blend in with the background.

Continued

STEP 11: Scroll through and find the shape that looks like paint splatters, as shown here (it's two shapes to the left of the American flag shape in the Shape Picker). Click-and-drag a large one of these out, and since it's on the 35% opacity layer, it automatically blends in. If you want to add another set of drips, add a new layer (as shown here), so once you drag out your drip, you can use Free Transform to rotate your shape (just move your cursor outside the bounding box until it turns into a two-headed arrow, then click-and-drag upward or downward in a circular motion to rotate), so it looks a little different (like I did here). Make sure you lower the new layer's Opacity to 35%, as well.

STEP 12: Now, get the Horizontal Type tool **(T)**, and add some text in white. I used the font Helvetica Bold Condensed—the small text is at a size of 17 points, and the large text (the middle line of each text block) is 44 points in size. Once your blocks of text are in place (like you see here), then use Free Transform to rotate your text counterclockwise so they look like what you see here. For the bottom block of text, I just duplicated one of the top Type layers, and used the Move tool to drag it to the bottom of the image. Then, I switched back to the Horizontal Type tool, highlighted the text, clicked on the color swatch in the Options Bar, changed the color to black, and typed in the fictitious name in all caps (as seen here) to complete the effect.

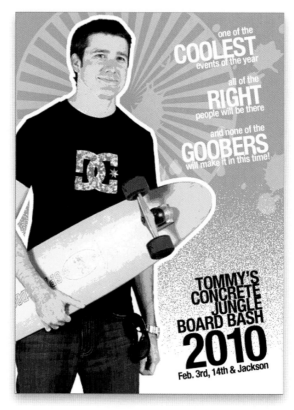

Creating Sparkle Trails

Photoshop genius-guy Corey Barker (my colleague and contributing author, who wrote the 3D chapter for this book) came up with this technique, and when he first showed it to me, I said, "Corey, you gotta let me include that in my new book." He was gracious enough to let me share this with you, and I've gotta tell ya—it rocks!!! It came from a Verizon Wireless ad that people emailed Corey about to ask if it could be recreated in Photoshop CS4. Well, it can (this is one you have to try for yourself to really fall in love with). Thanks, Corey, for letting me include your amazing technique in the book.

STEP ONE: Open the image you want to wrap a sparkle trail around (you can download the guitar image you see here from the book's downloads page, mentioned in the book's introduction). Press **D**, then **X** to set your Foreground color to white, then click on the Create a New Layer icon at the bottom of the Layers panel to create a new blank layer (this is where you'll test your trail to see that it looks right before you apply it).

STEP TWO: There's a specific brush you're going to need for this technique, but luckily it's already installed on your computer—you just have to load it into your Brush Picker. So, get the Brush tool **(B)**, then go up to the Options Bar and click on the Brush thumbnail to bring up the Brush Picker (shown here). Click on the right-facing arrow in the top-right corner of the Picker to bring up the flyout menu you see here, with a list of all the Photoshop brush sets you can load at the bottom of the menu. Choose Assorted Brushes to add that set of brushes to the Picker, then click Append in the warning dialog.

©ISTOCKPHOTO/SCOTT HIRKO

Continued

STEP THREE: Once they're loaded, scroll down in the Brush Picker until you find the 28-pixel brush (Texture 4) you see here. This is the brush you're going to use to make your sparkle trails, but the key to this trick is how you "hot rod" this brush.

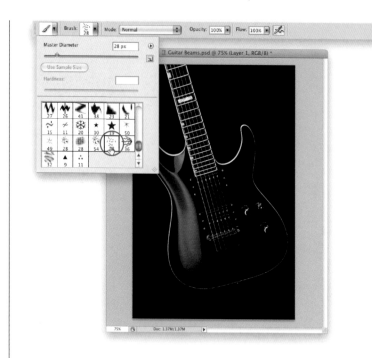

STEP FOUR: You're going to make your brush tweaks in the Brushes panel. To bring this panel up, click the button toward the far-right side of the Options Bar (seen in the previous step). When the Brushes panel appears (shown here), you're going to make changes in two different sections. First, in the list of options on the left side of the panel, click on Brush Tip Shape to bring up those options, then lower the Spacing amount to 1% (as shown here, circled in red). Now click on Shape Dynamics and, in the Control pop-up menu, you'll need to choose Pen Pressure, as shown here (you have to do this even if you're not using a Wacom wireless pen and tablet). Okay, that's all we have to do to the brush, but we've got some other tweaks coming up (don't worry—they're all pretty simple).

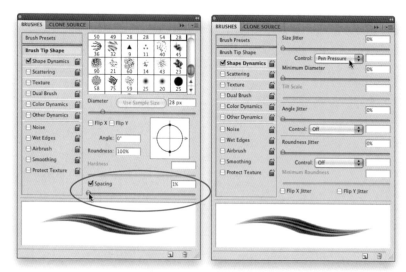

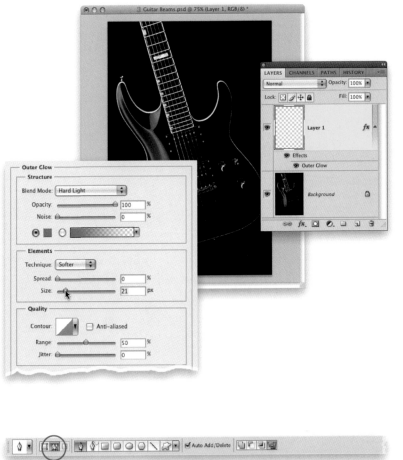

STEP FIVE: You're going to add an Outer Glow layer style to this layer, so when you draw your trail, it will get this effect added to it automatically (with layer styles, you're applying the effect to the entire layer—anything you do on this layer will get that effect). Click on the Add a Layer Style icon at the bottom of the Layers panel and choose Outer Glow from the pop-up menu. In the Layer Style dialog, change the Blend Mode to Hard Light, increase the Opacity to 100%, click on the color swatch and change the glow color to a bright magenta (I used R: 198, G: 0, B: 255), then increase your glow Size to 21 (as shown here), and click OK.

STEP SIX: Now you're going to draw a path with the Pen tool (don't worry, I'll walk you through it). Start by getting the Pen tool **(P)**, then go up to the Options Bar and click on the second icon from the left (the Paths icon—it's circled here in red). This sets the Pen tool to create a path only. Now take the Pen tool and click it once up near the top of the image, just to the left of the guitar neck (it's marked as #1 here). Move over to the other side of the neck, move down a little lower, and click, hold, and drag downward. As you drag, you'll see your curve appear (marked #2), and you can adjust the curve by how you move the little adjustment handle that appears. That's all there is to it—move your cursor to the left side of the guitar (marked #3), and just click to draw a straight line between the two. Now move over the guitar to point #4, click, hold, and drag, and so on, until you have the shape you see here. Once your points are in place, you can take the Direct Selection tool (the hollow arrow tool, press **Shift-A** until you have it), click on a point, and adjust the curve using the little handle points that appear, or you can just drag a point itself.

Continued

STEP SEVEN: You're going to have Photoshop automatically add a stroke along that path, and vary the stroke as if you had applied real pressure to the brush. To do that, first make sure your Foreground color is white, then go to the Paths panel (you can find it under the Window menu up top). When the panel appears, click the down-facing arrow in the top-right corner and, from the flyout menu that appears, choose Stroke Path (as shown here). This is where you tell Photoshop which tool to stroke the path with. In our case, we want it to be the Brush tool, so when the Stroke Path dialog appears, from the pop-up menu, choose Brush, then turn on the checkbox for Simulate Pressure (as seen here).

STEP EIGHT: When you click OK in the Stroke Path dialog, a white stroke is applied to your path, but since you've applied a magenta Outer Glow layer style to this layer, the white appears on the inside of the stroke, and the outsides have almost a neon-like glow to them (as seen here). You probably want to hide your path, so you can see just the stroke (after all, we're done with the path now anyway), so go to the Paths panel and click in the gray empty space below your Work Path to deselect your path. Now, let's add one more tweak to really take this technique to the next level.

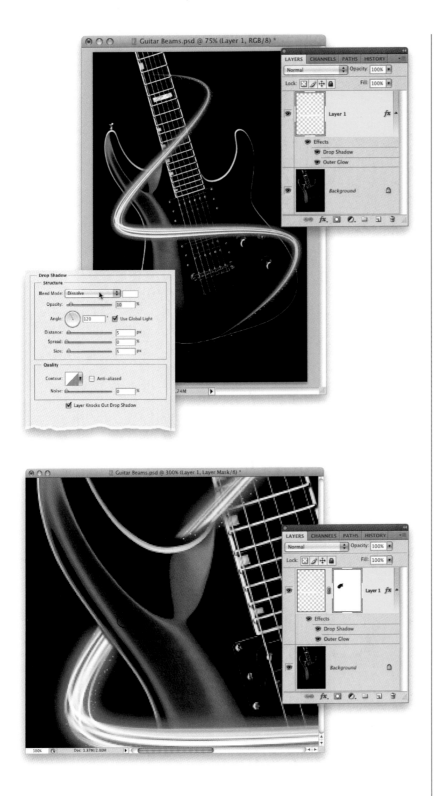

STEP NINE: Go back to the Layers panel and click on the Add a Layer Style icon again at the bottom of the panel, then choose Drop Shadow from the pop-up menu. You're going to add a slight drop shadow to your layer, but more importantly, you're going to change the blend mode of just the drop shadow, so it creates little sparkles that come off your stroke, that really enhance the look big time. When the Layer Style dialog appears, lower the Opacity to 10%, then change the Blend Mode of this drop shadow to Dissolve (as seen here), click on the color swatch to the right of the Blend Mode pop-up menu and change your drop shadow color to white, then click OK, and that creates the little sparks that come off your stroke.

STEP 10: To make your sparkle trail look like it's wrapping around your guitar, click on the Add Layer Mask icon at the bottom of the Layers panel, and press **D**, then **X** to set your Foreground color to black. Get the Brush tool, choose a small-sized, soft-edged round brush from the Brush Picker, then paint over the part of the stroke that appears over the top-left part of the body of the guitar (I switched to the Zoom tool **[Z]** and zoomed in here, so you could see that area easily). There will be a little spillover on the edges because of the glow, but that's okay—just paint over as much of the stroke in that area as you can (as shown here).

Continued

STEP 11: When you zoom back out, you'll see that your stroke looks like it's wrapping around the guitar, rather than just going over it. Now create a new layer, and put a copy of your two layer styles (Outer Glow and Drop Shadow) onto this layer by pressing-and-holding the **Option (PC: Alt) key** and, in the Layers panel, under your stroke layer, clicking-and-dragging the word "Effects" right up onto your new blank layer. This makes a copy of those layer styles and applies them to this layer. Let's create another path, a simpler one, on the other side (all the hard work's already been done, so once you draw the path, everything else happens in just a few clicks). Get the Pen tool, click it once up at the top of the left side of the guitar body, then click, hold, and drag to the other side of the guitar's neck, and down a bit. Click, hold, and drag once more, way down near the bottom of the image window, on the bottom-left side of the guitar (as shown here).

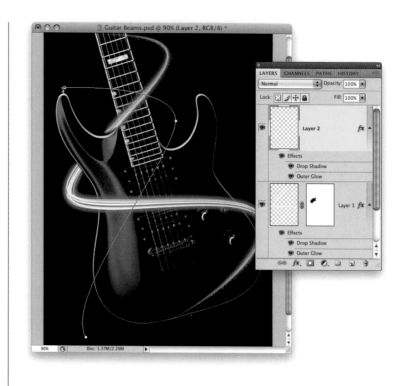

STEP 12: Now, make sure your Foreground color is set to white, go to the Paths panel and, from its flyout menu, choose Stroke Path. Make sure Brush is selected, and the Simulate Pressure checkbox is turned on in the dialog, then click OK to stroke your new path with a white-and-magenta stroke. Go to that layer in the Layers panel and double-click directly on the words "Outer Glow" to bring up the Outer Glow options in the Layer Style dialog. Change the color of your glow from magenta to a bright neon-green (I used R: 12, G: 255, B: 0), and click OK to change the color of your second stroke (as seen here). Go back to the Paths panel now and deselect that path, so you just see the stroke.

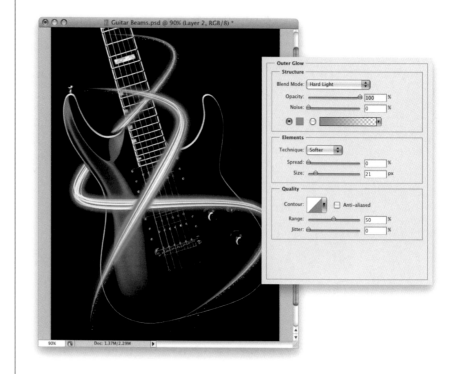

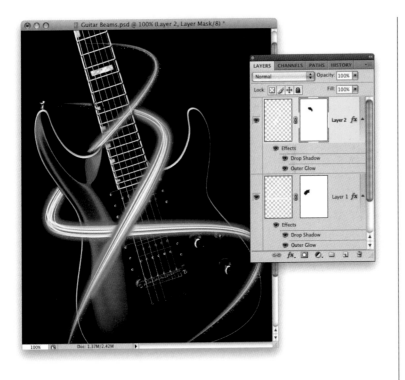

STEP 13: You're going to hide part of that stroke behind the guitar so, once again, it looks like you're wrapping the stroke around the guitar. Click on the Add Layer Mask icon, get the Brush tool, and paint in black over the part of the green stroke that appears over the neck of the guitar.

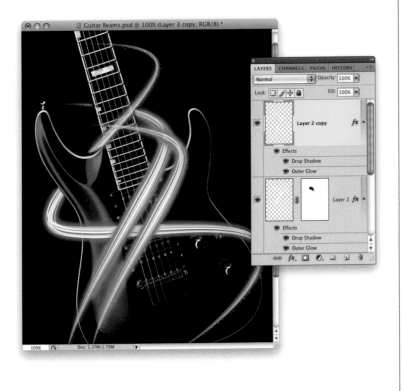

STEP 14: To really help "sell" the idea that sparkle trails are wrapping around the guitar, let's create a reflection of the green trail on the guitar. Press **Command-J (PC: Ctrl-J)** to duplicate your green stroke layer. Click on the duplicate layer's layer mask and drag it down onto the Trash icon at the bottom of the Layers panel. Click Delete in the warning dialog. Then get the Move tool **(V)** and drag your duplicate stroke down and to the right, as shown here (position it kind of like where a drop shadow would go if you were making it from scratch).

Continued

STEP 15: Add a layer mask, then paint over the parts of the reflection that extend outside the body of the guitar (that's a change, eh?), so that the reflection just appears within the body of the guitar (not on the background or neck). Now go to the Layers panel and lower the Opacity of this reflection layer to 30% (as shown here). By the way, if you wanted to do the same thing with the purple stroke layer, just follow the same steps (you can see I did that in the final shot below).

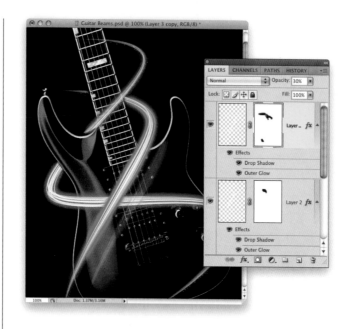

STEP 16: If you want to add a logo, or company name, I've got just the place—the bottom-left corner (seeing as both sparkle trails are aiming there). Get the Horizontal Type tool **(T)**, set white as your Foreground color, then add your text. I used the font Satisfaction from MyFonts.com. (It cost me 12 bucks. Cheap!) Once your text is in place, press-and-hold the Option (PC: Alt) key and drag-and-drop the word "Effects" (below the stroke reflection layer) right onto this new layer, so the glow and drop shadow effects are added automatically (as seen here). A final note: Once I had two reflections in place, the reflections seemed too busy, so I lowered the Opacity setting for both sparkle trail reflection layers to 20% for the final look you see here.

Two-Photo Quick Blend

This is a very quick Down & Dirty technique that's popular with portrait photographers for combining two shots into one collage. The technique has you shooting one shot that's farther back (so it's almost a full-body shot) and one shot nice and close (kind of a head-and-shoulders shot), and then using a simple layer mask trick to blend the two photos together.

SCOTT KELBY

STEP ONE: Start by creating a new document that is 800 pixels wide by 600 pixels high at a resolution of 72 ppi. Press **D** to set your Foreground color to black, then fill your Background layer with black by pressing **Option-Delete (PC: Alt-Backspace)**. Now open the first of the two images you want to blend together (the first one is shown here. You can download this same photo from the book's downloads page, listed in the intro of the book).

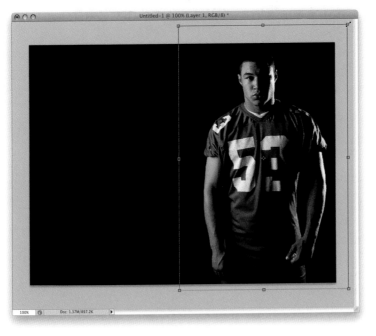

STEP TWO: Get the Move tool **(V)** and drag-and-drop this photo onto your black background, then position the player over to the far-right side of the image (as seen here). The image is larger than the background, so you'll have to scale it down in size. Press **Command-T (PC: Ctrl-T)** to bring up Free Transform, then press **Command-0 (zero; PC: Ctrl-0)** to expand the image window so you can reach all the Free Transform handles. Press-and-hold the Shift key (to keep him proportional), click on the top-right corner point, and drag inward to resize the image so its size looks like what you see here. When it looks good to you, press **Return (PC: Enter)** to lock in your transformation.

Continued

STEP THREE: Open the second photo (you can download this one too, of course), and with the Move tool, drag-and-drop it onto your main document, then position it over to the far left, like you see here. If you feel the photo needs resizing, use Free Transform again. Now, to create your blend, first click on the Add Layer Mask icon at the bottom of the Layers panel (it's shown circled in red here), then press **X** to set your Foreground color to black. Now, get the Gradient tool **(G)** from the Toolbox, click on the Linear Gradient icon up in the Options Bar (the first one on the left), then click on the down-facing arrow next to the gradient thumbnail to open the Gradient Picker, and click on the top-left gradient (Foreground to Background) in the Picker. Click-and-drag the gradient from just inside the right edge of the larger photo over to the left, until you almost reach his lips (as shown here).

STEP FOUR: Dragging that gradient creates the blend, and fades the right side of the larger photo into the left, to create the simple and quick composite you see here. If there's a particular part of the image you wish hadn't faded, you can bring back in just that area by switching to the Brush tool **(B)**, choosing a large, soft-edged brush (from the Brush Picker up in the Options Bar), pressing **X** to switch your Foreground color to white, and painting over that area on the layer mask, and that area will return to 100% opacity.

CHAPTER **9**

3D Jamboree

3D effects

I know this sounds like kind of a weenie title for my first-ever chapter on 3D effects, but if you think that's bad, what's worse is it's not really my chapter at all, because I brought in my buddy, and Photoshop 3D wizard, Corey Barker to write this chapter. The reason I asked Corey to do this is because I'm essentially a 2D guy. Things in my world don't have a backside (stop snickering), so I had to get some help, and since Corey actually works for my company, he was surprisingly willing to take on this project. Now, before we go on to something very important (which is breaking with the tradition of these intros being just strictly for a mental break), the chapter name "3D Jamboree" is taken from a 1956 movie short hosted by Disney's original Mouseketeers (including Annette Funicello), who intro a number of cartoons shown in 3D. Believe it or not, *3D Jamboree* was one of the better movie names. I could have gone with any of these actual movie titles: *3D Ant Attack*, *3D Frog Man*, *Bubsy 3D*, or *3D Tetrimania*. Anyway, the important part of all this is if you go up to Photoshop's menu bar and you don't see a menu named "3D," it means you don't have the Extended version of Photoshop (which, of course, costs more than regular Photoshop). Hey, don't shoot me, I'm only a 2D guy livin' in a 3D world.

True 3D Lights and Shadows

Here we are going to do something that you just couldn't do in any other version of Photoshop—we are going to create lights and shadows using the new 3D features built right inside Photoshop CS4 Extended. The fact that you can not only create 3D layers and shapes, but also create and manipulate lights in a 3D space, opens up so many creative possibilities that you will find yourself trying many different arrangements, once you find out how easy it can be.

STEP ONE: Begin by going under the File menu, choosing New, and creating a new blank document that is 9 inches by 6 inches at around 100 ppi.

STEP TWO: At the bottom of the Layers panel, click on the Create a New Layer icon to create a new blank layer. Fill this new layer with 50% gray by pressing **Shift-Delete (PC: Shift-Backspace)** to open the Fill dialog, then choosing 50% Gray from the Use pop-up menu, and clicking OK.

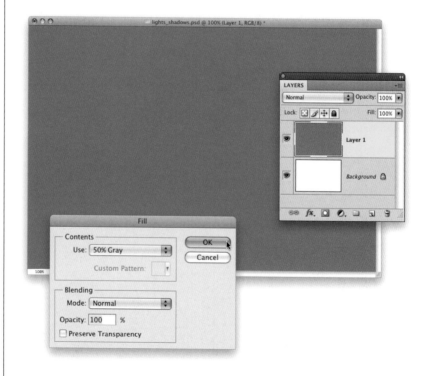

STEP THREE: Get the Horizontal Type tool **(T)** from the Toolbox, press **D** to set your Foreground and Background colors to their defaults of black and white, and then click on your document to create a Type layer. Here, I typed the word "NOW" using the font Georgia Regular. Get the Move tool (by clicking on it in the Toolbox), and then press **Command-T (PC: Ctrl-T)** to bring up Free Transform. Press-and-hold the Shift key to keep the type proportional, and then click on a corner point and drag inward (or outward) to scale the type to fit in the document, like you see here. Press **Return (PC: Enter)** to lock in your transformation. Now, center the type in the document by pressing **Command-A (PC: Ctrl-A)** to select your entire document, then click on the Align Vertical Centers and Align Horizontal Centers icons up in the Options Bar (both are shown circled here in red). Press **Command-D (PC: Ctrl-D)** to Deselect.

STEP FOUR: With the Type layer still active in the Layers panel, go under Photoshop's 3D menu and choose New 3D Postcard From Layer. This will turn this Type layer into a 3D layer. Do the same thing to the gray layer just below (you can tell that these are now 3D layers by the little cube icons that appear at the bottom right of the layer thumbnails).

Continued

STEP FIVE: With the gray layer still active, go to the Toolbox and select the 3D Rotate tool **(K)**, and then in the Options Bar, enter –90 in the X Orientation field. The gray in the layer will seem to have disappeared, but it has merely rotated on its side, which we can't see because it's flat. (*Note:* Go to the book's downloads page for a video tutorial on the basics of using the 3D tools.)

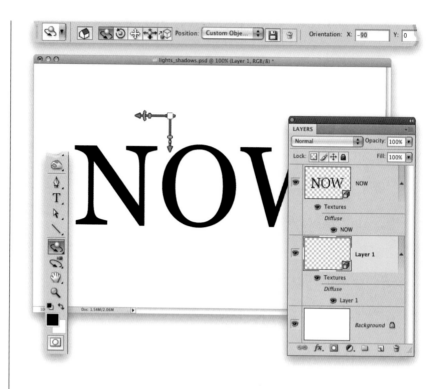

STEP SIX: Now, press-and-hold the Shift key and click on the Type layer, so that both 3D layers are selected in the Layers panel, then go to the 3D menu and choose Merge 3D Layers. This will combine these two 3D objects into one layer. However, we can still manipulate each 3D object individually using the 3D panel.

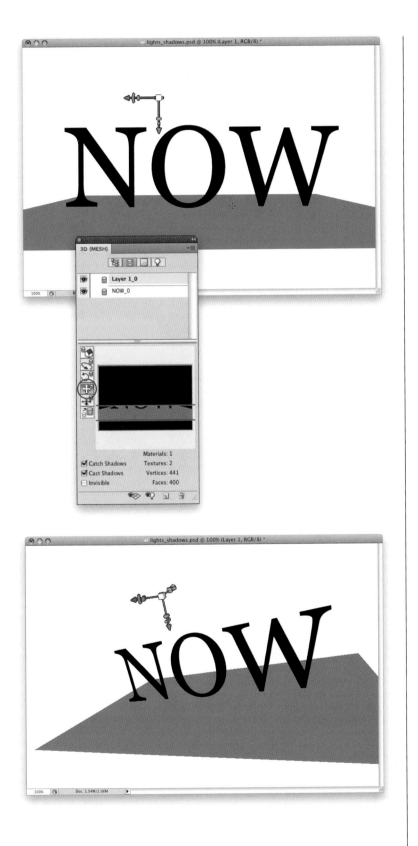

STEP SEVEN: Go under the Window menu and choose 3D to open the 3D panel, then at the top of the panel, click on the Filter By: Meshes icon (the second icon from the left), and the two objects in this 3D layer will appear near the top of the panel, with the Mesh options appearing below. With Layer 1_0 highlighted at the top, click on the Drag the Mesh tool (shown circled here) in the middle left of the panel. Press-and-hold the Shift key, then click-and-drag down in the document, until the gray 3D layer is right at the bottom of the letters.

STEP EIGHT: Now, get the 3D Rotate tool again, and rotate the object to get the most dramatic angle. This is one thing that is really cool about 3D—you can change the angle anytime. *Note:* That little red, green, and blue 3D icon on the document here is the Axis widget, which only appears when a 3D tool is selected. To reposition it in your document, simply hover your cursor over it and you will see a small gray bar appear above it. Click anywhere on the gray bar, and then click-and-drag the bar to reposition it (and the widget) within your document. The icon on the left end of the gray bar minimizes the widget to a very small icon. The icon on the right allows you to scale the widget to a custom size—just click on that icon and then click-and-drag, and the widget will increase and decrease in size.

Continued

STEP NINE: We'll need to enlarge the gray plane layer, so we can see the light hitting it. So, go back to the Mesh options in the 3D panel, and click on the Scale the Mesh tool (it's the bottom tool on the middle left). Now, click-and-drag straight up in the document to increase the size of the gray plane layer. Increase it so there is more area for the light's shadow to cast onto.

STEP 10: Now, in the Layers panel, click on the Background layer and then fill it with 50% gray, as well (using the Fill shortcut that you used in Step Two). This will make it seem as though the background is uniform with the 3D layer.

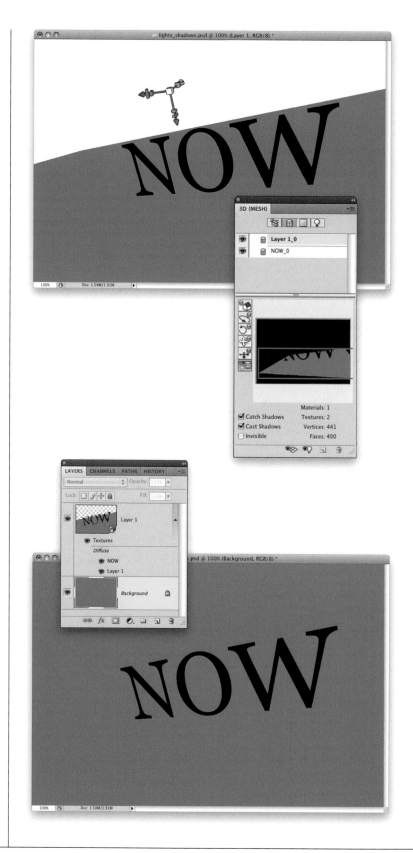

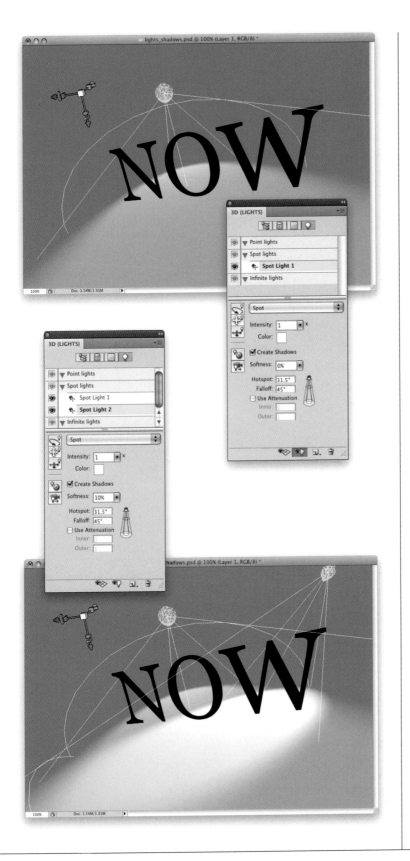

STEP 11: Click back on the 3D layer in the Layers panel, and then at the top of the 3D panel, click on the Filter By: Lights icon (it's the last icon on the right at the top of the panel). Now, click on the down-facing arrow at the top right of the 3D panel and, from the flyout menu, choose New Spot Light. This is where it can get tricky and may require some practice. First, turn on the wireframe of the light by clicking on the Toggle Lights icon at the bottom of the panel (it's the second icon from the left). We need to position the light behind the text and shining back towards us, and you do this by using the 3D Lights tools in the middle left of the 3D panel. You can choose from the Rotate the Light tool, the Drag the Light tool, or the Slide the Light tool. I would suggest just playing around with each one to get a feel for how they work. Fortunately, you can see the light on the object, so it helps to position it. Here, I have rotated the spotlight toward us using the Rotate the Light tool, then I used the Drag the Light and Slide the Light tools to push it back and above the type. (*Note:* Remember to go to the book's downloads page and watch the video on the basics of using the 3D tools.)

STEP 12: Next, create a second spotlight (by going under the panel's flyout menu again, or by just clicking on the Create a New Light icon at the bottom of the 3D panel, and choosing New Spot Light from the pop-up menu) and position it behind the lettering as we did with the first one, but position it on the right side and make it cross beams with the other spotlight.

Continued

STEP 13: Now, go back to the 3D panel and click on the Filter By: Whole Scene icon at the top (the first icon from the left) to access the Scene options. From the Preset pop-up menu in the middle of the panel, choose Ray Traced. This will render the shadows based on the lights in the scene.

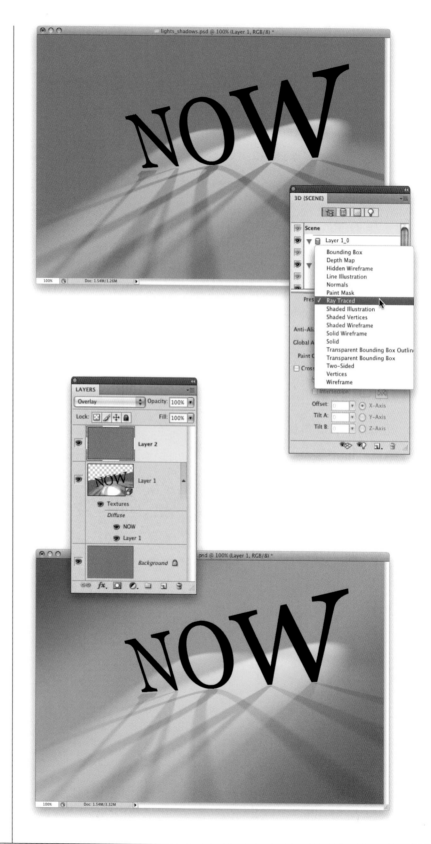

STEP 14: Go to the Layers panel, and create a new blank layer. Then, click on the Foreground color swatch in the Toolbox, choose a tan color (or really any color you like) and press **Option-Delete (PC: Alt-Backspace)** to fill the new layer with this color. Change this layer's blend mode to Overlay at the top of the Layers panel, and this will color the entire image to make it more interesting. (*Note*: Remember, you can change the color of the over-all image by filling this new layer with a new color.)

STEP 15: With the lights and color layer in place, using the 3D Rotate tool, you can rotate the 3D layer to a new angle and the lights will adjust accordingly, but the only thing is you'll need to change the Scene Preset pop-up menu in the 3D panel back to Solid before you change the angle, and then just set it back to Ray Traced when you're done to render the shadows.

3D Package Design

In order to create a 3D package design in earlier versions of Photoshop, you would have had to distort each side of a box individually and hope you got the perspective right. As smart as most applications are these days, why don't we let it do that kind of thinking for us? Here, we are going to take some existing label art and create a 3D package using the preset 3D shapes built into Photoshop CS4 Extended.

STEP ONE: It all starts with a label. Here, I have created a fictional label based on an obvious real product. While, in this tutorial, we are only going to be creating a backdrop and then applying this logo to a 3D object, you can download this image and view an online tutorial on how to create the entire label at **www.kelbytraining.com/books/CS4DD**.

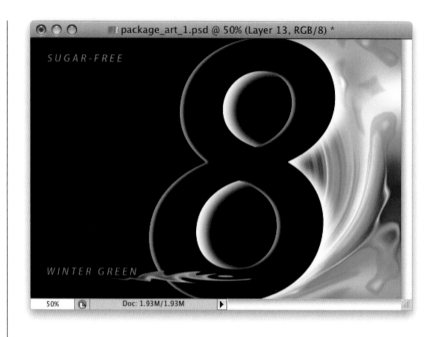

STEP TWO: Go under the File menu, choose New, and create a new blank document that is 7 inches wide by 5 inches tall at 125 ppi. (*Note*: If you're creating this for print, you will want to create it at a higher resolution.) Now, press **D** to set your Foreground and Background colors to their defaults of black and white, then press **Command-I (PC: Ctrl-I)** to Invert the white Background layer to black.

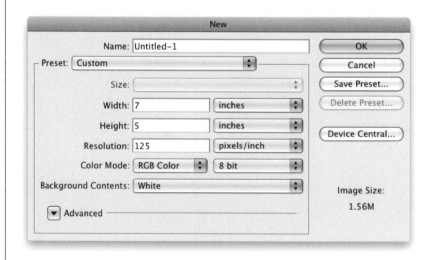

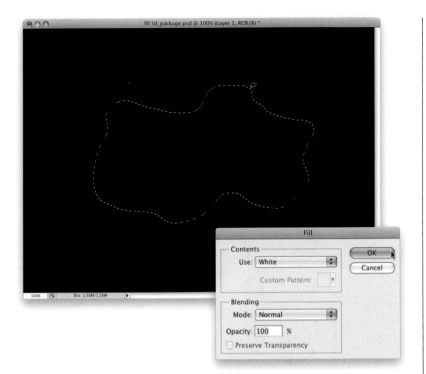

STEP THREE: Grab the Lasso tool **(L)** in the Toolbox and draw a very loose selection around the center of the canvas, like you see here, and then click on the Create a New Layer icon at the bottom of the Layers panel to create a new layer for this selection. Press **Shift-Delete (PC: Shift-Backspace)** to open the Fill dialog, choose White from the Use pop-up menu, and click OK. Now, press **Command-D (PC: Ctrl-D)** to Deselect.

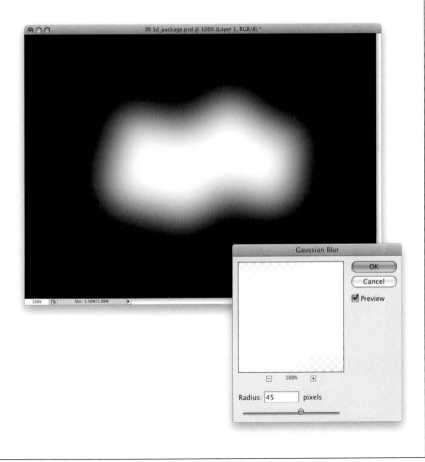

STEP FOUR: Go under the Filter menu, under Blur, and choose Gaussian Blur. Set the Radius to 45 pixels, and click OK.

Continued

STEP FIVE: With this layer still selected in the Layers panel, change the blend mode to Dissolve at the top of the panel, and then create a new layer beneath this one by pressing-and-holding the Command (PC: Ctrl) key and clicking on the Create a New Layer icon. Click back on the Dissolve layer, then click on the Layers panel's flyout menu, and choose Merge Down (or press **Command-E [PC: Ctrl-E]**). This will make the Dissolve permanent and change the layer's blend mode back to Normal, which we'll need to apply our next filter.

STEP SIX: Go under the Filter menu again, under Blur, and choose Motion Blur. Set the Angle to 0, the Distance to 250 pixels, and click OK.

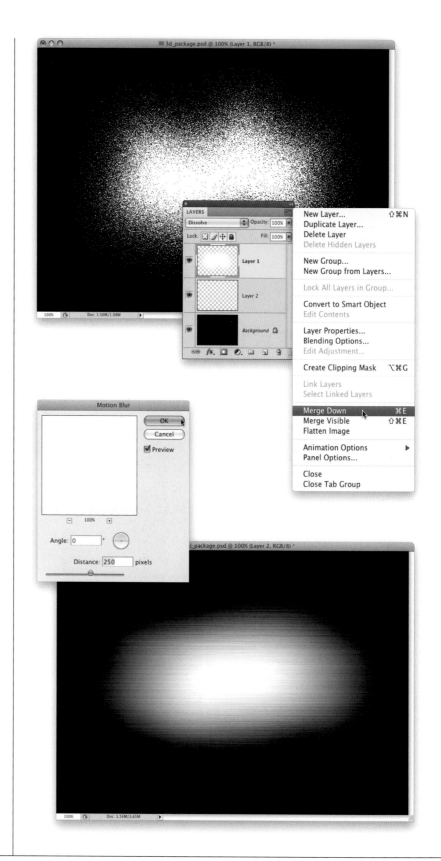

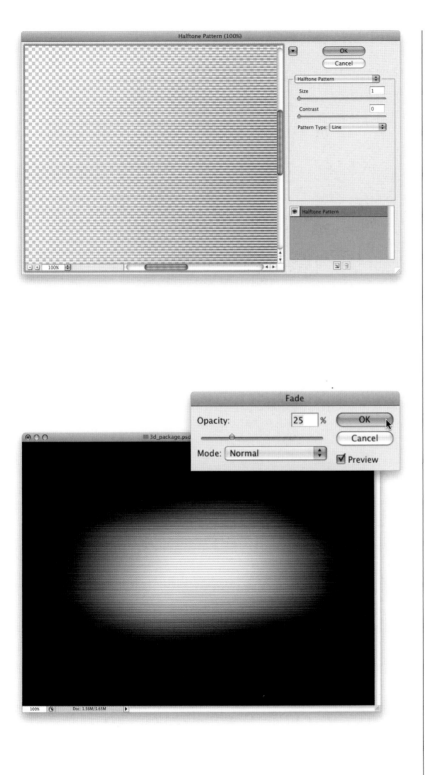

STEP SEVEN: Now, guess what? We're going to go under the Filter menu again, but this time, go under Sketch and choose Halftone Pattern. In this dialog, set the Size to 1 and the Contrast to 0, then from the Pattern Type pop-up menu, choose Line, and click OK.

STEP EIGHT: Next, go under the Edit menu and choose Fade Halftone Pattern—this option is only available right after you apply a filter. When the dialog opens, set the Opacity to 25% and click OK.

Continued

STEP NINE: In the Adjustments panel, click on the Hue/Saturation icon (it's the second icon from the left, in the second row). In the Hue/Saturation options, turn on the Colorize checkbox, set the Hue to 143, and then set the Saturation to 43 (as shown here). We are looking to get a green color similar to our original label. If you want to use a different color, simply drag the Hue slider to the left or right and use the Saturation slider to adjust the intensity of the color.

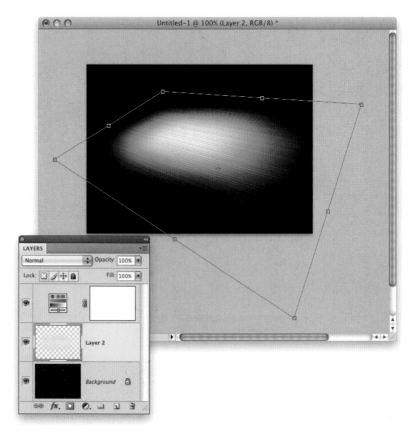

STEP 10: Now, in the Layers panel, click back on your shape layer (Layer 2), then press **Command-T (PC: Ctrl-T)** to bring up Free Transform. Control-click (PC: Right-click) inside the bounding box and choose Distort from the contextual menu. Using the corner handles, click-and-drag outward, creating the effect of a 3D plane, as you see here—don't worry about scaling it out of proportion as it is merely a background element. You can also use the middle handles to change the size of the shape, as well (if you can't see the corner handles when you enter Free Transform, just press **Command-0 [zero; PC: Ctrl-0]** and your image window will resize, so you can see them). When you're done, press **Return (PC: Enter)** to lock in your transformation.

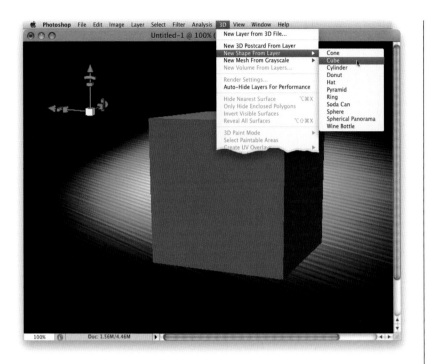

STEP 11: Let's now create the 3D object for our package. First, click on the top layer in your layer stack, and create a new blank layer, then go under the 3D menu, under New Shape From Layer, and choose Cube. This will produce a multi-colored 3D cube contained in a 3D layer.

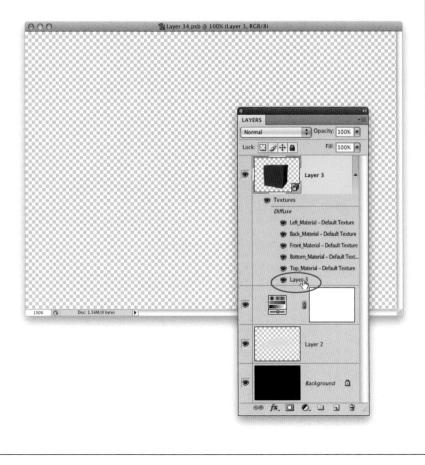

STEP 12: You will see that the 3D layer contains numerous sub-layers, which contain the texture files for each surface of the 3D shape. Go to the bottom of the list of sub-layers and double-click on the layer named "Layer 3" (circled here in red). This will open a separate file, similar to that of a Smart Object.

Continued

STEP 13: Open the file containing the label mentioned in Step One. Using the Move tool **(V)**, press-and-hold the Shift key, and drag-and-drop the label into the 3D texture layer document (holding the Shift key will place the image centered in the document). You'll see the label now appears on the cube in your main document (as shown in the next step). Use Free Transform to scale the label to fit the cube, if necessary. (*Note*: You'll need to press **Command-S [PC: Ctrl-S]** to Save the texture layer document in order to see the transformation in your main document. If it still doesn't look right, you can keep transforming and saving until it fits properly.) Once it looks good, save the changes and close the document.

STEP 14: The label may appear very dark on the object and this is because of the default lights applied to this 3D shape. Since we don't need the lights, go under the 3D menu and choose Render Settings. Near the top of the resulting dialog, from the Face Style pop-up menu, select Unlit Texture, and click OK.

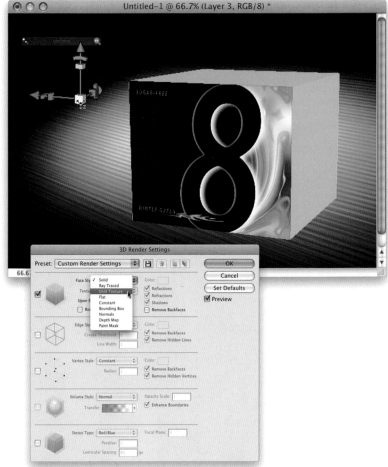

STEP 15: Now we need to make the cube a little thinner by modifying the 3D shape using the Axis widget, which only appears when a 3D tool is selected, so go ahead and press **K** to get the 3D Rotate tool. The widget allows you to modify different aspects of your 3D shape. You'll notice each line has three shapes: the arrow allows you to move the object only on that axis; the curved line isolates the rotation of the shape only to that axis; and the cube shape resizes the shape on that axis. Position your cursor over the cube on the red line and it will highlight in yellow (as shown circled here in the overlay). Then simply click-and-drag to the left to squeeze in the depth of the box.

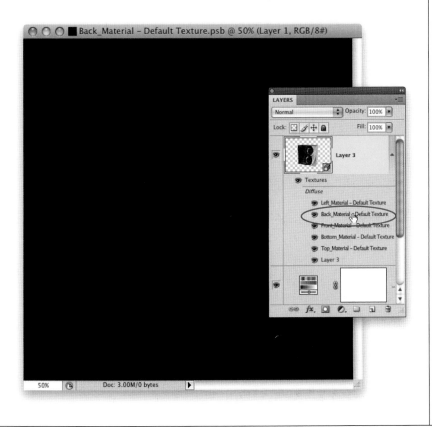

STEP 16: Next, we need to fill in the sides of the cube, so go back in the Layers panel, and double-click on the 3D sub-layer named "Back_Material-Default Texture." This will open a blank document. Press Shift-Delete to open the Fill dialog, select Black from the Use pop-up menu, and then click OK. Now, save the change, close this document, and this will fill in the top side of the cube.

Continued

STEP 17: Double-click on the sub-layer named "Bottom_Material-Default Texture." Select the gradient tool **(G)** from the Toolbox and then click on the gradient thumbnail in the Options Bar to open the Gradient Editor. Create a black-to-green gradient by double-clicking on the bottom-right color stop beneath the gradient ramp and sampling the green from the background in your main document, then in the Options Bar, click on the Radial Gradient icon (the second icon from the left). Starting at the bottom-right corner, draw the gradient up to the upper-left corner. Save the changes, then close the document, and this will fill the side of the cube. While I only did this to the sides that are visible (as you'll see in the next step), you can certainly continue to fill all the other sides, if you like.

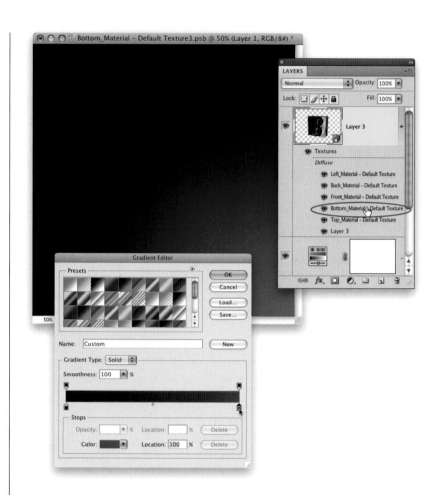

STEP 18: With the 3D Rotate tool, click-and-drag around the object to freely rotate the object to get the best positioning. You can also use the 3D Slide tool (press **Shift-K** until you have it) to push the object back in space. (*Note:* Go to the book's downloads page for a video tutorial on the basics of using the 3D tools.)

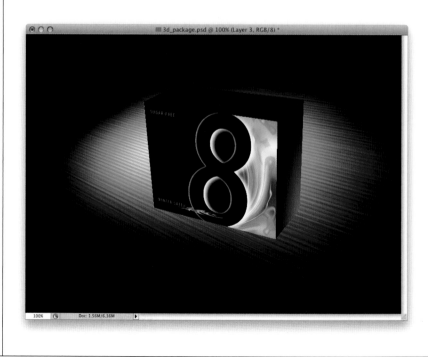

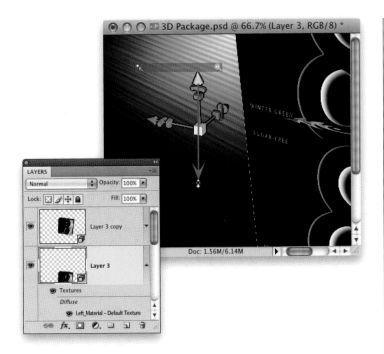

STEP 19: Create a duplicate of the 3D layer by pressing **Command-J (PC: Ctrl-J)**, then click back on the original 3D layer in the Layers panel. With the 3D Rotate tool, go to the Axis widget and click on the blue axis line arrowhead, then click-and-drag downward until the original and duplicate are edge-to-edge (as shown here). Since it is moving on a 3D axis, it makes for a perfect reflection. (*Note:* The copy that you just made will now be your original 3D cube layer; the original layer will now be used as the reflection layer.)

STEP 20: We do, however, need to flip the reflected label, so simply double-click on the 3D sub-layer named "Layer 3" (as shown here) and it will open in its own image window. Go to the Edit menu, choose Transform, and then choose Flip Vertical. Close this file and save the changes, and now the reflected image is mirrored.

Continued

STEP 21: Now, at the bottom of the Layers panel, click on the Add Layer Mask icon to add a layer mask to the 3D reflection layer. Select the Gradient tool in the Toolbox, and then press **X** to set the Foreground color to black. In the Options Bar, click on the Linear Gradient icon (the first icon from the left), then click on the down-facing arrow to the right of the gradient thumbnail, and choose the Foreground to Transparent gradient (the second icon from the left, in the top row) in the Gradient Picker. Start at the very bottom of the reflected image and click-and-drag up to the top of the reflection to have it fade away.

STEP 22: Finally, in the 3D panel (found under the Window menu), in the Filter By: Whole Scene options (they should appear by default. If not, click on the first icon on the left at the top), change the Anti-Alias pop-up menu from Draft to Best. This will clean up the jagged lines around the edges. Here's the final image, where I've also added some text (using the font HemiHead426).

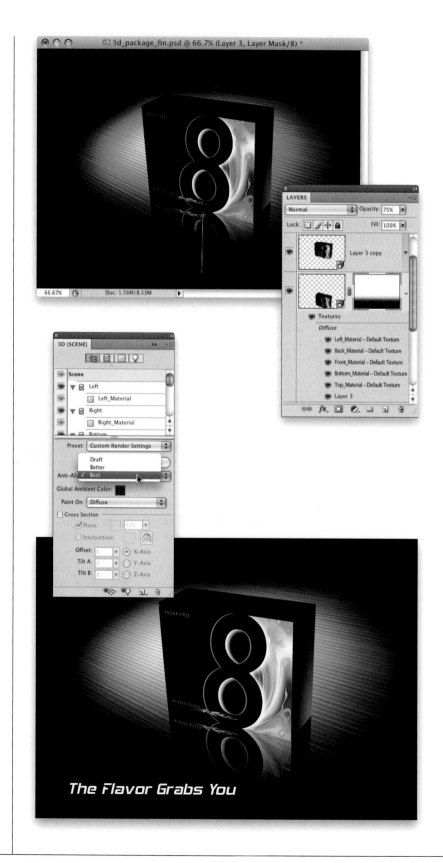

3D Filmstrip

Creating a filmstrip effect is nothing really new, although it still makes for a great design element. There have been so many different tutorials on creating a filmstrip, but perhaps not one quite like this. That's because we are creating it in real 3D right here in Photoshop CS4 Extended. Before we do that, though, we need to create the actual film graphic with photos in each frame, then we will create the 3D shape, complete with lights and reflections.

STEP ONE: Start by going under the File menu, choosing New, and creating a new document that is 16 inches wide by 3.5 inches tall at 125 ppi. Also, change the bit depth to 16 bit, as it seems that certain 3D effects tend to look better in 16-bit mode. Set the Background Contents pop-up menu to White, then click OK. Now, change the background to black by pressing **Command-I (PC: Ctrl-I)**.

STEP TWO: Click on the Create a New Layer icon at the bottom of the Layers panel to create a new blank layer. Grab the Rectangular Marquee tool **(M)** from the Toolbox, press-and-hold the Shift key, and draw a small square selection in the upper-left corner of your document (holding the Shift key as you drag maintains proportion). Press **Shift-Delete (PC: Shift-Backspace)** to open the Fill dialog, choose White from the Use pop-up menu, click OK, and this will fill your selection with white. Now, switch to the Move tool **(V)**, press-and-hold **Option-Shift (PC: Alt-Shift)**, and click-and-drag a duplicate of your white square to the bottom of the canvas, keeping it the same distance from the edge as the top square.

Continued

STEP THREE: Now, we are going to duplicate these shapes across the entire canvas. So, load these two shapes as a selection by Command-clicking (PC: Ctrl-clicking) on their layer's thumbnail in the Layers panel (it is important to have the objects selected in order to keep all the duplicates on the same layer, otherwise Photoshop would create a new layer for each). Press **Command-Option-T (Ctrl-Alt-T)** to bring up Free Transform in copy mode, press-and-hold the Shift key, and then hit the Right Arrow key four to six times to duplicate the shapes, creating space in between them as you see here. Press **Return (PC: Enter)** to commit your duplication. Now, press-and-hold **Command-Option-Shift (PC: Ctrl-Alt-Shift)** and keep pressing the **T key** until you have squares spanning the entire length of the document (as shown on the bottom here). Press **Command-D (PC: Ctrl-D)** to Deselect.

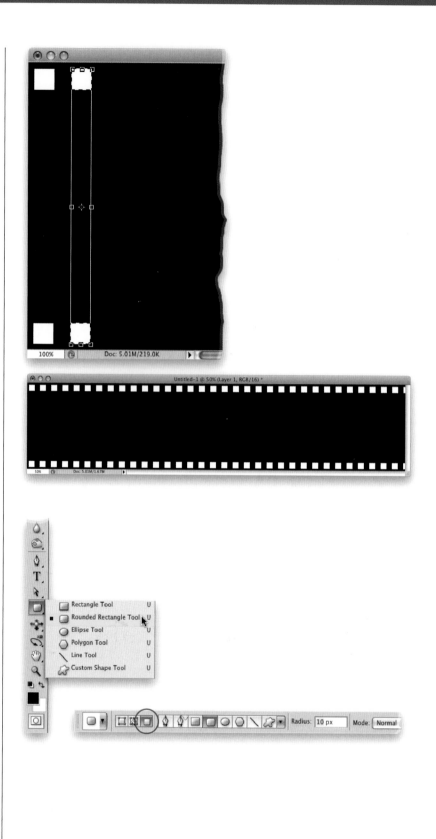

STEP FOUR: Get the Rounded Rectangle tool from the Toolbox (or press **Shift-U** until you have it) and then, in the Options Bar, click on the Fill Pixels icon (it's the third icon from the left, shown circled here in red), and set the Radius to 10 pixels.

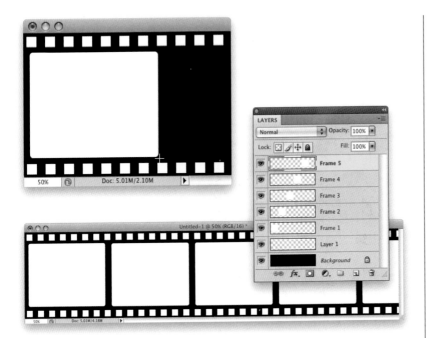

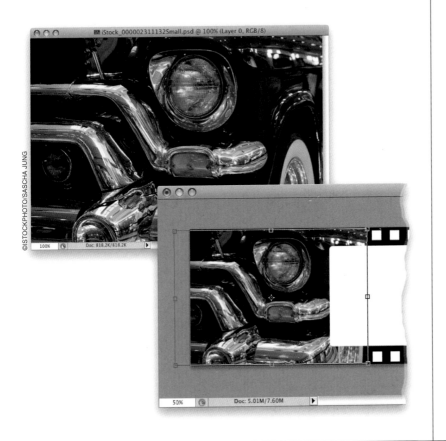

©ISTOCKPHOTO/SASCHA JUNG

STEP FIVE: Create a new blank layer and, with your Foreground color set to white, click-and-drag with the Rounded Rectangle tool to create a frame in the filmstrip (as shown here). Now, we need to create additional frames, so to keep the spacing the same, I would suggest doing the same thing we did in Step Three when we duplicated the small squares. Although, this time, don't Command-click (PC: Ctrl-click) on the layer's thumbnail because, in this case, we want each duplicate to be on its own layer. Just to make things easier as you go along, it might be a good idea to name each of the frame layers. Here, I have named them as they go from left to right "Frame 1," "Frame 2," etc.

STEP SIX: Click on the first frame layer in the Layers panel, and then open the image you want to place in this first frame. Here, I am going for a car theme. With the image open, get the Move tool, and drag-and-drop it into the film document. Press **Command-T (PC: Ctrl-T)** to bring up Free Transform, click on a corner point, and drag inward to scale the image down, then position it over the first frame (as shown here), and press **Return (PC: Enter)** to lock in your transformation.

Continued

STEP SEVEN: Now, to make this image visible only within that frame, simply press-and-hold the Option (PC: Alt) key and click right in between these layers in the Layers panel (as shown here). This will create a clipping group out of these two layers, leaving you free to move the car image around beneath the frame, so you can better position it.

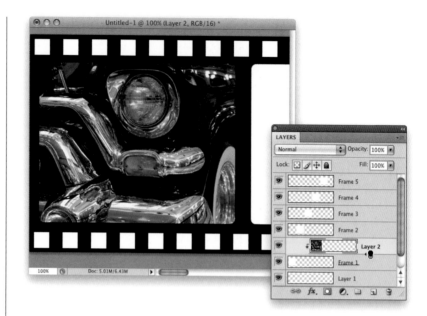

STEP EIGHT: Continue this process for each frame with a new image, or use the same image if you'd like. When you're done, you'll have an image clipped into each frame, like you see here.

©ISTOCKPHOTO

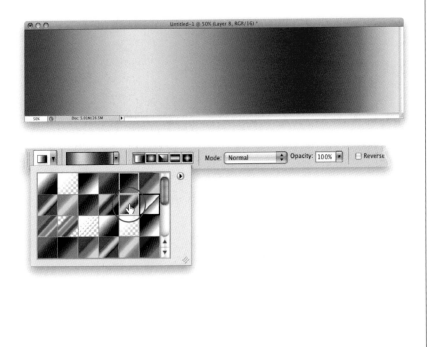

STEP NINE: Next, we want to merge all of these layers together without flattening the file, just in case we need to go back and change something. So, click on the top layer in the layer stack, press-and-hold the Option (PC: Alt) key, and from the Layers panel's flyout menu, choose Merge Visible. This will create a new layer with a flattened version of the image.

STEP 10: Create yet another blank layer, go to the Toolbox and get the Gradient tool **(G)**, and then click on the down-facing arrow to the right of the gradient thumbnail in the Options Bar to bring up the Gradient Picker. Now, normally, I might go ahead and create a new custom gradient here, but I discovered that the preset gradient called Copper worked beautifully for this effect, so choose that gradient (shown here). Click the Gradient tool on the left side of the canvas, press-and-hold the Shift key (to keep your gradient straight), and then drag all the way to the right side of the canvas.

Continued

STEP 11: Now, go under the 3D menu, under New Mesh From Grayscale, and choose Plane. What will happen is Photoshop will assess the grayscale values of the image. While we see it in color, Photoshop will interpret its light and dark tones—pushing darker areas further away and bringing lighter areas closer—resulting in a ribbon effect or, in this case, a film effect.

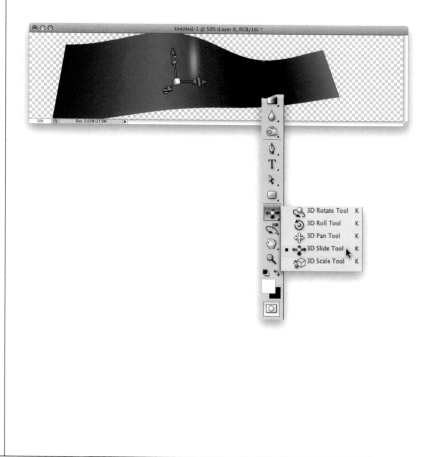

STEP 12: The object may need to be repositioned in its 3D space. So, get the 3D Slide tool (press **Shift-K** until you have it) and position the object inside the canvas—click-and-drag downward to slide the object closer and click-and-drag upward to push the object back. Next, grab the 3D Rotate tool (press **Shift-K** until you have it) and click-and-drag around to see how it makes the shape rotate around in 3D space. Position it where you think it will look best, but don't worry about getting it perfect—you can always change the angle later. (*Note:* To make it easier to reposition my 3D object, I hide all of the layers beneath my 3D object layer by **Option-clicking [PC: Alt-clicking]** on the Eye icon to the left of its layer. Go to the book's downloads page for a video tutorial on the basics of using the 3D tools.)

STEP 13: Next, create a new document that is 10 inches wide by 6.25 inches high at 100 ppi, and choose 16 bit for the bit depth. In the Swatches panel (found under the Window menu), click on the Pure Cyan Blue swatch (shown here) to set this as your Foreground color and get the Gradient tool again. In the Options Bar, click on the down-facing arrow to the right of the gradient thumbnail to open the Gradient Picker, and then click on the Foreground to Transparent gradient. Now, click on the Linear Gradient icon (the first icon from the left in the Options Bar) and draw a blue gradient in from the top-left corner to the center and then again, in from the bottom-right corner to the center.

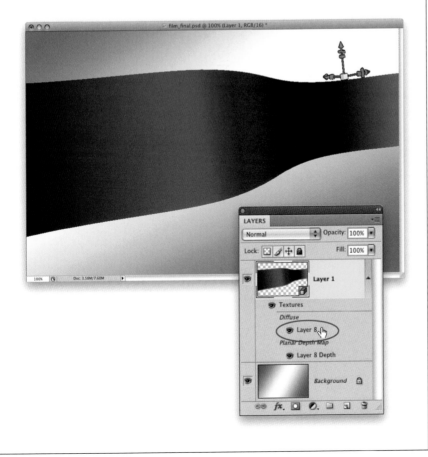

STEP 14: Go back to the filmstrip file, get the Move tool, and drag-and-drop the 3D object into this new document. Use the 3D Rotate, 3D Drag, and 3D Slide tools to position the shape in the composition. In the Layers panel, you can see the 3D layer contains a number of sub-layers. The sub-layer under Diffuse contains the actual art on the 3D layer and the sub-layer under Planar Depth Map contains the grayscale file that defines the 3D shape. Double-click on the Diffuse sub-layer to open the file and you will see the original copper gradient.

Continued

STEP 15: Now, go back into the film-strip file again, click on the merged filmstrip layer in the Layers panel, and then press **Command-A (PC: Ctrl-A)** to select the entire document. Go under the Edit menu and choose Copy, then go back into the copper gradient file, go under the Edit menu, and choose Paste. Now, just close this document, save the changes, and this will wrap the filmstrip onto the 3D shape (as shown in the next step).

STEP 16: Finally, we need to adjust the lights. Go to the 3D panel (found under the Window menu) and click on the Filter By: Lights icon (the little light bulb) at the top of the panel. You can see that there are three Infinite lights applied to the object. Click on the Toggle Lights icon at the bottom of the panel (the second icon from the left) to show the light wireframes in the canvas (the lines with the blue balls on the ends). With the first Infinite light in the 3D Lights options selected, use the Rotate the Light tool (the top tool in the middle left of the panel) to click-and-drag the light around, so it is in front of the filmstrip. You will see the light reacting to the surface of the filmstrip. Do this to each light, and position them so they illuminate and reflect on the film. (*Note:* The position of your lights may be different, depending on the angle of your 3D filmstrip.)

STEP 17: Okay, one more thing: the reflection. Create a duplicate of the 3D layer by pressing **Command-J (PC: Ctrl-J)**, then click back on the original 3D layer in the Layers panel (this is now going to be your reflection layer; the copy you just made will now be your main 3D object layer). Get the 3D Rotate tool in the Toolbox, then click on the arrow on the blue Axis widget line and drag down to slide the filmstrip reflection down, and position it so the top edge of the reflection touches the bottom edge of the original.

STEP 18: In the Layers panel, double-click on the sub-layer under Diffuse once more to open the filmstrip image, then go under the Edit menu, under Transform, and choose Flip Vertical. Now, click on the Add Layer Mask icon at the bottom of the Layers panel to add a layer mask to this layer and then grab the Gradient tool. Set your Foreground color to black and choose the Foreground to Transparent gradient from the Gradient Picker in the Options Bar. Turn off or throw away the copper gradient layer (by either clicking on the Eye icon to its left in the Layers panel or clicking-and-dragging it down onto the Trash icon at the bottom of the Layers panel), and then draw a gradient on the layer mask from the bottom of the document to the top. Close this document, save the changes, and you will now see this fade away your reflected filmstrip. You can certainly stop here (here is a final image, where I've added a little text, using the font Trajan Pro), but if you continue on to the next page, I will show you how to mask out the sprocket holes of the filmstrip in 3D.

Continued

STEP 19: In the Layers panel, click on the 3D filmstrip layer (Layer 1 copy), then double-click on the sub-layer under Diffuse (in this case Layer 8). This will open the original filmstrip file. Go under the Image menu and choose Duplicate to create a copy.

STEP 20: Grab the Rectangular Marquee tool and draw a selection over the images you added to the filmstrip, then press Shift-Delete (PC: Shift-Backspace), choose Black from the Fill dialog's Use pop-up menu, and click OK. Now, you can deselect.

STEP 21: 3D masking works similar to regular masking in Photoshop, where white reveals and black conceals. Since we want to hide the sprocket holes, we need to invert the colors, so go under the Image menu, under Adjustments, and choose Invert. From the Layers panel's flyout menu, choose Flatten Image, then save this document to your desktop and close it.

STEP 22: Finally, go back to your main filmstrip document and, in the 3D panel, click on the Filter By: Materials icon (the third icon from the left) at the top of the panel to access these options. Click on the icon to the right of the Opacity field and choose Load Texture from the pop-up menu. When the Open dialog appears, locate the mask file you just created and saved to your desktop. Click Open, and it will mask out the sprocket holes in 3D, and it will remain that way even if you change the 3D object's position. Simply follow these same steps to mask out the holes in the reflection layer, as well.

3D Sports Logo

These days, some of the coolest 3D graphics can be seen during major sporting events. Whether it's *SportsCenter*, *Monday Night Football*, or even the Olympics, these are a haven for ideas. I watch these events for the graphics as much as for the game. Sometimes more. What we are going to be doing here is creating a 3D sports logo all in Photoshop. By using multi-level 3D layers and light effects, we will be able to create a real sense of depth and dimension. As a bonus, I have provided a video tutorial on animating this very logo in Photoshop on the book's downloads page (you can find the address to it in the book's intro).

STEP ONE: Go under the File menu, choose New, and create a new document that is 12.5 inches by 8 inches at 72 ppi. (*Note:* The resolution may need to be higher if you are going to be printing this.) Set the Color Mode to RGB Color and the Background Contents to White. Click OK, then go under the Image menu, under Adjustments, and choose Invert to change the white background to black (or just press **Command-I [PC: Ctrl-I]**).

STEP TWO: Click on the Create a New Layer icon at the bottom of the Layers panel to create a new blank layer, and then get the Custom Shape tool from the Toolbox (or press **Shift-U** until you have it). Go up to the Options Bar and click on the Shape thumbnail to open the Shape Picker. Click on the right-facing arrow at the top right of the Picker and, from the flyout menu, choose Symbols. Click OK when asked if you want to replace the current shapes and this will give you a collection of familiar shapes to choose from. Select the shape named "Sign 2."

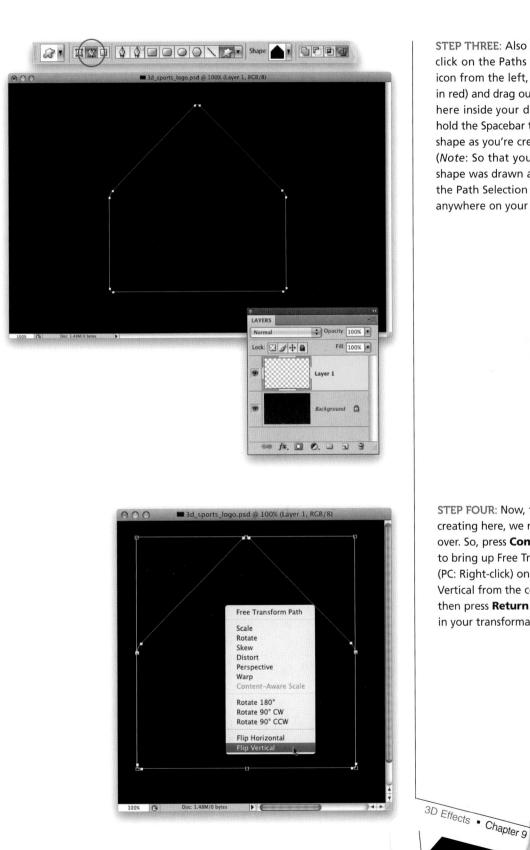

STEP THREE: Also in the Options Bar, click on the Paths icon (the second icon from the left, shown circled here in red) and drag out the shape you see here inside your document (press-and-hold the Spacebar to reposition your shape as you're creating it, if needed). (*Note*: So that you can see that this shape was drawn as a path, switch to the Path Selection tool **[A]** and click anywhere on your shape.)

STEP FOUR: Now, for the logo we are creating here, we need to flip this shape over. So, press **Command-T (PC: Ctrl-T)** to bring up Free Transform. Control-click (PC: Right-click) on the shape, select Flip Vertical from the contextual menu, and then press **Return (PC: Enter)** to lock in your transformation.

STEP FIVE: Get the Add Anchor Point tool from the Toolbox (it's nested beneath the Pen tool), and click at the center of the top path to add a point. Then, press-and-hold the Command (PC: Ctrl) key, and you will temporarily get the Direct Selection tool, which you will use to grab the new point on the path and move it slightly upward. This will give the logo a slight arch at the top (as seen here).

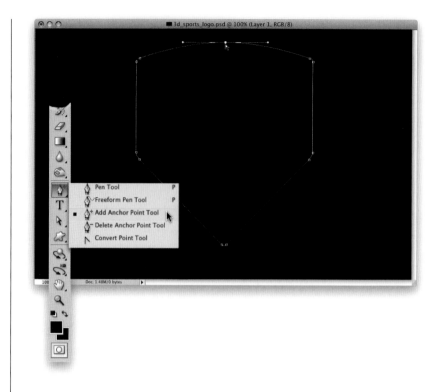

STEP SIX: After you have created the initial shape of the logo, press **Command-Return (PC: Ctrl-Enter)** to load the path as a selection. Go under the Window menu and choose Swatches to open the Swatches panel. Locate the swatch named Pure Yellow Orange (shown here), and click on it to load it as your Foreground color. Then press **Option-Delete (PC: Alt-** ackspace) to fill the shape with vellow/orange color and press **nd-D (PC: Ctrl-D)** to Deselect.

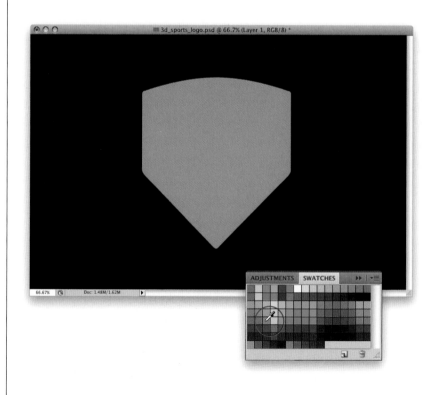

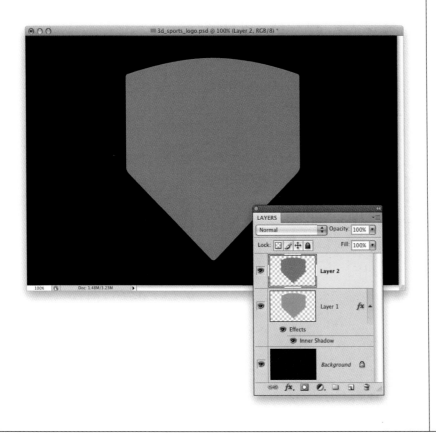

STEP SEVEN: Go to the Layers panel, click on the Add a Layer Style icon at the bottom of the panel, and choose Inner Shadow from the pop-up menu. In the Structure section of the Layer Style dialog, turn off the Use Global Light checkbox and set the Angle to 35°. Also, set the Distance to about 17. That's it in here. Click OK.

STEP EIGHT: We need to create another layer with this same shape, but with a different fill color. We can do this a number of different ways, but I like to load the current layer as a selection by clicking on the layer's thumbnail while pressing-and-holding the Command (PC: Ctrl) key. Now, create a new layer, press **Shift-Delete (PC: Shift-Backspace)** to open the Fill dialog, and choose 50% gray from the Use pop-up menu. Click OK and then deselect.

Continued

STEP NINE: Next, go under the Filter menu, under Sketch, and choose Halftone Pattern. Set the Size to 2 and the Contrast to 0. From the Pattern Type pop-up menu, choose Line, then click OK. Then, at the top of the Layers panel, set this layer's blend mode to Soft Light to blend it with the original yellow/orange shape.

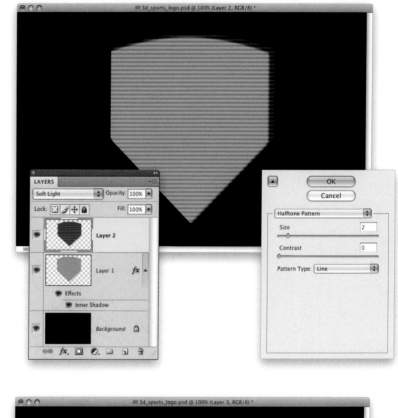

STEP 10: Load the shape as a selection as we did in Step Eight, create a new layer, then go under the Edit menu and choose Stroke. Set the Width to 10 pixels, click on the color swatch to open the Color Picker, enter R: 0, G: 111, B: 220, and then click OK. Finally, set the Location of the stroke to Center and click OK. Next, choose Bevel and Emboss from the Add a Layer Style icon's pop-up menu at the bottom of the Layers panel. Enter 250 for the Depth and 3 for the Size. Then, enter 29 for the Angle, turn off the Use Global Light checkbox, and enter an Altitude of 37° to get a more dimensional edge to the stroke. Click OK and then deselect.

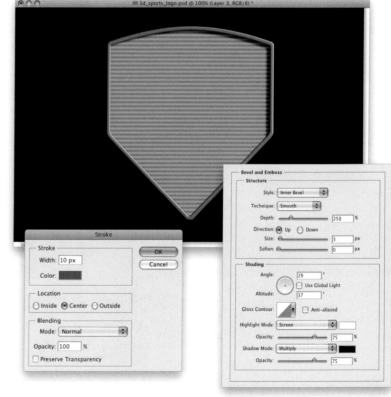

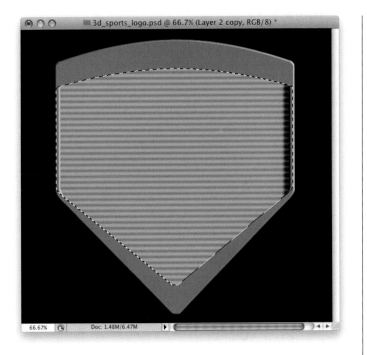

STEP 11: Now we are going to create another shape based on our current shape. Click on the second shape layer (Layer 2) and press **Command-J (PC: Ctrl-J)** to make a duplicate. Click-and-drag that duplicate layer to the top of the layer stack and change its blend mode to Normal. Click on your Foreground color swatch and change it to the same blue you used for the stroke in the previous step. Command-click (PC: Ctrl-click) on the duplicate layer's thumbnail to select the shape, and then fill it with your Foreground color. Go under the Select menu and choose Transform Selection. Grab the top-middle control handle, press-and-hold the Option (PC: Alt) key, and click-and-drag down toward the center of the shape. This will squeeze the selection vertically, leaving parts of the shape unselected. Press **Return (PC: Enter)** to commit the change, then press Delete (PC: Backspace) to knock out the selection, and deselect.

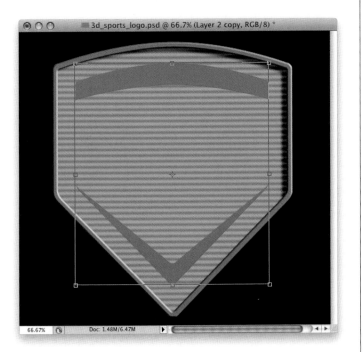

STEP 12: What you have now are two new shapes on a single layer that can be incorporated into this logo. Simply go into Free Transform, press-and-hold Option-Shift (PC: Alt-Shift), grab any of the corner handles, and drag in toward the center. Once the shapes are inset enough, lock in your transformation.

Continued

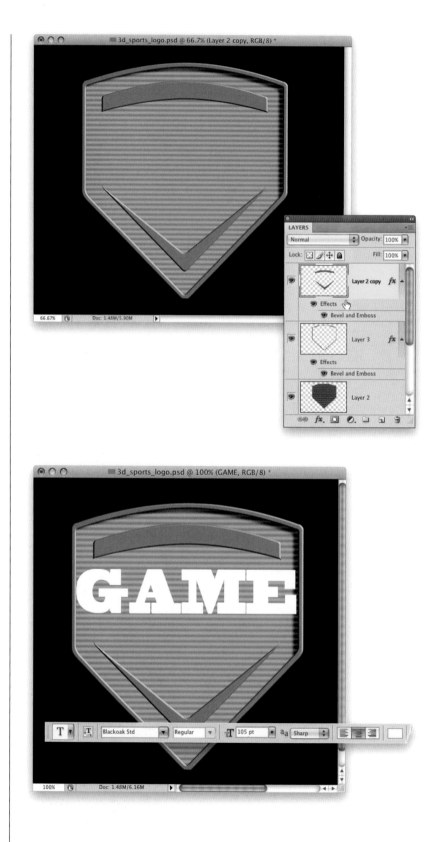

STEP 13: Now, apply the same Bevel and Emboss layer style that we applied to the Stroke layer by pressing-and-holding the **Option (PC: Alt) key**, clicking on the word "Effects" beneath the Stroke layer, and dragging-and-dropping it onto this layer.

STEP 14: Get the Horizontal Type tool **(T)** in the Toolbox, then select a really bold font from the font pop-up menus in the Options Bar. Here, I chose Blackoak Std Regular—because it's a nice, thick font—in white. Click in the document to create a Type layer and then type "GAME." Use Free Transform to resize and position your type, so it looks like what you see here.

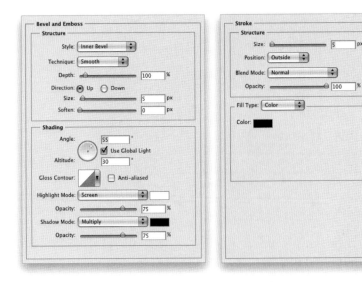

STEP 15: Click on the Add a Layer Style icon at the bottom of the Layers panel, choose Bevel and Emboss from the pop-up menu, and just change the Angle to 55°. While still in the Layer Style dialog, in the Styles section on the left, click on Stroke. Set the size to 5, the positioning to Outside, and then click on the color swatch and change the color to black. Click OK.

STEP 16: Create a duplicate of this Type layer, highlight the text, and then type the word "NIGHT." Switch to the Move tool, and scale and position it using Free Transform, if necessary. It already has the layer styles we added to "GAME," since we copied that layer to create this one.

Continued

3D Effects • Chapter 9   **319**

STEP 17: With the type set, click back on the GAME layer and then go under the Edit menu, under Transform, and choose Warp. In the Options Bar, you will see the Warp pop-up menu; click on it and choose Arc. Set the Bend amount to 15%, and then press the **Return (PC: Enter)** key twice.

STEP 18: Shift-click on the NIGHT layer, so that both Type layers are selected in the Layers panel, and then go under the 3D menu and choose New 3D Postcard From Layer. Now, click on the layer containing the inset shapes (Layer 2 copy) and again, choose New 3D Postcard From Layer from the 3D menu. Shift-click on the remaining three layers containing the rest of the graphic (everything except the Background layer, of course) to select them and choose New 3D Postcard From Layer from the 3D menu one more time. You should end up with three 3D layers (as shown here).

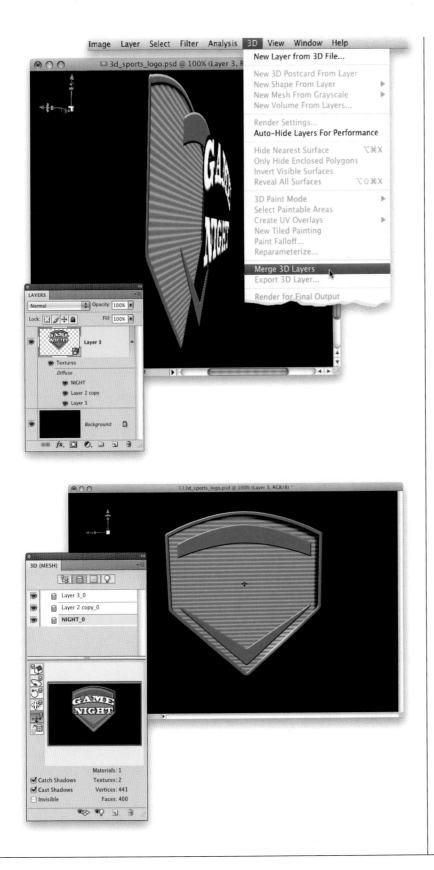

STEP 19: Okay, now select both the 3D Type layer and the 3D blue inset shapes layer in the Layers panel. Go under the 3D menu once again, but this time, choose Merge 3D Layers. Then do the same with the merged layer and the last remaining shape layer beneath it. While it appears that we have merged all the 3D layers together, this isn't quite the case. Each layer is actually separated by a few pixels. To verify this, grab the 3D Rotate tool **(K)** from the Toolbox and tilt the shape around, so you can see the separated layers. The problem is that the distancing between them is too far and we need to close it in a little. When you're done moving it around, go under the Edit menu and choose Undo to put the shape back in its original position.

STEP 20: Go to the 3D panel (found under the Window menu) and click on the Filter By: Meshes icon (the second icon from the left) at the top of the panel. Here is where you manage the position of each of the 3D objects within this one 3D layer. You can select the specific object by clicking on its layer at the top of the 3D panel and a red outline will appear in the panel's preview area where you have that object's mesh. However, this really isn't much of any help, unless you have diligently named your layers. A quick and easy way to determine which layer is which is to turn each one off by clicking on the Eye icon to the left of the layer. So, first, click on the layer containing the text, then click on the Slide the Mesh tool (the fifth tool down) in the middle left of the panel. Press-and-hold the Shift key, click inside the document, and drag upward gently. This will push the letters back a little bit. If you see it disappear (as it did here), you have gone too far. Now, select the layer in the 3D panel that contains the blue inset shapes and do the same thing.

Continued

STEP 21: Click on the Filter By: Lights icon (the light bulb) at the top of the 3D panel. You will see you can apply three different types of lights. From the 3D panel's flyout menu, choose New Spot Light. You will see the settings for the light appear in the panel. Click on the Toggle Lights icon at the bottom of the panel (the second icon from the left) to turn on the wireframe. If you don't see the light, it is probably behind the 3D object. Click on the Slide the Light tool (the third icon down) in the middle left of the panel. Then click-and-drag down in the document to bring the light forward. Continue to use the Slide, Drag, and Rotate the Light tools in the Lights options of the 3D panel, and position the light in the upper right of the document. (*Note:* Go to the book's downloads page for a video tutorial on the basics of using the 3D tools.)

STEP 22: Create a second spotlight and position it in the lower right of the document, so it illuminates the underside of the logo.

STEP 23: Finally, click on the Filter By: Whole Scene icon (the first icon on the left) at the top of the 3D panel to reveal the Scene options. First, choose Best from the Anti-Aliasing pop-up menu, then from the Preset menu, choose Ray Traced. This will render the shadows being cast by the objects (as you can see here with the type). Now, the cool part about this is that you can change the position of the logo quite easily. Before you do, however, you will need to set the Preset pop-up menu back to Solid. Reposition the shape using the 3D Rotate tool (as I have done here) and then choose Ray Traced from the Preset pop-up menu, again. Also, you can now click on the Toggle Lights icon, at the bottom of the 3D panel, to turn off the wireframe of the lights.

STEP 24: To finish up the background, create a new blank layer right above the Background layer. Get the Gradient tool **(G)**, and in the Options Bar, click on the down-facing arrow next to the gradient thumbnail, choose the Foreground to Transparent gradient from the Gradient Picker, then click on the Radial Gradient icon (the second icon from the left). Go to the Swatches panel and click on a blue swatch—here, I chose Pure Cyan. Starting at the middle of the canvas, click-and-drag out to apply the gradient.

Continued

STEP 25: Let's add one final background element here and this time we are going to fake 3D a bit. First, click on the Eye icon to the left of your 3D layer to hide it. Grab the Rectangular Marquee tool **(M)** in the Toolbox, create a new layer above your radial gradient layer, and draw a horizontal rectangle. Go under the Edit menu and choose Stroke. Set the Width to 3 pixels, set the Color to white, then set the Location to Inside, and click OK. With the selection still in place, get the Move tool, press-and-hold the Option (PC: Alt) key, and click-and-drag to duplicate your rectangle. Continue doing this over and over, overlapping the shapes as you go, until you have something similar to what you see here. Now, deselect.

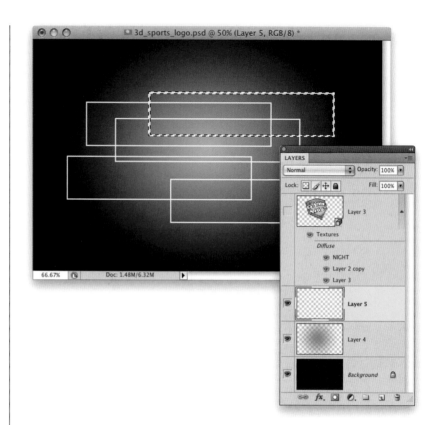

STEP 26: Go into Free Transform, Control-click (PC: Right-click), and choose Rotate. Tilt the graphic slightly to go along with the main logo, and then while you're still in Free Transform, go under the Edit menu, under Transform, and choose Warp. From the Warp pop-up menu in the Options Bar, choose Bulge, enter –20 for the bend amount, and lock in your transformation. Click on the Add Layer Mask icon at the bottom of the Layers panel to add a layer mask, then get the Gradient tool. Set your Foreground color to black and, in the Options Bar, make sure the Foreground to Transparent gradient is still selected in the Gradient Picker, then click on the Linear Gradient icon (the first one from the left). Now, just click-and-drag from the outer edges of your image in slightly towards the middle to fade the edges.

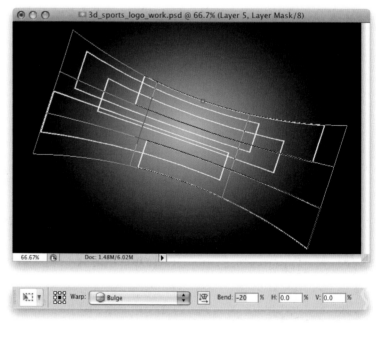

STEP 27: Finally, click on the Add a Layer Style icon at the bottom of the Layers panel and, from the pop-up menu, choose Outer Glow. Set the Blend Mode to Overlay, click on the color swatch and set the glow color to another blue (I used R: 45, G: 169, B: 255), set the Size to 250, and there you have it.

STEP 28: Now, the beauty of this logo being in 3D is that we can always modify it—for instance, let's modify the words. Let's say we wanted to change the text from "GAME NIGHT" to "BASEBALL NIGHT." Simply go into the Layers panel and double-click on the 3D layer's sub-layer that contains the text. Here, it is the sub-layer called NIGHT, and double-clicking on it will open the Type layer's file, where the text is editable. Using the Horizontal Type tool, just highlight "GAME" and type "BASEBALL." The warping will redraw as you type. Once you're done, close the document and save the changes. Go back to the original file and the text will be updated.

Index

W

Z

TOOLS
FOR
CREATION

CAMERAS
LENSES
LIGHTING
TRIPODS

Our knowledge comes standard.

When it comes to the B&H sales staff, knowledge and experience are a given. We offer unparalleled expertise and solutions for the Photography professional.

Visit our SuperStore in the heart of NYC, give us a call, or browse our newly expanded web site featuring live assistance, and experience for yourself the most knowledgeable and helpful sales staff anywhere.

Subscribe to our free B&H catalog
www.bhphotovideo.com/catalog

bhphotovideo.com
Shop conveniently online

Visit Our SuperStore
420 Ninth Ave, New York, NY 10001

800-947-9957
Speak to a Sales Associate

B&H
PHOTO · VIDEO · PRO AUDIO

The Professional's Source

 a **KelbyMediaGroup** company
the force behind creatives

Adobe, Photoshop, Lightroom, Illustrator, Photoshop Camera Raw, and Dreamweaver are registered trademarks of Adobe Systems Incorporated. Produced by the National Association of Photoshop Professionals.